PRAISE FOR *COAST TO COAST: MURDER FROM SEA TO SHINING SEA*

"A sterling collection of coast-to-coast crime stories dripping with local color—all of it blood red."
—Chuck Hogan, Hammett Prize winner and international bestselling author of *The Strain*

"Envelope-pushers! A truly *WOW* collection by the *best* mystery writers out there—full of surprises *only* they can pull off."
—Thomas B. Sawyer, bestselling author of *Cross Purposes* and Head-Writer of *Murder, She Wrote*

"An engaging collection from a stellar cast of award-winning mystery authors guaranteed to keep you awake all night."
—Hannah Dennison, author of the IMBA bestselling Vicky Hill Mysteries

"This intriguing collection of stories from these masters of suspense will keep you guessing from cover to cover *and* coast to coast."
—Raffi Yessayan, author of *8 in the Box* and *2 in the Hat*

PRAISE FOR *COAST TO COAST: PRIVATE EYES FROM SEA TO SHINING SEA*

"A tantalizing array of stories guaranteed to please fans of PI fiction. High fives all around!"

> —MWA Grand Master Bill Pronzini

"Tough, taut and terrific. This cross-country collection of sleuthing stories—from the best writers in the private eye biz—is wonderfully written, always surprising, and completely entertaining."

> —Hank Phillippi Ryan, Anthony, Agatha and
> Mary Higgins Clark Award-winning author

"A bang-up read of PI fiction from a gallery of impressive authors. Compelling, fun, and full of clever surprises. A treat."

> —Shamus Award-winning author John Shepphird

COAST TO COAST

Noir from Sea to Shining Sea

BOOKS IN THIS SERIES

COAST TO COAST

Noir from Sea to Shining Sea

Edited by
Andrew McAleer and Paul D. Marks

DOWN&OUT BOOKS

Down & Out Books
3959 Van Dyke Road, Suite 265
Lutz, FL 33558
DownAndOutBooks.com

The characters and events in this book are fictitious. Any similarity to real persons, living or dead, is coincidental and not intended by the author.

Cover design by Eric Beetner

ISBN: 1-64396-147-0
ISBN-13: 978-1-64396-147-7

For the noir writers and filmmakers who inspired us.

CONTENTS

NOWHERE MAN

Paul D. Marks

I

Venice Beach, California—1965

Are there things worse than death? Tim Stanton wasn't sure, but life came close. He brought a bottle of Night Train to his lips. Swigged. He used to enjoy coming down here to Venice, the Beach. Watching the roller coaster crest the summit of the highest hill at the Pacific Ocean Park amusement pier on the Venice-Santa Monica border. Now it was just a place to hang. To hide. On the beach or under the pier in the cool and the dark, where he could drink in peace. The rhythm of the waves lulled him into a false sense of tranquility.

Oil derricks pulsed nearby. Fog rolled in from the ocean. Fog rolled in from the Night Train. The mirage of a young woman washed across his mind. Memories. He used to enjoy them, reliving the glorious conquests of his past in the movie in his mind. Now they were thick and hazy like the fog.

The whine and wail of the air raid siren woke him from his reverie. They blasted out a test howl at 10:00 a.m. on the last Friday of every month. At least he didn't have to duck and cover any more like when he was in school. Yeah, hiding under his flimsy elementary school desk was going to save him from being nuked.

1

"How the fuck did I get here?" he grumbled, his mind somersaulting, spinning circles like the dryer at the laundromat. "How the fuck—"

II

Santa Monica, California—One Year Earlier

Tim had always been a snappy dresser. And if clothes made the man, clothes made Tim. Most of the men who worked with him bought their suits at the May Company, a mid-level department store. He went to Brooks Brothers. They had families, he was free. Free to date, free to spend money on clothes and cars instead of a mortgage. Free. He was well-built, decent looking and had good hair, slicked down with Brylcreem—*A Little Dab'll Do Ya*. And just a dash of Old Spice to finish things off.

Looking at himself in the Department of Motor Vehicle's plate glass window, he ran his comb through his hair, like Kookie on *77 Sunset Strip*, before heading inside to a cuppa and a quick glance at the *L.A. Herald Examiner* before settling into the job.

He wasn't one of those mindless robots who lived for his job. His real love: shooting up Pacific Coast Highway in his convertible Porsche Spyder, just like James Dean's, a gal in the passenger seat—hoping to avoid Broderick Crawford and the Highway Patrol. Listening to Elvis and, of course, Frank Sinatra, on the radio. The gals loved it, even if he was looking at other girls on the beach as they whizzed by.

His job at the Santa Monica branch of the DMV wasn't glamorous, but it paid decent. And there was a chance of upward mobility—isn't that what everyone in the country wanted? To move up and out, maybe to the suburbs—out to the San Fernando Valley. Have a station wagon and a lawn and a barbeque and a swimming pool. Someday, maybe. But now he was having too much fun. Dating two, three women a week. Spending money on them and on clothes and his car. And his apartment, which was okay, if not grand.

Tim normally had lunch at Zucky's Deli on Wilshire. Today he was meeting Bill Keller at Jack's at the Beach, Keller's treat. Jack's shared a pier with Pacific Ocean Park. One of his regulars, Keller was a private dick, who mostly did crappy little divorce jobs or runaways. For a few bucks Tim could often help him locate the people he was looking for in the DMV records. And like all his special *private* clients, Keller always paid for the meal.

Jack's sat at the far end of the pier. The sun streaked through the clouds, throwing long shadows on the pier's rough wooden planks. A sting of salt water slapped Tim as he grabbed the door, stepped inside. The hostess sat him at his regular table with a great view of the ocean. Keller joined him a few minutes later.

"Who is it today?" Tim said, shaking a Lucky Strike from the pack. Tapping it on the table. They didn't need small talk as they went through this routine at least half a dozen times a month, maybe more.

"Name's Liz Harris."

"Pretty ordinary. Why can't it ever be Zasu Pitts?"

Keller laughed. "'Cause that would make it too easy."

"I assume you have all her stats."

Keller pushed a piece of paper across the table. Tim looked it over.

"I'll see what I can do," Tim said.

Before they left, Keller shoved an envelope toward Tim. Twenty bucks. The going rate. Well, maybe twenty-five next time. They walked down the pier together, past a couple of kids wearing funny clothes and with those weird Beatle haircuts.

"This is what I fought in Korea for?" Keller sneered, glaring at the kids.

Tim nodded his agreement. "What's that smell?"

Keller sniffed the air. "Marijuana."

"Isn't that illegal?"

III

Tim took his life seriously, the part that began at five o'clock. The job was the job, but the nighttime was the right time. And tonight the right gal was Darla and a trip to the Ash Grove, Keller's twenty would come in handy. The Ash Grove always impressed girls. The folk music made them think Tim was deep, not just interested in getting them into bed. Maybe he'd even get lucky.

But he didn't. She was a dud. Turned into Cinderella right about midnight. Besides, he'd wanted to go see the James Bond flick *Goldfinger*. But she didn't want to see something with all the violence she'd heard about—too scary. So now here he was, alone in his apartment, with a glass of Jack Daniels, 'cause that's what Frankie drank, watching Johnny Carson on *The Tonight Show*. His apartment on Fountain in West Hollywood was decorated the way he thought Sinatra might decorate. Danish modern furniture. Splashy Neiman prints on the walls, though Frankie probably owned originals.

He had another lunch appointment tomorrow. Another twenty bucks, twenty-five if he could swing it—inflation, you know. Easy money.

He changed channels. *The Late, Late Show* on channel two droned on. Some old movie with Dana Andrews and Gene Tierney. He never did catch the name. The TV cast a flickering blue spell on the room. He fell asleep before the first commercial.

"Hello, Mr. Stanton? The usual, Harvey Wallbanger?" the hostess at Jack's said, leading him to his regular table. His new client was waiting for him.

"Tim? Tim Stanton?" The man looked like any other. Would hardly stand out in a crowd. Large man. Dressed in a loud Hawaiian shirt and pork pie hat with a wide band and a bright feather. The kind of hat that Frank wore—Tim liked that. "I'm Ken Dorsey."

Tim nodded. They shook hands, Dorsey nearly crushing Tim's. Made small talk, then the man finally came to the point.

"Bill Keller tells me you can help me out."

"Maybe," Tim said. He sloshed down his Wallbanger.

"I'm trying to find someone."

"Who?"

"Mary Singleton."

"Pretty common name. How will I know if I've found the right one? I don't like giving out everyone's info who has the same name as the someone you're looking for." He liked to believe he had some ethics left.

"I got all her stats here. Age. Hair color—"

"That can be changed."

"Don't I know it. I married a blonde once who turned into a mousy brunette six weeks after the wedding." Dorsey's ruddy face turned even redder. He smiled, but it was more of a snarl or a sneer. He seemed friendly enough—on the surface. But he wanted something from Tim, so maybe it was an act.

Tim made a show of hemming and hawing. Should he help the guy out? It wasn't really ethical—but that was just the game he played with himself to ease his conscience. Of course it wasn't ethical—it never was. He could get in trouble, even lose his job. But in the end he always ended up taking the money and enjoying the lunch. The guy probably knew he was faking it. It was a game, a dance. Everybody knew their parts. After all, this was Hollywood or damn close to it. And everybody in L.A. was an actor.

"Twenty-five," Tim said.

"Keller said it was twenty."

"Twenty-five for new clients."

Dorsey yanked an extra fin from his wallet, shoved it into a crinkled, dirty white envelope, slid it across the table.

Tim ordered abalone, the most expensive thing on the menu. Man, it tasted so damn good and went down so damn smooth.

5

IV

He got back to the office around one-thirty; did what he always did. Went to the army of file cabinets, found the "S" drawer. He stole a quick glance around to see if anyone was looking. But really, what did it matter? He had a right to be there as part of his job. One of these days the department would get one of those fancy computer-things, something called UNIVAC, and it would be even easier to look someone up.

He snatched the card for Mary Singleton.

"Piece of cake," he muttered. He set the card on his desk, took his seat.

The photo on Mary Singleton's card caught his eye—actually her eyes caught his attention. The most stunning, beautiful eyes he'd ever seen. The picture was black and white; the card said they were blue. He imagined them to be a cerulean blue to go with her soft blond hair and perfect oval face, with the Max Factor Hollywood-flawless skin. He didn't know her, probably never would, but he thought he could fall in love with her. At the very least, he was in love with her picture.

He leaned back in his chair, letting his mind wander—to picket fences and kids on swings and in wading pools. Even a dog. And Mary Singleton in an itsy bitsy teenie weenie yellow polka-dot bikini on a lounge.

Stop!

Why should he feel this way about her? He didn't know her—never would.

Was he that lonely? With all the women he was dating, still that lonely?

He wished he was closer with his family, his parents and his sister.

He wished he didn't live in L.A., where everyone was a movie star—or wanted to be.

But he didn't know if he could ever break his pattern. He was having fun, at least he thought he was. Still, every once in a while he thought there should be something more, something deeper.

He didn't know why he saw all of that in Mary Singleton.

Except that maybe it was those eyes.

He picked up the card, looked at it closer. Read her address and phone number to himself.

Should he?

He'd never done it before.

Should he call her out of the blue?

It was a crazy thought.

Or maybe he could accidentally bump into her? Find out where she shopped, probably near her home.

Why not?

Because if anyone found out he'd lose his job, that was certain.

Still, there were those eyes. And the card claimed she was single—*Miss* Mary Singleton.

So, why not?

Because it was crazy.

No, he'd just do what he always did. Turn the info over to his client, Dorsey this time, and forget about it. Move on to the next one and the next twenty bucks.

V

One of the women in the office had left a copy of *Look* magazine in the break room. Tim skimmed through it, shielding his eyes against the harsh glare of the fluorescent lights. Lots of those long-haired kids filled the pages. And it seemed every girl in the world had a crush on Paul McCartney from the Beatles, and just about every other long-haired guy out there. Tim thought about growing his hair longer, letting it fall down over his forehead, but he didn't want to look like a fag. Still, if it would get him more women, well, why not?

"Hey, Tim, you see the paper today?" said Nate Marlowe, Tim's best friend at the office. Once in a while they double dated, but Marlowe's speed was too slow. He was a Ford Country

Squire wagon to Tim's Spyder.

"Not yet."

"Some girl got killed. They say it's the worst murder of a woman since that Black Dahlia thing twenty years ago. Probably one-a them filthy hippies did it." Nate put a match to a Chesterfield.

"Hippies?"

"I heard it somewhere, on TV I think. Hippie, one-a them long-haired punks. Too many nutcases out there these days. "

"Are there really more crazy people or do we just hear more about them?"

"Dunno, but this is a pretty gruesome murder."

Nate walked off, leaving his copy of the *Herald Examiner* with Tim. He felt bad for the girl that had been killed, but didn't want to spoil his day with bad news. Figured he'd check out the sports page. See how Maury Wills and the Dodgers were doing.

He uncrinkled the paper, slapped it open. The photo of the woman on the front page caught his eye. He knew her immediately—the eyes. Her eyes. He focused on the caption below her face—Mary Singleton, as if he needed confirmation.

Blood rushed to his head, his temples feeling like they would explode. A piercing pain seared his chest, a knife twisting inside him. Is this what a heart attack felt like? His whole body sagged; his head felt so light he almost fell over.

"Damn. Goddamn!" He slammed his fist on the Formica tabletop, hard enough to get a boxer's fracture, he learned later. It can't be, he thought. That guy—what was his name? Dorsey. Bill Keller had vouched for him. It's gotta be coincidence.

He'd never felt so alone in his life.

VI

Tim's heart raced as fast as if he'd swallowed a handful of bennies or dexies. He cancelled his date for that night. And his carton of

Lucky Strikes didn't last long enough. The carton had been half full when he started in on it the minute he got home from work. He didn't eat. Didn't drink. Just smoked and smoked, the TV droning in the background: *Rawhide*, *Red Skelton*—he didn't laugh like he usually did. *The Late Show* and *The Late, Late Show*, which didn't go late enough.

No sleep.

No dreams.

No escape.

He sat on the edge of the bed in a square of cold light, the rest of the room filled with dark patches and shadows. Got out of bed, went to the wet bar in the living room. Eyed the bottle of Jack D.

"No," he said.

Went back to the rumpled covers of his bed.

Three days of this was enough. What was going on? Was he finally developing a conscience? He didn't kill that girl. He didn't cause her to get killed.

Still, for twenty bucks—twenty-five—she was dead. Even if he didn't know it would happen.

"What do you mean you don't know him?"

Bill Keller's crappy little Venice storefront office was suffocating Tim with its cheap wood paneling, three black telephones, four non-descript beige file cabinets, papers, old, used coffee cups, paper and ceramic. Stench of stale coffee, cigarettes and sweat. The couch looked like it came from the No-Tell Motel, stained like it too—so much so that Tim wouldn't sit on it. The yellowed fluorescent lights in the ceiling cast a ghostly pallor about the room. Some new Beatles song screamed from the tinny transistor radio on Keller's desk—there was always a new Beatles song on the radio these days.

"I don't know Dorsey," Keller said.

"Then why'd you send him to me?"

"I was too busy to deal with it myself."

"So he just walked in here one day? Just like that." Tim had tried looking up Ken Dorsey in the DMV files. No such man in the age range that his Ken Dorsey would fit.

"Just like that." Keller was cool. Not even a bead of sweat on his forehead or a quiver of the lip. He just didn't seem to give a damn.

"You think he did it?" Tim pointed to the *Herald Examiner* splayed across Keller's desk.

"Looks that way, don'tcha think?"

"So what do I do now?"

"Why do you have to do anything?" Keller slugged down some coffee.

"Because I gave him the info he used to find her and kill her."

"You're not responsible, he is."

"You don't feel any guilt, nothing at all?" Tim said.

"Nothing. I didn't kill her. Neither did you. You got too much guilt, too much conscience."

"Yeah, I'm overdosing on conscience."

"You never had it before."

"Never needed it. Nobody we ever looked up got killed—murdered." Tim lit up a Lucky Strike, only today he wasn't feeling so lucky. "Will you help me find Dorsey?"

Keller smirked. "Go have a drink or smoke some reefer like those, what're they called, hippies. You're getting in over your head."

"Maybe. Maybe—"

Tim didn't know where to begin.

The only clue he had to go on was Mary Singleton herself. He called in sick, got into the Spyder, drove over to her Carthay Circle neighborhood. She lived on a typical street in that neck of the woods, lots of Spanish-style stucco duplexes and fourplexes built before the war. Nice, spacious. Two police prowlers sat in front of her apartment building. No way he could talk his way past them. He wondered how long they'd be there.

Next stop was her next of kin contact from her DMV card. He drove to Los Feliz. More Spanish architecture, but at least no cop cars here.

His heart beat an executioner's riff through his shirt and his armpits were soaked through as he knocked on Mrs. Singleton's door. An attractive woman of maybe fifty-five answered. What Mary would look like in middle age. Her eyes were red, probably from crying.

"Mrs. Singleton?"

"Yes."

"I'm—"

"If you're from the press—"

"My name is, uh, Bill Keller." He handed her Keller's card that he'd copped from Bill's desk. It read "William H. Keller, Private Detective".

"A private eye?"

"May I come in?"

Barbara and Ed Singleton's Spanish-colonial living room looked like something out of one of those old crime movies Tim fell asleep to every night, heavy damask drapes, dark wooden furniture that had a Mediterranean feel to it, wrought iron bannister leading upstairs—like something from, what was that movie, *Double Indemnity*. Pictures of Mary, no siblings. Only child. Ed wasn't home. Tim was just as glad.

"How can you help us, Mr. Keller?"

"I want to find your daughter's—"

"May I ask who you're working for?"

"I'm sorry, I'm not allowed to reveal that. It's confidential." Tim had read a few detective stories, some Raymond Chandler, some Mickey Spillane, seen some movies. He knew that was the dodge.

"I understand. It's been very rough, you know."

"I'm sure it has. And I know that even if I can help bring this perpetrator to justice that it won't bring your daughter back. But hopefully it will give you some peace."

"I don't think I'll ever know peace again. My husband is even more of a basket case than I am. He works at Columbia; they'd let him have some time off without docking him now that Mr. Cohn is passed. But he goes to work so he doesn't have to be home."

She offered Tim tea. He never drank tea but graciously accepted.

"To be honest with you, Mrs. Singleton, I don't even know where to begin. Do you have any idea who might have wanted to harm your daughter?"

"The police think it was random."

Tim knew otherwise.

VII

Tim slipped Bill Keller's card back into his wallet. He had surreptitiously pinched it off the end table where Mrs. Singleton had left it when she went to refill his tea. He didn't want her calling the real Keller for a variety of reasons.

Regret gnawed at the edges of his consciousness, like termites eating the timbers that held up a house. If he didn't do something about them, at some point his *house* would fall down.

Barbara Singleton hadn't given him much to go on, just Mary's best friend's name and work info: Sheila Sorrentino.

Twenty minutes later, Tim pulled up in front of a medical office building on Wilshire in the Miracle Mile.

Sheila bounced into the waiting room; he flashed her the same William H. Keller, Private Detective card he'd used on Mrs. Singleton. She tugged on a cigarette as they went down to the lobby atrium. Sheila looked like a party girl. She twirled her hair with her finger—maybe she didn't remember that her friend was dead. In another life, Tim might have tried to hit on her. But in this life, his current tortured life in hell, it didn't even cross his mind. Right now, he didn't care about partying or Sinatra or girls. He just wanted to find Mary's killer. This wasn't him. Something had happened, something changed. Maybe unintentionally being party to a murder did things to a guy.

"How'd you find me?" She sucked down smoke. "Oh, yeah. I guess you'd know how. What can I do for you?"

"I'm hitting some dead ends. Where did Mary hang out? With who?"

"How do I know you're not the guy who killed her?" she winked.

"Look, I'll buy you lunch. Will you talk to me?"

She took an early lunch and they went to Nickodell, across from Paramount and the Desilu Studios. She liked seeing the stars at the dark, red-boothed restaurant.

"My dates never take me to nice places like this. I'm lucky to go to Dolores' Drive-in," she said. "Look, there's Little Joe, Michael Landon from *Bonanza*. He's so cute."

She ordered a vodka gimlet; unbuttoned the top button of her blouse. He didn't care.

"Why should I talk to you?" she said, in between sucking on the cigarette and downing her gimlet.

"Because you want to find Mary's killer." He stared into her eyes.

"What're you looking at?"

"You have really gorgeous eyes," he said, pouring on the charm.

"Really?"

"Would I lie to you?" Of course he would. Some bought the BS, while others saw right through it. He knew Sheila was the type to buy it. In reality, she had average eyes. Nothing like Mary's luminous eyes that haunted him day and night.

"There was a creepy guy who hit on Mary at the Whiskey A-Go-Go one night. We went there to see the Byrds, I think it was the Byrds. I got a little high, you know. That David Crosby sure is the cute one." She sipped her drink. "Mary was kinda square. Left the Whiskey early."

"What was the guy's name?"

"I-I'm not sure. The police might have it. Mary probably has it written down in her apartment."

Fat chance he could get any info from the cops.

"In her phonebook?"

"I doubt he made it that far. On a piece of paper. Before people made it into her book she'd keep their names on slips of paper in a bowl in the kitchen."

"Can you describe him?"

"He was kinda lanky, growing his hair out, you know, to be cool."

That didn't sound much like Dorsey, if that was even his real name.

"Anyone else? Did she date a lot?"

"She dated. Not as much as I do. She was more serious. Y'know, looking for Prince Charming to come swooping in on his white horse."

"Where did she like to go?"

"Tiki clubs, you know, Don the Beachcomber, Trader Vic's in the Beverly Hilton."

"Mary's eyes were blue?" he said, abruptly.

"Yeah, blue. Fair hair and blue eyes. If you like that type."

Blue eyes crying in the rain, Tim thought. And they weren't the only crying eyes.

He could hardly get his steak sandwich down. He just wanted outta there—wanted to be on the hunt. Sheila lingered over a cigarette and a third gimlet. He couldn't figure out how she'd get her work done, but that wasn't his problem. Two people sitting in the same space, at the same table—they might as well have been on different planets.

VIII

Tim grabbed a flashlight and a large screwdriver from his glove compartment. Looked up and down Mary's street. After midnight on a moonless night. The fog that blanketed the city caused the streetlamp's light to halo out in concentric circles. Eerie, Tim thought, as he stole down the driveway to the back of the eightplex. Mary's apartment was ground floor-rear—that made it pretty easy. Most people in this neighborhood would be long asleep.

There was enough light from the streetlamps and the service light over the garage at the end of the driveway that he didn't have to turn on the flash. He slid the screwdriver under the double hung window, slid it up and slipped inside. Now the flashlight went on. He was in the kitchen.

He quickly found the bowl that had held the scraps of paper Sheila said Mary used before someone's name went in her phone book. The bowl was empty. He was surprised the cops didn't take the bowl too. He knew it would be futile looking for her phonebook. That would be the first thing the cops grabbed. So what the hell could he find that would help him?

He started a methodical search of every room, bathroom included, though he knew he had to be out of there before the sun came up. The cops may or may not be back, but he didn't want anyone seeing him leaving the building. Hell, they might think he killed her.

I guess in a sense I did, he thought.

Nothing! Nothing in her damn apartment. Either the cops had nabbed it all or there just wasn't anything worth shit. The only things he took were a color photo of her that the cops must've missed and a scarf that was hanging on her dresser mirror. He just wanted something of hers to hold.

By the time Tim got home *The Late, Late Show* was over. There was nothing on the goddamn television except test patterns. An Indian head, numbers and circles within circles. A high-pitched tone ringing in his ears. He shut the damn TV off, flicked on the radio. Joe Pyne was prattling on about how the country was going to hell in a handbasket. Turning the dial he landed on KHJ, the singer singing that yesterday all his troubles seemed so far away. No shit.

He caught himself staring at her picture. Daydreaming about her—not the way a private detective would. More like a lovesick lover. Sick. She was dead.

The color photo he'd taken from her apartment was a thousand times better than the crummy DMV black and white. A perfect five-by-seven glossy. Her eyes were, indeed, blue. Perfect face, frosted lips, like she might be wearing some of that hip Yardley or Mary Quant makeup he'd seen Twiggy or Jean Shrimpton selling in one ad after another.

He stared at Mary's picture, his mind a whirl of images. Conjuring up who she was, who she might have become. Images of him and her together, at the pier in Santa Monica, Disneyland. Going to a movie. Her making dinner for him. Him throwing some steaks on the grill for her. Mowing the lawn. He shook his head to clear it. No dice.

Still, there were those eyes.

This was crazy.

Why?

Because she was dead.

Damn! He couldn't get her out of his mind.

He grabbed the bottle of Jack D. from the wet bar. Nursed it through the night. Hell, it was better company than *The Late, Late Show* any time.

He called in sick again the next day.

"When you comin' back? We miss you, buddy," Richard Dale, his boss, said.

"Soon. I just have to get over this bug."

Tim didn't bother to shave, just a quick shower and he was out the door.

The library was just opening as he arrived. A school day. No kids. Just some old geezers and him. He perused every L.A. paper, the *Times*, the *Herald E*, the *Van Nuys News* and *Valley Green Sheet*, several others. Either the cops were holding back or there was nothing to report on Mary Singleton's murder. No leads. No nothing. Tim dropped his head to the table. A couple of minutes later the librarian tapped him on the shoulder.

"No sleeping in the library, sir."

He thought about hitting Mrs. Singleton again, thought better of it.

"What the fuck do I do now—I'm no fucking detective."

From Sheila, Tim had learned that after work Mary liked going to Don the Beachcomber's in Hollywood. And that's where he was, sitting in the Spyder, watching the busy bees drive by in their Fords and Chevys. "Five O'Clock World" by the Vogues came on the radio—how appropriate. Maybe because it was five and worker bees were pouring out of their offices and into the happy hour bars. Normally he would watch the women as they headed for the bar—normally he wouldn't be here at all. Today he watched the men. Looking for anyone who even vaguely resembled Dorsey. Zilch.

After an hour of watching, he decided to go inside, something he'd hoped not to have to do. Now he wished he would have shaved this morning. He also wished he had more of Keller's cards.

The inside of Don the Beachcomber's looked like some movie art director's idea of a Hawaiian hangout. Bamboo everywhere, tropical plants, large queen-fan wicker chairs. Ceiling fans that looked like palm fronds, doing nothing special, just agitating the cigarette smoke. All as real as anything else in Hollywood. Kyu Sakamoto's "Sukiyaki" streamed from hidden speakers. *Tiki-tacky*, Tim thought. What, no singing birds like the Enchanted Tiki Room at Disneyland?

"Excuse me," he said to the young hostess dressed in a vibrant sarong.

"Yes?" A smile lit her face. It always did when he talked to a girl. They liked him. Since they didn't know him it had to be his looks. Lucky.

"My name's Bill Keller," he flashed the card; it was starting to fray around the edges. "Do you know this woman?"

She looked at Mary's picture. "I've seen her around."

"Do you know anyone she hung out with?"

"No, I don't think so."

"Maybe a guy named Ken Dorsey. Six feet, broad shouldered, wide face. Brown hair. Dresses like he belongs in this place, Hawaiian shirts, pork pie hat, like Sinatra wears."

"Sorry."

He talked with several other women. Even some men. No dice.

A quick trip home. Shower, shave. Then a drive to Trader Vic's, where he went through the routine again. Mary had liked tiki joints and mai tais. They weren't really Tim's cup of tea. He'd rather take dates to Scandia or Tail o' the Cock for Welsh Rarebit. But if tiki joints were where Mary wanted to go that was okay with him.

But the tiki joints turned up zip.

Same thing the next day and the next and on the weekend.

He hadn't been to work in a week. Was now into his vacation time, having used up his sick days. Fuck it!

He drove down to the Santa Monica Pier. The dividing line between L.A. and Santa Monica had been marked by a layer of low hanging clouds. He'd felt a couple of droplets of water hit his cheek in the open Spyder. It was like going from one world to another. Surreal, like in that movie *Carnival of Souls*. Was he in some kind of purgatory without knowing it like the woman in that flick?

He watched the moms and kids dance in and out of the water. Grabbed a quick lunch at Sinbad's on the pier. Walked down to the end, staring off into the ocean, to distant shores. At the horizon, he saw Mary's face. Mary's eyes. They never left him. And never left him alone.

Who the fuck is that guy, Dorsey?

Where can I find him?

How?

He bought a paper. Mary Singleton's murder was on page five now. Still no leads. He crumpled the paper, threw it into the ocean, headed down the heavy wood-plank steps to the sand. The briny tang of the water stung his nose. He kept walking and walking.

A crowd of kids surrounded a roped off area on the sand. Television cameras inside the wire. A rock band playing—lip syncing. All those kids with their Moe Howard, er, Beatle haircuts.

"What's going on?" he asked one of the longhairs.

"They're filming *Where the Action Is*. It's a TV show."

"Who's the band?"

"Paul Revere and the Raiders. Dig it."

"I dig Elvis. Sinatra."

"Who?"

Tim stumbled off in the soft sand, heading south, dodging waves, passing Pacific Ocean Park, finally coming to Windward Avenue, Venice's main drag. Cars slanted into diagonal parking spaces. The arched colonnade along the building fronts looked like Hollywood's version of Venice, Italy—everything in L.A. looked like Hollywood's version of somewhere. And in fact that's what they were supposed to be. Abbott Kinney built Venice of America around the turn of the century, complete with canals. He had high hopes for his Venice, and wanted high culture, a cultural renaissance. Now the buildings were decaying and most of the canals had been filled in. The ones that were left were in bad shape. Venice used to be the Coney Island of the Pacific, now it was a flophouse, and a shooting gallery, for beatniks and hippies. It was so decrepit that Orson Wells used it in his movie *Touch of Evil* to double for that sinkhole Tijuana on the Mexican border. Kinney must be rolling over in his grave.

Fog serpentined through the colonnades. Bars' neon lights cast spooky iridescent glows. Tim saw himself in the plate glass window of one of the bars. His face still unlined, good hairline. No shadows or bags under the eyes, well maybe a little but only as of the last couple of weeks. But in the eerie, flashing neon he looked like something out of a horror movie and, though whole on the outside, he felt like Dorian Gray rotting on the inside.

He wished he had someone he could talk to, share his thoughts with. Maybe get some ideas how to proceed. But he was alone—totally alone.

He considered going to the cops. But they'd probably finger him for the murder, especially once they found out he was selling info from the DMV. Nope, Sgt. Joe Friday wouldn't give him a chance. They had no leads and they liked to tie things up nice, neat and tidy, even if they got the wrong guy. And that wrong guy might be him. Nope, the cops were out.

IX

Three weeks chasing every lead he could think of. Back to Sheila's four times, Mrs. Singleton's twice. Checking everything and everyone they told him about. Interviewing them. Hanging out at Trader Vic's and Don the Beachcomber's until last call, hoping to run into Dorsey. He might as well have really been a detective. Should have been, because on Monday of the fourth week he got a call from Richard Dale.

"Yeah, Rich, I've been meaning to call you."

"I'm sure you have. I'm also sure you've been meaning to get me a doctor's note like I've asked for several times."

"Yeah, I will. I promise."

"Don't bother. You're being let go. Since you won't deign to join us at the office you'll be getting a pink slip in the mail."

"But—"

There were no buts. He was out of a job.

* * *

Tim sat at the bar in Don the Beachcomber's, Hawaiian music swirling in the background. Without a job his finances were draining as fast as the mai tai in his hand. He didn't even care about picking up women, which didn't mean they didn't catch his eye. Mostly he thought about drowning—walking out into the Pacific. He pictured the scene from that Frederic March movie, *A Star is Born*, where he walks out into the ocean, out and out and out, until he drowns, on an endless loop in his mind.

Every sip of his drink stirred up a memory. Boating with his grandparents in MacArthur Park, then called Westlake Park. Going to Kip's Toy Store in the Farmer's Market with his mom. The time his father took him to his first baseball game—before the Dodgers even came out to L.A. It was the Hollywood Stars, at Gilmore Field on Beverly Boulevard. Triple A ball. But fun, maybe even more fun than the pros. His first girlfriend, Susie. His first kiss, behind the spook house ride at Beverly Park Kiddieland, with a girl who worked there.

What the hell had become of him? He'd been voted most likely to succeed in high school. But he wanted to have fun, not work. The easy way out his father had said—always the easy way. Look what it got him.

Something caught his eye. The sharp light from the restroom illuminating a man in a Hawaiian shirt, just exiting.

"Jesus H. Christ."

The man headed for the front door, Tim close behind him. If that wasn't Dorsey, Dorsey didn't exist. Same build. Same hair. Tim's knees caved—too much rum and curaçao. The door swung closed. A hostess helped him up. He steadied himself. Hobbled out the door. A candy apple red car pulled away from the curb, one of those jazzy new Ford Mustangs, leaden gray smoke trailing from its muffler. Dorsey at the wheel. Tim squinted at the license plate, California, but it was too dark to read the numbers and letters and soon the Mustang was lost in a sea of other cars.

Damn!

"Who was that guy?" Tim shouted at the valet.

"What guy?"

"Guy who just drove off in the red Mustang."

"I dunno. Good tipper though."

"You seen him before?"

"He's been in a couple-a times. Don't know his name."

"Know anything—anything at all about him?"

"Nada."

Another valet brought up the Spyder. Tim jammed into his car, tore into traffic to the sound of honking horns. He sped down McCadden, burning rubber onto Hollywood Boulevard, zipping in and out of traffic—sideswiping a Caddie parked on the side of the road. He didn't even care about the scratch he knew would be on the Spyder, and cared even less about the Caddie.

Shit, which way had Dorsey gone? He drove around Hollywood and Beverly Hills, circling. Looking for that damn candy apple red car.

At one thirty in the morning, just before last call, he headed back to Don the Beachcomber's, talked to the hostess and bartender. They looked at him funny and claimed they didn't know Dorsey from Adam.

He slunk home and into bed to the droning sound of the test pattern. Got out of bed in the morning to see an envelope under his door. He didn't have to look at it. He knew it was an eviction notice.

He downed a slug of Jack D, watching the second hand on the clock tick by, as if in slow motion. Waiting until nine o'clock. At nine o'five he dialed the office.

"Nate."

"Yeah. Tim, that you?"

"Listen, Nate, you gotta do me a favor."

"You're persona non grata around here, buddy."

"I'm persona non grata everywhere," Tim said.

"At first Dale wanted you back. Now he just—anyway, whaddaya need?"

"I need you to run a plate for me."

"I could get fired."

"It's not really a plate. I don't have a license. Just need a list of all the red Mustangs with California plates."

"What? Are you crazy?"

"Getting there, buddy. Getting there."

X

Nate took a little persuading but he came through. Tim now had a list of every Mustang in California. Popular new car. The list could keep him busy for ages. He divided it into locales. He started with Santa Monica and L.A. City, then county, then Ventura and Orange Counties. He crossed off all female names. Looked at every man who was within the age range of Dorsey. Who had his hair color. There were hundreds. He set out to knock on all their doors. It was futile and turned up nothing.

He hung out at Don the Beachcomber's and Trader Vic's at night, even after he'd had to sell the Spyder.

A man in a loud voice and louder shirt was holding court at Vic's.

"Hey, Mister," Tim said.

The man in the Hawaiian shirt turned around. Not Dorsey. Damn, he sure looked like Dorsey from behind. They all did. And none of them ever were.

He never stopped looking, but he never saw Dorsey again. At least not the S.O.B. that met him at Jack's. But every man in a Hawaiian shirt was Dorsey...until he turned around. Every man in a pork pie hat was Dorsey...until he got a close-up of his face. And in Los Angles there were a lot of men in Hawaiian shirts, and plenty in pork pie hats. Dorsey was a phantom, the delusion of an obsessed mind. He was everyone and no one, everywhere and nowhere. Just like Tim.

XI

Venice Beach, California—1965

He might never find Dorsey, but he could always find Mary in a joint he copped from one of the hippies on the beach. He saw her face in the smoke or the haze from the dope. Young and pretty, with those striking blue eyes, as it always would be. As he aged day by day, fading with each day, she remained the same. And he'd wish he could go back and change things. Do it over again. Give her her life back. But he knew he couldn't.

He'd think about how they could have gotten together. Gotten that house in the Valley, with the green grass and kidney-shaped pool in the backyard. A couple-a rug rats running around. Sometimes he could stay on that street, in that house for hours at a time. If he worked it, days. That was the place he liked best.

Tim stumbled up the beach, squinted against the glaring golden hour Venice sun. He eyed himself in the plate glass window. Long, stringy hair. Paisley shirt. Bell-bottoms and boots. He looked just like one of those hippies now, though he didn't feel much like one on the inside. Still, they had become his friends. His only friends. He hung with them on the beach, smoked their dope. Shared their food.

An image flashed across the plate glass. Tim jerked around. Darted after the man in the Hawaiian shirt. Dorsey. Another guy in green and white baggies. Dorsey. He lurched after another man in cutoffs and sandals. Dorsey. Everyone was Dorsey. Ghosts of Dorsey snaked through his vision. Every little floater in his eyes, on the periphery of his vision: Dorsey.

He saw Dorsey around every corner. Under every bed, if he ever had a bed to look under anymore.

Dorsey was everywhere.

And Dorsey was nowhere. A shadow.

Always with him—like Mary.

A ghost that haunted him.

If he had a choice he'd rather live with the ghost of Dorsey than the ghost of Mary. It was less torturous.

Tim joined his hippie buddies on the beach. They passed joints and a bota bag of wine. And when the crimson knife of the sun sliced the horizon and the fog rolled in, he walked down the shore, past the Del Mar Beach Club, and over to the oil derricks where Orson Wells filmed that *Late, Late Show* movie *Touch of Evil*.

A forest of gantries reached skyward, ticking like an army of crazed crickets. Tangled metal beams, America's answer to the Eiffel Tower.

Tim dodged pools of black, slimy oil, fields of muck, crawled under Derrick #7, his home. He reached into the grimy pocket of his jacket, gently pulled out a wax paper sandwich bag and slipped the picture of Mary from it. The utility light on the dilapidated rig shed just enough light for him to see her face— her eyes. He stared at her until his eyes went blurry. Slipped it back into the wax paper and gently returned the little bag to his pocket. Dragged some newspapers up over his body and let the tick-tocking of the well lull him to sleep. Each tick and each tock a life sentence.

PANDORA'S BOX

John Shepphird

September 1983—Los Alamos, New Mexico

Brooke thought there was nothing much to see in Atomic City—a mundane supermarket, gas station and video rental store among a smattering of suburban homes. The VW bus puttered through the town. She shared the back seat with June. Daryl drove and Vic rode shotgun.

There was a fence and guard shack at the main gate of the Los Alamos National Laboratory. Daryl gave it a long look before he spun a U-turn. He explained how the Manhattan Project was developed here. "This place was personally chosen by Oppenheimer to be a top-secret city."

"Who's Oppenheimer?" asked Brooke.

"The father of the atomic bomb," said Daryl.

With the exception of the canyons, mountain pines and view of the Sangre de Cristo Mountains, this could be a small town in her home state of North Carolina.

Two hours later the foursome watched hidden in the trees as Dr. Lundquist pulled his Chrysler LeBaron into the driveway of his home. He got out and went to the mailbox. The man wore a short sleeve, button-down shirt and high-water Dockers. He was in his early-thirties and Brooke imagined he would have been much older.

"Is that the dude?" Vic asked, studying through binoculars.

Daryl checked against the photo in his hand. "Looks like it."

Dr. Lundquist thumbed through his mail and went inside.

Later that day, as the sun set over the Black Canyon Campground in the Santa Fe National Forest, they practiced their heist.

"No, that's wrong," Daryl said. "You're the bump. Everything relies on the set up."

"How am I doing it wrong?" Brooke asked. She really wanted to get this right.

"You can't be afraid to get physical," Daryl said. "Press your ass up in there. Feel the heat of his body."

Playing the victim in the rehearsal, Vic tipped his straw cowboy hat at her with a smile. Meanwhile June waited for her cue. Daryl put a loving arm around Brooke and led her over to Vic. "Get in there," he said, "distract this guy enough so I can hook." With his other hand, Daryl lifted a hard plastic nametag out of Vic's back pocket. "And then I'll pass," he said just as June walked behind him. She grabbed the badge and walked off. "Say our mark feels something. If he does, and turns to me, well..."

Vic feigned reaching into his back pocket with surprise before playfully confronting Daryl, grabbing him by the collar, fist raised. Daryl turned his palms up and said, "Got nothing, pal."

June victoriously held up the prize, a wry smile on her face.

"It has to feel natural," said Daryl. "Bump, hook, pass. That's how a whiz mob works."

"I'll get it," Brooke said, hopeful that she would. The smile Daryl gave her basked her in warmth. Brooke had crushes on boys in high school but Daryl was her first true love. He was so charismatic, and all she wanted was to share every moment and be at his side. He listened to her. Nobody had ever done that.

With a Bic lighter, Vic lit a joint. He got it going and passed it to June.

Brooke asked Daryl, "In the movies why are pickpockets just one guy?"

"That's mostly fiction," Daryl said, "but this is how it's really done, as a team. The Gypsies in Europe never work single-handed, and they're the best in the world." Daryl stepped over and took the joint from June. "Consider this is your first class in the School of Seven Bells," he said before taking a toke.

"What's that?" asked Brooke.

"Mythical pickpocket academy," said Vic.

"Really?"

Daryl nodded.

"Why seven bells?"

Vic explained, "Bells clipped on the practice mark. If one rings, the student fails."

As Daryl held smoke in his lungs he managed to utter, "We'll work on it until you get it right."

June asked, "What's the big deal with this guy's badge, anyway?"

Daryl exhaled and passed the cigarette to Vic. "It's his key to the kingdom. We lift the thing and put it in that case for a while," he said pointing to a black briefcase set away from the campsite and leaning against a gnarled pinion tree, "and it will change the color of the film on his badge. We slip it back without him knowing and the Los Alamos National Laboratory will think he got nuked."

Vic said, "We don't need no stinkin' badges," in a voice mimicking the Mexican desperado from the movie *The Treasure of Sierra Madre.*

Daryl and June laughed. Brooke had never seen the movie and didn't get it. Daryl said, "He's some kind of subatomic-particle mathematical genius. Taking him out of whatever project he's working on is our client's goal."

"Who's our client?"

"A man by the name of Sam. That's all I know," Daryl replied. "Let's try again."

* * *

Boulder, Colorado

"I don't want your sandwich, lady" he said, blond dreadlocks dangling under a ratty knit cap, "but if you can help me out with a few bucks that would be greatly appreciated." The young man held a cardboard sign that read "We're hungry" next to a bowl—loose change inside. A drowsy Labrador with a bandana as a collar lounged on the pavement nearby.

"You don't want it?" Ellen said, holding out the wrapped deli sandwich.

"We need bus fare."

Ellen doubted a dog would be allowed on a bus. "Are you sure?"

"Just trying to get home."

She was standing at the crosswalk just outside campus. The young man sat strategically positioned near the signal button. Ellen put the turkey sandwich back in her bag, one of the few she ordered at the bakery while picking up the cake.

He jiggled his bowl, egging her on.

Ellen thought he was far too young and able-bodied to be begging on the street. She suspected if she gave him money it would go towards booze or drugs. Boulder had that kind of reputation—the university deemed a party school. It had given her pause when her daughter decided to attend college there. In Brooke's senior year she'd fallen in with a new set of friends and that concerned her too. And doing Brooke's laundry one day, she'd found a pot pipe in the pocket of her jeans. But Dartmouth and Tulane had that kind of reputation, and they were good schools. It went with the territory.

The light turned green and she crossed Broadway. "Have a nice day," he said flippantly, and then under his breath, "thanks for nothing."

Today was Brooke's birthday and Ellen had come to surprise her. She'd caught a flight out of Raleigh, rented a car and walked into the campus. She dodged a few students playing a game of Ultimate Frisbee.

It was two months ago that she'd helped Brooke move into the dorm and remembered where it was. She found Elliott Hall and climbed the stairs to the second floor. At Brooke's door she knocked. Her roommate Sara answered. Ellen didn't see her daughter. Instead a petite Asian girl sat at Brooke's built-in desk.

"Hey Sara," said Ellen. "It's Brooke's birthday and I've come to surprise her."

"Mrs. Connor," Sara said, surprised. "I, uh..." She stammered before she said, "Brooke moved out."

Ellen could see that all of Brooke's things were gone; the drapery treatment they'd bought, her flowery bedspread.

The Asian girl eyed her with concern.

"Where'd she go?"

"I don't know," said Sara. "It was weird. She didn't say anything and then split."

"When?"

"A few weeks ago."

That didn't make sense. Ellen had just spoken to her daughter two days ago. She didn't mention that she'd moved out of her dorm.

Sara went on, "I came back one day and all of her stuff was gone. Nobody knows where she went, not even the RA down the hall."

"A few weeks ago?" Ellen asked.

"Yeah."

Ellen thought about the phone conversations she'd had with Brooke. In the beginning of the semester she'd offered various details about freshman life, the dorm food and classes, but in the last few weeks there had been less and less of that. If anything, Brooke had been much more aloof and had often cut the calls short. Ellen felt awkward standing there with the boxed cake in hand.

Her next stop was the administration office. She stood at the Student Affairs window as a pale, bespectacled young man said,

"It appears she dropped out three weeks ago." He shuffled papers inside a file folder.

"That doesn't make sense."

He pulled out a document and handed it over. "Is this your daughter's Social Security number?"

Ellen examined and confirmed.

"Then it's her."

"She would have told me."

"It happens all the time, students dropping out and not telling their parents." He found a receipt and showed her. "The university returned her tuition and housing fee pro-rated for the time she was in the dorm."

"I don't understand," Ellen said. "This has to be a mistake. The fees were returned?"

He pushed up his glasses and squinted at the paper, "By check, made out to Brooke Connor."

Next Ellen marched to the Campus Police. She told an officer at the counter the issue and she seated her in a conference room. Two officers met with her. Nelson was in his mid-thirties and athletic. Lieutenant King was the polar opposite, hefty beer gut hanging over his tooled-leather belt. King asked, "When was the last time you spoke with her?"

"Two days ago. She never said she dropped out."

"Has there been any conflict between you two?"

"No." Ellen got the impression he didn't believe her.

"Her father?"

"We're divorced," Ellen said. "Brooke's father is not part of her life. He hasn't been for many years."

"At all?"

It pained her to say, "He lives in Boca Raton and has another family now."

"Could she have gone to him?" asked Officer King.

Ellen swallowed hard. "The last time Brooke saw her father was over ten years ago. He stopped sending Christmas gifts and birthday cards long ago. He's a ghost."

"Is Brooke mad at you for any reason?" Nelson asked.

"No. She has been a little more distant, but we're not fighting."

"What do you mean by *distant*?"

"I don't know. In the last few weeks she seemed preoccupied. I asked her if everything was okay and she said she was fine."

"Is she romantically involved?"

"Not that I know of."

King asked, "Was there anyone back home she may have gone to see? Or was she homesick in any way?"

"She had friends from school but most of them went off to college themselves. Brooke was accepted to Vanderbilt but she chose the University of Colorado because of the skiing."

King and Nelson shared a knowing look before Nelson explained, "Every year there's a number of students that start the semester but once it starts snowing take off and find employment as lift operators and burger flippers up at the resorts."

"They become ski bums," Lieutenant King said. "We see it all the time."

"Brooke would have told me. She was a good student in high school, too smart to drop out. And it's not snowing yet, right?"

King said, "This town has many distractions. We've got Buddhist Temples, Transcendental Meditation, Hare Krishnas...did she speak of anything of a spiritual nature?"

"No."

"You mentioned money was missing," King said.

"We'd paid for the fall semester and put down a deposit for the spring. The school confirmed they refunded it by check." She explained how Ellen's late mother had passed down the money to be used for Brooke's education and Ellen combined it with her own savings. "Before she started school we set up a bank account in her name."

"A lot of money at a teenager's disposal," King said.

"Yes, but the sooner we established Brooke as a resident of Colorado, the sooner she could apply for in-state tuition. Proof includes a driver's license and a bank account."

The cops shared a look before Lieutenant King said, "I'm sorry, but there's nothing we can do. Your daughter is an adult and can legally make her own decisions. The money is technically in her name and since you spoke with her recently she's not necessarily a missing person."

Nelson added, "Consider going home and waiting by the phone until she calls again."

Ellen thanked them and walked back to her rental car feeling nauseous.

To go back home and wait by the phone? Was that her only option? She needed to find Brooke and made the decision not to go back to North Carolina. She'd call the phone company and have them forward her calls.

The job came as a referral a few weeks before Daryl met Brooke. He learned about it from a lawyer who got an old friend out of a Possession with Intent to Distribute charge. The defense attorney knew a guy who knew a guy that had a lucrative opportunity for someone with Daryl's special skill, no questions asked.

The meeting was set at the historic Broadmoor hotel in Colorado Springs amid the mountain foothills below famed Pike's Peak. Daryl avoided the valet and self-parked. He was clearly underdressed for the place in torn jeans and a ratty Rolling Stones T-shirt.

Daryl met Sam Unger in the hotel bar with a view of the golf course. Sam appeared to be the country club type, middle-aged with paunch, but broad-shouldered and seemingly fit, ex-military as far as he could tell. He sipped coffee, asked Daryl what he preferred. Daryl ordered a Lowenbrau.

After questions that were clearly aimed at sizing Daryl up, Sam got down to business "There have been accidents at the Los Alamos National Laboratory over the years and they take safety very seriously. If anyone working at the lab is exposed to

34

a level of radiation deemed unsafe they're no longer allowed to work there."

"Radiation?" Daryl questioned.

"Exposure over time becomes a health hazard. It's the same for radiologists and X-ray technicians. Think of it as a sunburn, but on the inside."

"A burn that never goes away," Daryl said.

"Unfortunately, that's right. There is vested interest to keep Dr. Lundquist out of New Mexico."

"What would that be?"

"To delay the project he has been hired to lead. Taking him out will temporarily accomplish that."

"Temporarily?"

"Eventually they'll realize he hasn't been exposed, but it will some take time. Or he may never return. I'm not entirely certain what this project is, but I understand it has something to do with fusion."

"The nuclear reaction of joining of atoms," Daryl vaguely remembered that in high school science class, "as opposed to fission which is breaking them apart."

"Apparently so. The client is offering two hundred thousand dollars."

Daryl was blown away but tried not to show it. He sipped his beer and asked, "Who's the client?"

"I'm not at liberty to say."

"Why not?"

"It's a liability for both of us."

"Why the cloak and dagger?"

"It's the way it has to be."

"I don't work for someone unless I know who they are."

Sam shifted his weight before he said, "You're welcome to not take this job. Nobody is stopping you, and no hard feelings."

Daryl needed to hear more and said, "Go on."

"As the broker on this deal my fee is fifteen percent. If you agree, you'll be paid in stages, first a ten-thousand-dollar retainer and then a fee for successfully taking Lundquist's security badge and returning it to him undetected. A final payment will be made if Lundquist is taken off the project."

The sheer idea of that amount of money put Daryl back on his heels. He figured he could pay the crew a pittance and walk away with a small fortune. No more lifting wallets from middle-aged conventioneers. No more home burglaries, hot prowls and the stress of fencing stolen goods.

Sam explained the mechanics of the heist included "a briefcase with traces of plutonium in order to taint the badge." He assured as long as the case was not left open for an extended period of time he'd be "entirely safe."

It was only because Sam had the cash retainer with him that Daryl took the job. Sam explained he'd be given the briefcase later. "Let me know where you'll be and we'll deliver it to you when it's ready. I understand you follow the Grateful Dead," Sam said.

"That's right."

"It just so happens, Dr. Lundquist is a big fan and they'll be performing in September in Santa Fe. I'm betting he wouldn't miss the show. He saw every performance in Boston when he attended MIT."

"And he'd have this security badge on him?" asked Daryl.

"Lundquist carries it at all times."

The pair of Santa Fe performances were not news to Daryl. It was true, he had been following The Dead on and off over the years. As long as he was smart about keeping his drugs stashed, the roaming caravan allowed him a method of slipping in and out of towns. He and his crew picked pockets and burglarized homes before moving on. Jewelry stolen in Ohio and fenced in California was virtually untraceable.

Over the last few months they'd taken a break from the road and Vic and June were chilling out in Boulder because The Dead would play Red Rocks in a few weeks. From there, they'd already planned on falling in with the tie-dyed pilgrims on the trek down to New Mexico.

Daryl took the eight thousand, five-hundred-dollar retainer—ten grand minus Sam's fifteen percent.

With his newly acquired cash he felt like treating himself. The majority of Dead enthusiasts preferred marijuana and psychedelics. Cocaine was Daryl's favorite. It made him the king of the world—but it was expensive. He knew a guy in Denver and bought an ounce.

The money also afforded Daryl a stay at the Hilton Harvest House, a full-service hotel steps from the University of Colorado campus in Boulder. On Friday afternoons, the hotel hosted a popular courtyard happy hour with live music and that's where he met Brooke. She had a great body and liked to party. Daryl had money to spend and time to kill so Brooke was a welcome distraction. They holed up for days in his hotel room snorting coke and having sex.

He liked that he could control her.

One day, when Brooke was in class there was a knock at the door. Sam delivered the briefcase and said, "Whatever you do, don't lose this." He handed Daryl an envelope, "After you've completed the task you'll deliver the briefcase to this location, alone. Is that understood?"

"Got it," Daryl said. He couldn't believe how heavy the briefcase was. Sam explained how it was armored with lead.

"Good luck."

As the Red Rocks date approached, Daryl convinced Brooke to drop out of school and join him on the road. Even better, she agreed to pull her money out of the bank and give it to him for safe-keeping.

He bought even more coke.

Daryl, Brooke, Vic and June attended all three nights of the Grateful Dead performances at Red Rocks Amphitheatre. The plan was to follow the band to New Mexico for this pickpocket job and then continue from show to show which included one in Austin and Madison Square Garden in New York City. Ultimately they'd drive back across the country for the band's hometown Halloween performance at Marin County Veteran's Auditorium in San Rafael, California.

Vic was hesitant to bring a new member into their crew. Daryl convinced him it was only fair. Vic and June were a couple and Daryl deserved a companion too. Daryl had a history of party girls that tagged along. He realized somewhere down the road he'd get bored with Brooke and find another partner in crime, probably after her money ran out.

In the meantime it turned him on to turn her out.

Pojoaque Pueblo, New Mexico

At the junction of the Los Alamos Highway and Interstate 285 the crew waited for the Chrysler LeBaron outside a general store. Through the loophole of tribal sovereignty, tobacco products could be purchased tax free on reservation land. This establishment sold discount cigarettes by the carton with signs of popular brands displayed in the window.

The plan was to follow Lundquist to The Downs at Santa Fe and tail him throughout the day. When the opportunity presented itself, they'd lift the badge, let it sit in the briefcase for a while and then return it undetected. If getting it back to Lundquist appeared to be too difficult, plan B was to place it on the seat of his car as if it presumably fell out of his pocket. Daryl clearly didn't want to do that.

Brooke was hesitant to be part of this but she couldn't admit it to Daryl. She'd nicknamed the briefcase "Pandora's Box" and said to all, "You know, in Greek mythology Pandora opens the box and releases evil upon the world. Do we really want to do that?"

With edge in her voice, June said, "Total bullshit. Like Eve tempting Adam with the apple, it's always a woman's fault in these stories."

"What are you talking about?" said Vic.

"Femme fatales and witches, it's just a way to marginalize women and blame them for everything wrong in a man's world."

"Enough with your Women's Studies feminist theory bullshit."

"It's true."

"You took one class. What do you know?"

"Don't be a dick."

"Quit your bickering," Daryl said. "You guys are overthinking this. All the bad shit in the world is already out there. All we're doing is putting a little stink on this guy's nametag."

Vic repeated his *Treasure of Sierra Madre* quote, "We don't need no stinking badges."

Brooke had always been superstitious and believed there was a kernel of truth behind mythology. She was mindful not to cross paths with a black cat and careful with mirrors. She made sure not to leave a hat on the bed or open an umbrella indoors. You never know. The Pandora briefcase spooked her.

When June lit a joint Daryl snapped, "No partying until the job's over. We've got to play it cool. We're on a reservation."

"Which means?" she asked.

"Tribal police."

June looked around nervously and said, "Really?"

Brooke didn't like it that Daryl was so stressed out. She yearned for the other Daryl, the one who was fun and affectionate. She wanted to get this over with so they could party at the show and relax. She spotted a pay phone and asked if she could call her mom.

"And tell her what?" said Daryl.

"Just to say hey. It's been a few days since we talked and she's probably worried."

"Let her worry."

"No. She'll be pissed."

Daryl gave in. Brooke dug out the roll of quarters she used for laundry and crossed the clay parking lot to the phone. She noticed the few shacks and adobe structures scattered about—

clearly homes of poor people. Jeans and T-shirts hung out to dry on makeshift clotheslines. Rusty vehicles sat abandoned in the weeds. Home appliances were out on porches and a barefoot toddler chased a squalid dog. It reminded Brooke of the shanty neighborhoods back home in North Carolina. Poverty looked the same everywhere.

It took three dollars in quarters to call home. Her mother picked up on the second ring, "Brooke?"

"Hey Mom."

"Where are you?" she asked, concerned.

"At school."

"They said you dropped out." Ellen explained how she'd come to Boulder as a surprise. Brooke knew she'd have to eventually tell her mom but didn't expect it to be so soon. Ellen asked, "Honey, are you alright?"

"Everything is fine. I'm with friends."

"Who?"

"Just friends."

"Where?"

"New Mexico. We're going to a concert."

"Where are you calling from?"

"A payphone."

"I've been worried sick," Ellen said with emotion building. "What concert? Where are you?"

Daryl leaned on the horn. This startled Brooke. She turned to see the Chrysler LeBaron drive past them.

"I've got to go, mom," Brooke said. "I'll call you later." She hung up. Tears welled in her eyes as she ran back to the van.

Boulder, Colorado

On one hand it was a relief to hear from her daughter, but on the other Ellen was incredibly concerned.

Why had Brooke lied?

The phone company was able to successfully forward calls from North Carolina. At first she'd gone to hotels but those calls would come through a front desk switchboard. That wouldn't work. She needed a dedicated line and found the solution. Ellen paid cash to a pair of graduate students to sleep in their guest room on a lumpy futon, but with its own phone. What she didn't count on were all the cats. Her allergies flared, and she was miserable.

What concert could Brooke be going to in New Mexico?

Ellen called around. The Oak Ridge Boys were playing in Albuquerque. Brooke wouldn't go to that. Through the Chamber of Commerce she learned the Grateful Dead was playing two dates in Santa Fe, starting tonight. That had to be it. From the map she purchased it appeared to be a six-hour drive.

Tesuque Pueblo, New Mexico

Following Lundquist's Chrysler down Interstate 285 it became clear the VW could not keep up. Its 1.6-liter, air-cooled engine was no match for the mighty General Motors V-8. Daryl cursed in frustration.

Brooke tried her best not to cry in front of the others.

"Who's that with him?" asked Vic.

They'd made out a woman in the passenger seat. "Hell if I know," Daryl said, and then to June, "You're going to have to distract her."

"No problem, chief," June said. She dug out a Kleenex and handed it to Brooke.

They reached The Downs at Santa Fe and pulled into the parking lot. Searching for the LeBaron, Brooke spotted it first. "There."

Lundquist and a brunette woman had the trunk open with foldable metal chairs set out, a cooler between them. They were drinking beers, eating a sandwich and sharing a bag of chips.

To Brooke the woman appeared to be studious, thick glasses and hair tied back. They looked like they were tailgating at a North Carolina Tar Heels football game rather than a Grateful Dead concert.

Daryl parked and they all got out.

Brooke recognized a few of the Deadheads they'd seen back in Colorado; the ones Daryl introduced as Peyote Bob, Melissa Rose and Pigpen.

Peyote Bob approached and said, "'Shrooms, hashish, peyote, acid...whatcha need?" This was the same sales pitch Brooke had heard back at Red Rocks.

"We're all set, Bobby," said Vic.

"Got 'ludes, too."

"We'll catch up with you later."

Peyote Bob shifted his eyes and scratched the back of his head before he drifted off.

The way Daryl explained it to Brooke—to afford the travel from show to show you need to either deal or have a trust fund. Dealing was dicey. Sell to an undercover cop and it's jail time. "There are far less risky ventures, if you're smart about it."

Daryl turned to his crew, "Okay, we'll keep an eye on them and look to make our move over by the gate. He's supposed to keep the badge opposite of his wallet, on the right side." He asked Brooke to go to the back of the van and get the briefcase.

She obliged, and couldn't believe how heavy it was. "This thing weighs a ton."

He set it inside the van's sliding door.

They studied Lundquist from afar until he placed the chairs and cooler into the trunk of the Chrysler.

Daryl took Brooke by the arm. "You ready?"

"Yeah." Her heart skipped. She *so* wanted to get this right.

"Stick your hot ass right up in his crotch, just like we practiced."

"Okay," she said.

As Lundquist strolled to the entrance, they followed.

Security guys were checking bags. This crowded the entrance. Daryl kept his arm around Brooke as June and Vic walked on the other side of Lundquist.

When all were at a standstill Daryl whispered, "Now."

Just as she'd practiced, Brooke darted out in front of Lundquist. She raised her arms as if she had spotted someone up ahead. "Lisa!" she shouted to her imaginary friend, jumping up to see over the crowd.

She threw herself back into him. He grunted. She spun, inches away and could smell the beer on his breath. "Oh, I'm so sorry," Brooke said with forced laughter, "I'm such a klutz."

"No problem," he said.

Lundquist's female companion eyed Brooke with daggers. Brooke said to her, "Sorry, but I got separated from my friend." She turned back as if searching ahead. "There she is," and Brooke darted off.

She hadn't seen Daryl. Had he gotten the badge?

Brooke circumvented the crowd by the gate but could not find them. Had they gone in? Brooke returned to the VW to find Daryl and June. From the look on Daryl's face she wasn't sure if it had worked.

"You get it?" she asked.

"We got something," Daryl said. He held up the badge.

"Where's Vic?"

"He followed Lundquist in to see where he's sitting. We're not done yet, one more thing." He handed Brooke the badge. "Go put this in the briefcase."

"You want *me* to do it?" she said.

"It's your initiation."

Brooke could see embossed within the hard plastic security badge there was a photo of Lundquist beside a black chip.

Daryl opened the vehicle's sliding door, "We'll get the tickets. Meet us at the gate," he said and moved on.

Brooke had second thoughts. She knew whatever was in that briefcase was dangerous and could bring bad luck, but she couldn't back out now. The man she loved would be mad at her.

As quickly as she could, Brooke popped open the latches and placed the badge inside. She closed it and stepped back. Had she felt something strange, some sort of evil escaping? She didn't think so, but couldn't tell.

When she met them at the gate the music had already begun. Daryl checked his watch and said, "In a half hour we'll go in, after the badge gets its stink."

She asked, "How dangerous is what's in there?"

"You've got nothing to worry about." Daryl reached into his sock and pulled out a tab. "Take this."

"What is it?"

"Something extra special."

"Will it make me paranoid?"

"It will make you brave."

Again she was hesitant but didn't want to anger him. She'd eaten mushrooms but hadn't dosed LSD.

"Come on," Daryl urged.

She ate the paper and when it was time to retrieve the badge she was starting to feel the effect of the drug. All she wanted to do was to get this over with. Again she opened and closed the briefcase as fast as she could, but this time she thought she'd felt something, her throat tightening. She wondered if it was all in her mind. She wished she hadn't taken the acid.

Walking back to the gate, she could see the color of the chip on the badge had gone from black to a dark red. The distant music beckoned her. Brooke gave the badge to Daryl. He kissed her on the forehead and they entered.

Finally, thought Brooke.

By the time Ellen arrived in Santa Fe the sun had set to a brilliant cobalt blue sky. She found The Downs at Santa Fe racetrack but the show had ended and only a few dozen cars remained in the parking lot. There would be another tomorrow. She hoped

Brooke would be there.

She asked around showing people Brooke's student ID photo. The Dead enthusiasts stuck out like a sore thumbs in their hippie attire and Birkenstocks. Those she asked hanging out in the Santa Fe Plaza offered no help. Ellen needed a place to stay but because of the concert the moderately priced accommodations were all booked. She had no other choice than to check into the historic La Fonda Hotel in the heart of downtown. Surrounded by rustic, adobe architecture she felt like she'd travelled back in time. The accommodations were elegant, the linen plush, but she was so worried about her daughter Ellen barely slept a wink. *Had I been too strict? Where'd this rebellion come from?* All she wanted was to be assured that her child was safe.

Brooke woke inside the VW in her sleeping bag at dawn to the smell of campfire smoke. Much of the show was a blur in her mind. She could remember sitting on an Indian blanket with June and then later driving back to the campsite. Brooke remembered the campfire and the sweet tasting wine she drank from a bota bag. She recalled having sex with Daryl by firelight.

She could see he was up and stoking the fire. This reminded her to dig through her purse for the birth control pill. Brooke pulled on her jeans, joined him and asked, "Did you get that thing back to Lundquist?" she asked.

"You don't remember?"

"No. What was that you gave me?"

"Got it from a dude."

"I don't like blacking out."

He put his arm around her and said, "It took me a while, but mission accomplished."

She stared at the flame and asked, "What do we do now?"

"After the show tonight I'll return the briefcase, collect our money then meet you guys in Austin. Next show is at Manor Downs, another racetrack."

Brooke asked, "What do you think is going to happen to Lundquist?"

"He'll probably freak out," Daryl said, laughing to himself. "Wouldn't you?"

"I guess."

"You did good. You should be proud."

Brooke didn't feel proud, said, "All I did was stick my ass into a guy's crotch." She didn't want to believe the briefcase was Pandora's box.

When Vic and June awoke they all packed up the campsite. Vic said, "Boy Scout rule, leave it better than you found it," and insisted everyone scour the grounds for trash. Brooke found a lone silver and turquoise earring. She cleaned it off with water and wore it, a souvenir from New Mexico. She imagined it had a superstitious power to bring them luck. And since the job was done, she could finally relax.

The big surprise was seeing her mother at the entrance of the show.

"Brooke?"

All Brooke could think to say was, "What are you doing here?"

"You've had me worried sick," Ellen said, tears in her eyes.

Brooke introduced "my mom" to Daryl, Vic and June.

Ellen said, "You need to come back to school."

"But I'm doing this now," Brooke said.

"Doing what?"

Brooke motioned to the others with, "Living my own life."

"Why didn't you tell me? And what have you done with the money?"

"I was gonna." Tears welled in Brooke's eyes.

Ellen took her daughter by the arm. "Let's go home."

"No." Brooke pulled away and went to Daryl's side. "I'm with him now."

Daryl reached out for a shake, pouring on the charm, "Nice to meet you Mrs. Connor. You've raised a wonderful daughter."

Ellen did not shake his hand. She had always imagined that one day Brooke would bring home a young man she'd met in college, a page out of a modern romance novel. She never thought it would be someone so ragged, long-haired and despicable. She said to her daughter, "Brooke, let's go."

"I'm not going back to school. You can't make me."

At that moment Peyote Bob walked past. In his raspy voice he pitched, "Acid, 'ludes, 'shrooms, hashish, whatever you desire I've got the magic fire."

"I'll call the police," Ellen said.

Peyote Bob scurried off.

Daryl said, "We're not doing anything wrong."

Ellen gave Brooke a long, hard look.

Brooke said. "I don't want to go to school anymore."

"But we talked about this," Ellen said.

"No, *you* talked about it. I tried to talk but you wouldn't listen."

"What's that mean?"

"It means I can make my own decisions, and you can't stop me," said Brooke. "College is your dream, not mine."

"Then come home, Brooke."

"No."

Ellen's heart sank. Daryl led her only child to the gate. She wondered at what point had she failed as a mother.

The next day at the Santa Fe Greyhound Bus station Daryl bought the tickets. Brooke pleaded to go along but he explained he had to return the briefcase alone.

"To who?"

"Our client Sam."

After the bus departed, Daryl followed the map and made the three-hour drive to the Whataburger fast food restaurant in Truth or Consequences, New Mexico. The cocaine kept him alert for the drive.

He recognized the Whataburger chain restaurant from its signature A-frame architecture. Sam climbed out of a black Mercury Cougar. Daryl pulled the briefcase out from under the VW's seat.

Daryl said, "The strip on the badge turned dark red, just like you said."

"And Dr. Lundquist had no idea?"

"We had it back in his pocket before the encore."

"We?" asked Sam.

"I mean me. I got it done,"

Sam went to the car and came back with a shoebox. He said, "Don't spend it all in one place."

"When do I get the rest?"

"When Dr. Lundquist is taken off the project I'll follow up with the balance."

"Cool."

Daryl opened the shoebox and it happened in a flash. Sam was suddenly behind him and locked Daryl in a military-style stranglehold. Daryl struggled, kicked at the pavement but the relentless pressure on his carotid arteries made his head spin and weakened him greatly. A gray fog rolled in and Daryl fell. The next sensation was the prick of a needle in his neck before all went black.

Brooke, Vic and June arrived in Austin and checked into a motel on South Congress Avenue with the money Daryl had given them. When Daryl did not meet them at the show, Vic and June feared he'd been arrested. Brooke was optimistic. "He probably just got delayed."

They waited but Daryl never arrived.

The three of them bought bus tickets and travelled to the next Dead show at the Nevada County Fairgrounds in Grass Valley, California. Daryl was not there either.

Brooke was heartbroken. She wondered why he'd betrayed

them. Was it because her mother threatened to call the cops? He'd taken all of her money. She felt like a fool.

Vic and June made plans to steal a car and drive back to Boulder. Brooke wanted nothing to do with that. Instead she called her mother for help. Ellen wired her money for the flight back to Raleigh.

As much as Brooke apologized, Ellen would not forgive her. "Why'd you do it?" Ellen asked.

"Because I loved him."

The movie *Silkwood*, the true story of a nuclear whistleblower and labor union activist, wouldn't be released until the end of the year and when Brooke saw Meryl Streep's horrific shower scene it chilled her to the bone. Would her fate be a radiation-induced cancer that would cut her down? That deep anxiety is what motivated her to go to the police.

They took her story and it escalated to a point where she'd met with men from the FBI and Nuclear Regulatory Commission. Doctors tested her. The results determined there were slight traces of radiation but Brooke's limited exposure was deemed non-harmful.

She wanted to believe them.

She pressed them for details and learned the VW bus had been found at the bottom of a New Mexico canyon, a decomposed Daryl inside.

So he hadn't abandoned her.

Apparently he'd missed the turn and the bus tumbled into the canyon below, hidden in the trees until it was discovered by hikers. She asked about the briefcase and stashed money. Neither had been found. But why was Daryl there? The canyon was nowhere near Truth or Consequences, New Mexico and he would have been travelling in the wrong direction if he was driving to meet them in Texas. It didn't make sense.

"What about Dr. Lundquist?" she asked and learned they tested him for exposure and the results came back negative. Dr. Lundquist returned to work so their big caper had failed. All of it, she thought, was for nothing. She gave the men a description of Vic and June but would never see or hear from them again.

As the years passed, Brooke would go on to attend the University of North Carolina and earn a teaching certificate. She'd get married and have a daughter of her own. Grandmother Ellen would spoil the child.

For Brooke, the thought of that briefcase and the fear of radiation would haunt her. It was made worse from movies like *Pulp Fiction*, *Kiss Me Deadly* and *Repo Man*. All those films had scenes with unexplained briefcases containing some sort of mysterious, deadly bright light. What did it mean?

Someone clearly masterminded the scheme to disrupt Dr. Lundquist's work. Brooke wondered who it could have been and for what purpose. Was it big oil? The Russians? An international conspiracy? Who was this guy Sam that Daryl talked about?

Brooke would also wonder if she'd released the curse that killed her first love by opening Pandora's box.

LOOK YOUR LAST

Colleen Collins

July 9, 1955—Denver, Colorado

The click click of high heels stopped outside the glass-paneled door stenciled with the black letters *Doyle Investigations*. Julie Doyle checked the time on the cream-faced desk clock. Seven-thirty in the evening. Late for a visitor, but then it was Saturday night when people did stupid things that usually included booze and women other than their wives.

The doorknob rattled. "Coming," Julie called out.

Her dad had rarely locked the door, but then few people had wanted to tangle with a beefy Irishman with fists the size of small hams. Heading to the door, she fluffed her short hair off her neck. Damn it was hot. Maybe if her office was on a higher floor she'd get some cool breezes through the open window, but on the fourth floor the best she got this time of year were tepid wisps of air. The metal rotating fan creaked and thrummed, but it was no match for the July heat.

She opened the door, and for a surreal moment, saw her mother's wavy blond hair, sunset-blue eyes.

"You Julie Doyle?" the woman asked. "The private eye?"

Julie's mother faded. In her place stood a woman about five-five, Julie's height. Brassier shade of blond than her mother's hair, muddier blue eyes. She appeared to be peeved, or maybe determined, likely the unfavorable effect of over-plucked

51

eyebrows. She looked dipped in blood, from her scarlet lipstick to her low-cut red halter dress and matching ankle-strap sandals.

"I am. Please come in." The woman strolled inside, her perfume smelling like something that had once been a flower.

Julie closed the door and crossed to the far side of the metal desk, catching the woman's up-down assessment of her simple cotton top, plaid capris, and moccasins. She sat down, shifting the lampshade so the burn spot didn't show, half-ready to apologize for her casual attire. Although she lived in the other room, the office was still a place for business.

"Sorry about your dad, honey."

The words hit hard, but then they always did. It was three years ago this month that her father had been murdered, a ghoulish story resurrected in *The Denver Post* every year this week as the killer had never been found. Never failed that some reporter regurgitated the history of Julie Doyle, nineteen, being the one to find his body in the wee hours on the front lawn of their family home. As always, the article dutifully requested that anyone who had a tip about the murder to call the D.A.'s office. The D.A. had called Julie, as he did every now and then, but she still had nothing to add, just the same story. How she'd woken up after hearing muffled voices outside, went to her parents' bedroom, but only her mom, ill with cancer at the time, was in bed. Not finding her dad in the kitchen or den, Julie had looked outside, saw his body sprawled on the lawn, his face contorted in the moonlight.

From the street below, a male voice yelled something incomprehensible, followed by the sound of breaking glass. Julie put on her best it's-nothing-just-ignore-it look. "Saturday night on Larimer Street," she said with a shrug. "Whattaya gonna do?" Larimer was a Mecca of dive bars. The good part was rents were cheap in this part of town.

The woman fished a silver lighter and cigarette out of her black clutch bag. "I bet it's not easy being a woman in a man's profession."

"It's not easy being a woman in a man's world."

"Touché, honey." The tobacco hissed as she touched the flame to the cigarette tip. "But women are smarter than men when it comes to digging up the truth, right? 'Cause we're quiet like smoke, can seep through cracks, glide under doors. Men? They blast like a furnace, makin' a mess of everything."

"Well, people don't expect a woman to be a PI, which can play in my favor." Julie pushed an ashtray toward her. "What's your name? How can I help you?"

"Sandy." She blew out a stream of bluish smoke. "I think my husband's cheating on me."

"This must be very difficult for you." Words that often triggered tears, but not for Sandy.

"He's a jerk." Shrug of the shoulders. "He'll be at the Rossonian later tonight, probably with some girl. Know the place?"

Julie nodded. The Rossonian Hotel and Lounge was in an area of Denver called Five Points as it sat at a five-corner intersection. The area was also called Harlem of the West because of the predominantly Negro residents who'd been banned from living elsewhere in Denver. Jazz greats like Duke Ellington, Louie Armstrong, and Billie Holliday often performed at the Rossonian, whose doors were open to Negroes and whites alike.

"Can you be there by nine-thirty?"

"Kinda last-minute..."

"Didn't know his plans until an hour ago." Sandy pulled an envelope out of her purse and handed it to Julie. "How's two hundred?"

Excessive, but from the rock on Sandy's ring finger, she could afford it. Made up for two almost-clients this week who'd walked out of Doyle Investigations after learning there was no suit, just a skirt.

"Thank you." Julie slipped the envelope into her desk drawer. "I'll scout out the jazz lounge, follow them afterward. If they leave separately, I'll follow her, try to ID her. Let me get some information." She grabbed a steno pad and pen, asked questions, wrote down Sandy's answers. She was married to Spiro Contos, who owned Spiro's Taverna down in Greek Town. Sandy showed her a black and white photograph of a man in his thirties, dark wavy hair, olive-skinned. *Good lookin', yeah? Like all Greek men, he's a lady charmer. In Greece, that game of charm is called "kamaki," the harpoon used to catch a fish in one swift stroke. He's six foot, acts like he's seven. Always wears his gold Orthodox cross necklace and pinkie ring.*

After Sandy left, Julie dressed in a dark skirt, pink blouse, low-heeled pumps, started to put on lipstick, then paused, staring at her mouth in the mirror. Some bastard had forced her father to drink poison that long-ago night. The D.A. thought it was a signature Smaldone mob hit, because it was neater, quieter than a shooting—*They don't like things messy*—although it was never proven.

She sometimes wondered if her father owed the Smaldones money as his last months had been spent grieving over his dying wife, unable to keep up with mounting medical bills, juggling creditors. She still found cryptic messages he'd written to himself, scrawled on slips of paper or matchbooks. Some she couldn't interpret, like *"2 at 2"* or *"blue tile"*. But one had stood out— *"$4,200"*—because it was the only one with a monetary figure. Did they murder him because he couldn't pay it back?

Maybe she should've left Denver, like her kid brother had, after their mother died. Maybe Julie had stayed and worked at her father's old PI office to honor him, or maybe she'd made it into a shrine that she couldn't leave. Sometimes she wasn't sure who had become the ghost: her father or herself.

Twenty minutes later she parked her dad's '42 blue Chevy on Welton, then walked up the sidewalk past Marie's Records and Gift Shop, the 711 Club, and crossed the street to the triangular brick and stone building, the name Rossonian in sparkling lights over the entrance. Whenever the wooden door to the club opened, cigarette smoke rolled outside, mixing with the stench of car exhaust. Nearby, a crowd cheered at a neighborhood ballpark.

She checked her wristwatch. A few minutes after nine. She could wait outside for his nine-thirty arrival and follow him inside, but she looked conspicuous, being the only woman standing alone.

"Hey, baby, want some company?"

A thirty-ish guy in jeans and a checkered shirt, a pack of cigarettes jammed in the front pocket, slouched next to her, a sloppy grin on a face that let him get by with cheesy come-ons.

"Was supposed to meet someone..." She looked around as if there really was a someone.

"Don't waste your life on no-shows, baby. On this lilac evening, let's enjoy life, kicks, and the music. I'm Jack, by the way."

"Julie."

"What light through yonder window breaks?" He gestured to the lights seen through the round glass in the club door. "It is the jazz, and Juliet is my sun."

"Let me guess. You're a poet?"

"I just struggle to sketch the flow from my mind, baby." He crooked his arm.

He'd obviously been tippling more than a few, and could use a comb through his hair, but otherwise the guy seemed harmless. She folded her arm over his. She'd blend in better with a date.

Moments later, they strolled into the smoke-hazy, piano-banging jazz lounge. To Julie, the women looked like a sea of Sandys—candy-red lips, red polka-dot dresses, scarlet strapless numbers—laughing and dancing with uniformed servicemen and men in plaid ties and suspenders, all careful not to slip on the rust-red-and-teal-tiled floor. The place reeked of booze, cigarettes, and shrimp Creole, the special of the evening. In the center of the room, a woman, her skin bronze against a sultry white dress, played the piano.

They sat at a small table and ordered two beers, fifteen cents a pour. After the drinks arrived, Jack toasted her. "To Juliet. Mind if I call you that?"

"Actually, my mom named me Juliet, but Dad always called me Julie, and the name stuck. He thought Juliet sounded frail, wanted his daughter to grow up strong." She made that last part up. When her mother grew sickly, a teenage Juliet had felt powerless to help her. One day she insisted everyone start calling her Julie because it sounded more grown-up, but really because it sounded stronger, something she couldn't make her mother be again.

"Your old man got that wrong. Juliet was a helluva lot tougher than Romeo. He took poison, she took the dagger. He went all poetic in his last minutes, too. *Eyes look your last, arms take your last embrace*...and on and on, killing time first. But Juliet got *down* to it. *Oh, good, a knife! My body will be your sheath.*"

She felt shaky, took a long, cold swig of beer to calm herself. *Never should've told him my real name's Juliet.* Over the rim of the glass, her gaze caught on a familiar sight. Sandy, in her red halter dress, sitting in a leather-tufted corner booth with a man, light sparking off his gold necklace. The two of them were staring at her.

Ice skittered down her spine. She set down her glass too hard, banging it against the table.

"You okay, baby?" Jack asked.

Sandy disappeared down a hallway. Spiro, in a cream polo shirt and brown trousers, weaved through the crowd toward Julie. He had presence, all right. Looked like an ocean liner crossing a lake. He paused to shake a hand, then continued walking her way, smiling as if she were an old friend. This was crazy. She grabbed her purse to leave, but too late.

"Hello, Julie." The warmth in his voice cooled when he addressed Jack. "Time's up, buddy."

"Guess your date arrived." He grabbed his beer and left. Spiro sat down in Jack's place.

Julie kept her voice low. "What's going on? Your wife—"

He barked a laugh. "No, no. Not wife. Sister-in-law. Not good for me to be seen going into a private eye office. Many people know Spiro." He rolled his Rs like there were four for every one. "Word gets around, could hurt my business." He opened his hands and looked upward as if only God understood Spiro's dilemma.

The piano player pounded a pulsing rhythm while wailing about love gone bad. Spiro leaned closer, put his large hand on hers. His cologne, a heady mix of juniper and leather, cut through the stench of cigarettes and booze.

"Plus I wanted to see how you present yourself in a bar." His smile was all teeth as he looked her up and down. "A chrome-plated knock-out. Exactly what I need for a job. Join me for drinks and I tell you all about it. Keep the two hundred for the trouble I put you through tonight. You get another two for the real job."

The song ended. People clapped.

"I don't like being played," she said.

He looked surprised, as if nobody ever talked to him like that. Then he screwed his eyes up, as if trying to read her thoughts. After a few moments, he said, "Two hundred and fifty dollars."

For four hundred and fifty, she could set aside her grudge. As her father used to say, "Private eyes don't have morals, they have rates."

"One rule," she said.

"And that is?"

"I'm in charge. I'll listen to ideas, maybe ask for your feedback, but I'm in the driver's seat."

After a beat, he clapped his hands together and bellowed a laugh. "I like you, Julie! We are—how they say?—*birds of a feather*. I like driver's seat, too, but for you, I'll be passenger. Hungry?"

"Starved."

"Good! Let's eat, my lovely driver."

Over the next hour, she sat in his corner booth, nursing another beer and eating shrimp Creole while Spiro told her about a man named Bobby who used to deliver fruits and vegetables to Spiro's Taverna in the early mornings. Six months ago, Spiro came to work, discovered the safe in his office had been emptied.

"I'd worked late the night before, so of course it happened earlier that morning, before taverna opened. Told cops it was Andre, my restaurant manager, because only him and me knew safe combination." Spiro blew out a disgusted breath. "But cops made—what's the word?—ah, *chaos*. You know, mess of investigation. Bobby, my one hope for a witness, and cops, they screwed it up. Friends said cops made Bobby think he was guilty! So stupid."

He reached for the crusty loaf of bread, looked around the table with a scowl. "They serve bread but won't spent fifty cents on a good bread knife. Lucky that Spiro lives in a kitchen." He pulled out a knife, snapped it open. Light played on the long blade. "Fish knife, but good for everything." He sliced off a hunk of bread.

"How much money did your manager steal?"

"I don't know…a thousand, maybe two." He put away his knife. "So cops scared Bobby, and he stop deliveries. Won't answer my calls. Went to his house, no answer. I just want to know if he saw Andre, or his car. If not, okay. But if he saw Andre, I have my witness. Then I hire a lawyer, who takes my case to D.A. Your job? Help set up meeting for Bobby and me."

She'd met people like Spiro. They'd been screwed over, needed help righting a wrong. As for Bobby, cops could've scared him, or maybe he just didn't want to get involved in somebody's legal case. She'd dealt with her share of reluctant witnesses. Just like Spiro's experience, they'd refuse her calls, not answer their door.

"Sure," she said. "I'll try to set up a meeting."

"Wonderful!" He squeezed her hand. "First, we finish eating. Then, pretty lady, I escort you to your car, tell you my idea."

Twenty minutes later, they left the Rossonian. Breezes

brushed past them, carrying scents of barbecue and cabbage from the Yuye Cafe down the street. Cars streamed past, filling the night with fragments of laughter and music. Spiro put his hand protectively on her back as they walked.

"Bobby once told me he likes going to a bar in Central City on Mondays, his day off. Here's my idea. You flirt with him, invite him outside—beautiful girl like you, he'd follow you any-where—and I finally get my chance to talk with him."

"What if he's not there? I always have a backup plan."

"We go back the next Monday."

They crossed the street to her car. Trees cast deep shadows across the closed storefronts. An overhead streetlight spotlighted a gash of rust on the hood.

"Needs paint job." He eyed a cracked side mirror. "Maybe time to trade her in."

"I'm not ready for that. It was...my dad's car."

Spiro paused, leaned against a tree trunk, his dark silhouette speckled with moonlight. From the angle of his head, she could tell he was watching her.

"I read that article," he said.

"Along with the rest of Denver." She looked up at the moon. "God, I hate July. Another ghoulish story in the paper. The D.A. wanting to revisit the voices I heard that night, do I recall footsteps, maybe a car engine? The worst is the night when I see the moon as my father last saw it—the man in the moon, almost sliced in half. Hurts like hell, but in a strange way, it brings me closer to him. Like I'm sharing his last moments, I guess." She swallowed, hard. "I've never told anyone that. Guess I'm tired. It's late."

Spiro stepped closer, captured her hands and pulled her closer, placed her palms flat against his chest. Through his shirt, she felt his heart pumping, steady and strong.

"I want you." His voice, husky and low, reverberated through her.

Hazy moonlight slanted across his face, not enough to clearly see his features, but enough to see the line of his jaw, the mass of his shoulders. A melancholy swept over her, as unsettling as the prickly summer breezes. For too long she'd felt like a ghost in her own life. She wanted to be alive again, to feel. She raised her head, parted her lips...

A shriek jolted her from the haze of arousal. A drunken couple stumbled past them on the sidewalk. The girl shrieked another laugh that turned into a raspy scream as she lost her balance and pitched forward toward the cement sidewalk. Spiro lunged, caught her, helped her back to her feet.

The couple offered slurred thanks before staggering off into the night.

"I don't like women who can't hold their booze. If I had not been here, she would have cracked her silly head open on the cement. Dead. Just like that."

Spiro pulled a pack of cigarettes from his pocket, offered Julie one, clicked open his gold lighter. The diamond in his pinkie ring sparkled in the periphery of the flame as he lit their cigarettes.

Her nerves were jangled after that drunken episode. Her body was still shaking from what had preceded it. She dragged smoke into her lungs, blew it out, needing to regain her own equilibrium. "What's the name of this bar in Central City?"

"Earl's"

It jogged a memory. "Heard it has ties to the Smaldones."

He snorted in disgust. "Bunch of thugs. Got their start running booze during Prohibition, no surprise they still dip their dirty hands in local bars. Gambling, mostly. But you'll be fine there, it's a public place."

Occasional news stories popped up about the police busting a Smaldone gambling ring, bookmaking or loansharking operation, but charges were usually dismissed for insufficient evidence. Many Denver citizens were amused by the Smaldones, viewing them as small-time gangsters. Clyde Smaldone, who headed the mob family, had even been called a "gentleman" by arresting officers and acquaintances alike, including the state governor.

But Julie had heard darker stories from her father about the Smaldones being ruthless killers. Once they shot a man, inches from his face, with a shotgun for double-crossing them. Nevertheless, some people were in awe of the Smaldones. Because they donated so much money to the Roman Catholic church, they had earned the privilege to carry the statue of St. Rocco through the streets of Denver. They also gave money and groceries to those in need, from orphanages to families.

A cold realization seeped through her skin, settled like ice in the pit of her stomach. After her dad's death, gifts of food, sometimes money, had been left at their house. Nineteen-year-old Julie, battered with grief, had been struggling to be a parent to her kid brother, a nurse to her dying mother. She numbly accepted whatever was left for them. Once she caught sight of a green pickup truck as it drove away, the driver, maybe late forties, wiry dark hair shot with gray. There'd been a red lion, the symbol embraced by Italians in North Denver, painted on the truck tailgate. It had looked like a business name painted on the driver's door, but she hadn't been able to read it from that distance.

"Did Bobby drive a green pickup truck on his deliveries?" she asked.

"Yes."

"Red lion on the back?"

"Think so. Why?"

"Thought I saw it parked outside a restaurant once," she lied. "If I were to see it parked near the bar on Monday, I'd know for sure he's there."

Spiro had just confirmed that it was Bobby who'd dropped off the gift of food and money that day, and probably other days, too, as the vegetables, fruits, even the amounts of money were similar. Gifts from the Smaldones. The bastards pretending to care about Max Doyle's wife and kids.

But no gift could salvage their fractured world. Her mom gave up fighting her cancer, let it have its way. Her kid brother started hanging out with a rough crowd, racked up assault and theft charges, could've ended up at the Lookout Mountain School for Boys if a judge hadn't felt sorry for the boy whose father had been murdered. Julie could barely keep herself together, much less her family. Sometimes the only thing that kept her going was the hope to one day find her father's killer. After three long years, maybe that day had come.

A plan began forming in her mind.

They reached Central City around five Monday afternoon. Once Colorado's oldest, and most famous, mining camp, it now attracted tourists and opera buffs who traveled from all over the state to the Central City Opera House. They drove down Eureka Street, a winding street flanked by stone and red brick buildings that housed restaurants, lodges, a gas station. Green hills rose in the distance. Gray, swollen rain clouds hovered overhead. Afternoon storms were common in the mountains.

Spiro pulled his two-tone Chevy Bel Air next to Mine's Hotel. "Earl's is right around the corner. I'll be parked at the end of Eureka, behind that old mine shaft."

Today he wore a short-sleeve shirt covered with tiny, flighty bluebirds, all of them overpowered by the hefty cross around his neck. She leaned over and kissed him. "See you in twenty or so."

"With your classy chassis, you'll have him bagged in five." He trailed his finger down her tight white sweater and beige shorts, along her bare leg. "Afterward, a repeat at my place, eh?"

She gave him a knowing smile, exited the car, and headed down the street to Earl's. She wore a pair of sturdy black flats, her favorite shoes when she had a lot of walking to do on a case.

A few minutes later, she walked into Earl's, pausing to make it obvious she was alone. She adjusted her hat, a small beige turban that covered all but her bangs, a trendy style since Audrey Hepburn wore it in last year's *Sabrina*. She'd been heavy-handed with her make-up—darkly outlined eyes, smoky eye shadow, bright red lips. In her purse she carried lipstick, cigarettes, a fake ID identifying her as twenty-two-year-old Nancy Williams from Des Moines Iowa, and her father's .357 Magnum.

After seeing a few heads turn to check her out, she took a seat at the polished wooden bar, which a sign described as having been hand-carved and hauled by ox team from Iowa City to Central City in the 1880s. The place smelled like sawdust, cigarette smoke, and bleach. Hunting trophies of deer and elk were mounted on the walls. From the jukebox, Dean Martin crooned "That's Amore."

She ordered a beer and sipped it while checking out the room in the large mirror behind the bar. Spiro had described Bobby as late-forties with "goombah brown skin," blue eyes, skinny with muscled arms from carting boxes of fruits and vegetables for years. None of the men at the bar, or sitting at any of the dozen or so round tables, fit that description.

Then she saw him. He and another man were laughing as they entered the bar through a door in the back. Bobby wore a yellow-and-black plaid shirt, gray trousers, black loafers. He still had wiry, graying hair, just less of it. When his gaze caught hers in the mirror, she smiled.

A flash of thigh, a story about wanting to visit that old cemetery down the street, supposedly haunted by a woman dressed in black, but Julie was too scared to go alone, and she and Bobby were headed out the door. By the time they reached the end of Eureka Street, Bobby had his arm around her shoulders. From the corner of her eye, she caught Spiro standing at the back of the mine shaft across the street, watching them. He'd be frosted at her change in plan, but she wasn't making it a secret. Easy for him to catch up. Meanwhile, she'd get a few moments alone with Bobby.

She and Bobby walked up the short dirt path to the old cemetery at the top of the hill. Specks of blue and yellow wildflowers grew amid rocks and old granite headstones, some broken or leaning. A grove of aspens blocked their view of the road below.

When thunder erupted, she cuddled closer to Bobby, pressing herself into him as they kissed, running her hands around his torso, buttocks. No gun.

She squealed when a gust of wind blew off her hat. Bobby chased it a few feet, caught it, turned and held it up victoriously. He froze, releasing the hat, when he saw the gun in Julie's hand.

She walked closer, stopped. "I have a few questions."

"Christ, are you nuts?"

"You work for the Smaldones, right?" When he didn't answer, she notched the gun higher, targeted it at a spot between his eyes.

"Take it easy, okay? I do book. Pick up money, take bets, drop off winnings. I'm just a bookie."

Fat drops of rain began to fall. Beyond the aspen grove, lightning crackled and hissed.

Picking up money. Dropping off winnings. Then it clicked. "Bet you enforce loans, too," she said. "Drop by people's businesses and homes, strong-arm them to pay back their loans from the Smaldones. Loans so bloated with interest, sometimes people can't keep up with payments."

A form appeared about fifteen feet behind Bobby. Spiro, his face a tight mask of rage, had walked up the other side of the small hill. He walked briskly, holding a gun.

Bobby followed her line of vision, cursed when he saw Spiro.

"No, Julie!" Spiro called out. "Not the way to be in charge."

"Julie?" Bobby cocked her a look. "Said your name was Nancy."

"Julie Doyle. Max Doyle's daughter." She caught a look of recognition on his face. "You delivered groceries and money to us after my father was murdered. I'm beginning to think you also did 'book' at my father's office, or maybe dropped by to pick up loan payments..."

The look of recognition soured. His arms dangled at his sides, hands clenched. He looked like a skinny, dark snake, ready to strike.

Spiro walked slowly, rocks crunching under his shoes, stopped off to the side of Bobby. "Julie, put your gun away—"

"I'd hold onto it, Doll," Bobby said. "Our pal here has set both of us up. He's afraid one of us is gonna clue in the D.A. that he and I were there when your old man was killed."

Time seemed to slow to a crawl. His words sluggishly replayed in her head, like a movie soundtrack on low speed. *He and I were there when your old man was killed.* Her gaze drifted to Spiro, who looked completely floored, then back to Bobby, who stared at her with fierce blue eyes. The men's voices she'd heard that night had spoken in such hushed tones, she couldn't make out what was being said, had always assumed there were two men, her father and his killer, but *three*?

Time snapped back to reality as Spiro spoke.

"Don't fall for his lies, Julie. He is scum, just like the rest of the Smaldones."

Bobby barked a laugh. "I'm telling it to you real, Julie. Spiro got us to this isolated place because he wants to kill us both."

"But he didn't know I was bringing you here," Julie murmured.

Thunder growled across the sky. Aspen leaves clattered as winds blustered through the grove. Raindrops drizzled.

Spiro glanced at the darkening clouds. "Storm coming in. Julie, we need to go."

In a burst of movement, Bobby lunged, rammed his head into Spiro's gut. With an explosive grunt, Spiro stumbled backward, the gun skittering out of reach. As Bobby scrambled after it, Spiro heaved his body onto Bobby, who screeched like a small animal caught by a bird of prey. They wrestled, throwing wild blows. Julie jogged to Spiro's gun, picked it up, and turned to the men.

Spiro, a vein throbbing in his forehead, yelled something at her, his hands clenched around Bobby's neck. A flash of lightning turned the sky neon blue.

In the short time they'd been up here, the temperature had dropped significantly. She walked toward the men, her legs stiff from the cold, stopping a few feet from them. Bobby, his face flushed with exertion, was straining to pull Spiro's hands off his neck. Spiro, sweating and cursing, mouthed something at her. She pointed her gun at Bobby. "Come on, snake, let's rattle."

She pulled the trigger. Once. Twice. His head lolled back, mouth flapping for air. Above his dull blue eyes, the hole in his forehead oozed blood and brains.

"*Skata!*" Spiro yanked loose his hands and looked up at her, oblivious to the falling rain. "Go to the car. It's close, just down the hill over there." He pointed in the direction. "Wait for me there. Go!"

Carrying both guns, she hurried away, rain stinging her skin. The sky had shifted, taking on a surreal, metallic hue. She shivered, sucking in breaths of brittle, cold air. Before she descended the hill, she looked over her shoulder and saw Spiro dragging Bobby's limp body into the aspen grove.

Minutes later, Spiro, his face wet, his shirt sticking to his skin, got into the driver's seat and slammed shut the door. He ran a hand through his hair, muttered, "*Gamo teen Panagia sou.*" He looked at Julie. "You okay?"

"It all happened so fast...what if..."

"No, no, can't think that way." He turned the ignition key. The engine rumbled to life. "We need to leave. Anybody know you two went to cemetery?"

"No."

"Good. They won't look for him until after the storm passes. Unless somebody saw you two walking up the hill, they might not check cemetery for days."

Rain pummeled the windshield as they drove down the mountain road. Pines and aspens bent and swayed under the force of the lashing winds. Spiro had turned on the heater, which was drying their clothes and hair, but Julie continued to tremble. She'd shot her father's gun plenty of times before.

Warnings. Shooting bottles for practice. Once she nicked a guy who'd threatened her. But she'd never killed a human being.

She didn't doubt that she'd done the right thing. Bobby had admitted his guilt. But she'd always believed avenging her father's death would be a relief, a sense of victory, but instead she felt empty. Gutted. Maybe, with time, she'd feel differently.

They left the storm behind them as they neared Denver. Rain sprinkled to a stop, swirling clouds opened up to blue skies. At one point, Spiro pulled over and stashed their guns in a concealed space under the floor of the trunk. *Doubt police will pull us over, but just in case.* He suggested they go someplace public in Denver so they could be seen, have an alibi. Again, just in case. She suggested Elitch Gardens, a popular amusement park in North Denver.

By the time they reached Elitch Gardens the sun was setting, gold and orange, in a dusky sky. She fluffed her hair with her fingers, slicked on more red lipstick. He combed his hair, made a joke about the poor wrinkled little bluebirds on his shirt. But she didn't laugh.

"There's blood on your shirt." She pointed to the rust splatter on the far side of his stomach, the dots on his sleeve. On the drive down the mountain, she'd been caught up in her thoughts, hadn't noticed.

"*Gamo*," he muttered, checking his shirt.

She looked down at her top and shorts, stupefied they'd stayed pristine.

"You were far enough away," he said, answering her unspoken question. "Me, too close. But I am lucky, have sweater in trunk. You cold? Then I give it to you, you go inside, buy Spiro a cheesy shirt in gift shop, bring it back."

She almost smiled at the thought of Spiro wearing a cheesy anything. He was all about the flash. "No, I'm fine."

* * *

A short while later, they were strolling through the gardens, hand in hand, like any other couple out for the evening. Spiro wore a light-yellow pullover. He'd pulled the collars of the bluebird shirt over the neckline of the sweater. There was no blood on the collars, but it bothered Julie that he hadn't taken off his shirt. Of course, Spiro was all about appearances, and didn't want anyone he knew seeing him take it off, even in the semi-privacy of the backseat.

A lifetime ago, her family would come here on summer evenings. She and her kid brother would ride the brightly colored horses in the carousel, play pinball machines at the arcade. Her parents liked to sit in the picnic area, her mom sipping a cocktail, her dad a beer. Just like then, the air was rich with scents. Roses and lilacs, popcorn and hotdogs. Beyond the carousel, the Wildcat, a wooden roller coaster, loomed over a corner of the park. The clackity-clack of the wheels on rails, punctuated by screams from its thrill-seeking riders, resonated throughout the park and beyond.

"Hungry?" Spiro asked.

His voice pulled her out of her reverie. In the time they'd been walking, the sky had darkened and the stars were out. Not a cloud anywhere. A little girl ran past, squealing happily, gripping a cone of fluffy pink cotton candy.

"Julie? Hungry?"

"I don't know."

He cradled her face with his warm hands, looked deeply into her eyes. "We've walked enough," he said gently. "Let's find a place to sit and rest."

He steered her to a picnic table underneath a leafy canopy of trees. Moonlight spilled through the leaves, spotting the ground with dark silver. He brushed off a place for her to sit, and guided her there as if she were a child. Normally she hated men treating her this way, as if she were helpless, but tonight she didn't care.

She dutifully sat, placed her purse next to her on the bench.

He sat across from her, his dark form dappled in moonlight. "I will never tell anyone what happened."

"Me, neither," she whispered.

"Wish you had told me your plan. We both wanted truth from him, maybe we could have done things differently." He shrugged, his large shoulders were two dark mounds of movement. "But the more I think of it, my idea not so good. So what if I got the chance to ask questions? Bobby would've lied to me."

She released a shaky breath. "I brought a gun to intimidate him...didn't plan to..."

"Guns are messy. Always invite trouble."

"But...you had one."

With a groan, he turned his face upward, as if beseeching God to intervene, then looked back down and took her hands. "Julie, when I saw you and Bobby walking up that hill, I was afraid for your life! The Smaldones destroy people. If a bar stops paying protection money, they torch it. Somebody defaults on a loan, they kill 'em. Does not matter if they owe two hundred or four thousand two hundred. I had to protect you. Grabbed a gun I keep in glove compartment, prayed to God I wasn't too late."

She rubbed the sudden goosepimples on her arms. From across the park, shrieks and screams surged from the roller coaster.

"Time to relax." Spiro stood, looked across the grassy area at a series of lighted buildings next to the midway. "There's a bar over there. I'll bring back drinks."

She watched him walk away, thinking how Sandy was right. Six foot, but he seemed seven because he exuded a primal, bold confidence, like a gorilla owning its part of the jungle. But Spiro's true power was a shrewd, decisive mind. He bought people, calculated their worth, paid for their loyalty. His world was all about the numbers.

Her stomach clenched. *Numbers.* He was always precise about numbers. Paying her two hundred, then up-ing it to two hundred and fifty dollars. Griping that the Rossonian was too cheap to spend fifty cents for a bread knife. That the Smaldones didn't care if someone owed them two hundred or four thousand two hundred. *That* number—*four thousand two hundred*—was what her father had written on the scrap of paper. No way Spiro snagged that precise number from thin air.

Also damning was Spiro's inability to recall how much money had been stolen from his safe. *A thousand, maybe two.* Bullshit. Caught off guard by her question, he'd tossed out some random, vague amount because *the theft had never happened.* He'd made the damn story up.

Bobby hadn't lied. He'd told her the truth about Spiro's part in her father's murder. Wanted her to know that Spiro had plotted to silence them both, the two people who could pin him at the scene of her father's murder. She didn't have any dirt on Spiro, but he didn't like that she regularly talked to the D.A. What if she recalled something that implicated him? Easy solution: kill her.

For a moment, she felt dizzy, sick. She took a deep breath and released it slowly. This wasn't the time to panic. She'd worked cases that had taken an ugly, surprise turn—some frightening, even life-threatening—and she'd pulled her ass out of the fire each time. She needed to focus, think.

Spiro, a drink in each hand, was walking back to the picnic table. Strains of organ music emanated from the distant carousel. Sounds of laughter, bells, and whistles floated from the midway.

She mentally reviewed the backup plan she'd created in the off chance she didn't have ready access to her gun with Bobby. One thing in her favor: waiting in the darkened picnic area, her eyes had adjusted to the night shadows, while Spiro, having just been in a well-lighted bar, wouldn't see as well for the next few minutes. She scanned the table, spied the dark lump of his cigarette package, and tossed it on the ground underneath her bench just as he approached the table.

"For you, my beautiful Julie." He carefully lowered the glass until it set on the table in front of her. "A very nice single malt Scotch." He fumbled to find his seat before sitting down across from her. He raised his glass. "To us."

She raised hers, eyeing the murky liquid. Had it been this easy with her father? A phony celebratory toast? Or had they forced him to drink it.

"To truth," she said.

As he took a swig, she coughed, at the same time dropping her glass on the ground. "God, I'm so clumsy. I'm sorry."

He was quiet for a moment. "No problem. Have a sip of mine."

She accepted his glass and gingerly sipped. The scotch had a bite, warmed its way down her throat. She handed it back, steering it into his hand.

After a few moments, Spiro began patting the table. "Can't find my cigarettes."

"Maybe you left them in the car."

"No, no. I'm certain I brought them."

"Probably dropped on the ground while we were walking. But you're in luck!" She'd purposefully used the word *luck*, one he effusively used whenever he'd found a solution. "I have a cigarette or two in my purse." She extracted one, guided his hand to it. "For you."

"You're the most, Julie." He clicked his lighter, brought the flame to the tip of the cigarette. The tobacco sizzled orange. He inhaled deeply, blew it out.

She quietly got up, stepped away from the table.

He took another drag, held it in his lungs, coughed out the smoke. "Tastes...different."

"That's from the chamomile tea. Accidentally left my cigarettes next to a bunch of tea bags." She eased back another step.

He inhaled again, and then his body buckled. He doubled over, fell with a heavy thud onto the ground. He gasped, his body buckling again. "What—?"

"Strychnine," she answered. "Rat poison for a rat. That's what you put into my father's drink."

She hadn't been sure if strychnine, tamped down with tobacco into a cigarette, would work. Then she read that it could be inhaled, and similar to drinking it mixed into a liquid, the poison would be rapidly absorbed through the mucous membranes of the mouth and lungs, a direct line to the heart and blood.

He writhed on the ground, moaning. She turned, started to walk away.

A force felled her to the ground, knocked the air out of her. Spiro, panting, shoved her onto her back. Snap. Moonlight silvered along a blade. Pain sliced deep, splintering her insides, setting her nerves on fire. He stumbled away a few steps, collapsed, his body jackknifing.

She tried to cry out for help, but it came out in a thin wheeze. With great effort, she looked down at Spiro's knife embedded in her chest, the dark ooze spreading over her white top. Fighting for breaths, she looked up at the sky, watched the shadows crowding the half moon. Weakening, her life force draining, she stared at it, holding it in her gaze…

She felt the cool grass under her cheek.

Caught the scent of lilacs.

And smiled.

THE LONG ROAD

Dave Zeltserman

Tim's arms ached and his hands were all pins and needles as if they'd been tied behind his back for hours, if not longer. He felt Jenny staring at him. Reluctantly he turned toward her. Her face showed bone-white, but it was her eyes that particularly frightened him. He'd never seen such intense dread before.

"We need to get out of here," she whispered, her voice death-like.

He woke up then, his pulse racing and a sheen of sweat coating his body. For a long second he was too disoriented to realize where he was, and during that moment he had the sensation of falling from a great height. He regained his bearings and reached blindly over to Jenny's side of the bed.

It was empty. Good. If she weren't in the room he'd be able to get the notepad he kept hidden so he'd be able to write down the fragments that remained of the dream. If he didn't do it soon they'd be lost and he didn't want to lose them. He needed to hold onto everything that he could so he could make sense not only of this dream but the others.

"Are you okay?"

He pushed himself into a sitting position and squinted against the early morning light. Jenny stood by the foot of the bed, already dressed for her job as a cashier at the local market. She was trying to smile, but it was a sad, fragile smile. She was only twenty-seven and normally very pretty, but at that moment she looked worn-out. She'd been looking worn-out a lot over the last three months since she found out about his dreams, which was why he was trying so hard to keep them from her.

"I'm okay, I just slept funny on my arm," he said, his voice froggy from just waking. He clenched and unclenched his right fist several times. "I must've cut off the circulation. My hand's all numb."

Her smile weakened. She knew he was lying. "Hon, it's already six thirty. You should get out of bed if you're going to be at work by seven."

He watched as she left the room. Once the door closed behind her, he snuck out of bed and padded over to the closet. There was a loose board in the back of it, and that was where he hid his notepad. Carefully, he pushed aside clothing and shoe boxes so he could lift up the board, but his heart sank as he saw that his notepad was gone. He needed all those fragments he'd been collecting from his dreams if he were going to make sense of what was behind them. But as much as he wanted to understand his dreams, Jenny just as badly wanted them forgotten and thrown away.

He and Jenny had been sweethearts since their first year of high school. Actually, well before then. Their families had lived on the same country road, and even though he wouldn't have been able to articulate it at the time, he'd become smitten with her when they were seven and he pulled one of her pigtails as she sat in front of him during their second-grade class. She didn't tattle on him, and he figured years later it was because she was just as smitten with him.

When they were nineteen they left their small, rural Kansas town for New York City. The rest was a mystery to him. He had no memory of what happened during their trip, only that seven months later he woke up in the bed in his family's home that he was raised in. According to Jenny, they got in a car accident two weeks after they left Kansas, and the accident left him in a coma. He was flown back to a Topeka hospital and after the hospital did all they could for him, he was brought to his parents' home only to wake up four days later. Doc Shoal, who'd been seeing him since he was a baby, came over to the house a dozen or so times to check on him and told him he might have trouble remembering things, but given time he'd be just fine.

He had no reason to doubt that events had happened the way Jenny said they had, but he couldn't shake a nagging feeling that something else had happened. Two years ago he'd started having those dreams, although Jenny only found out about them much later. They were wisps of memories. Barely anything at all, but they left him feeling that it wasn't a car accident that had left him in a coma. That instead something violent had happened. Other vague wisps he remembered involved guns and violent men. Over the last six months he'd been remembering more of his dreams each night. Still little more than fragments, but enough to know there was something in his subconscious fighting to break loose. He wondered whether he could've been kidnapped and that was how he got injured. Or maybe it was Jenny who was taken and his injuries happened while rescuing her.

Tim regretted losing his notepad of dream fragments, but there was no point in crying over spilt milk. It didn't really matter. He had another way of finding out what happened. A year ago he'd gotten the idea of hiring a private investigator and he started putting aside whatever money he could without Jenny knowing about it. Three days ago he had enough to pay a Topeka detective named Don Gannon a one-week retainer. If it took Gannon more than a week, Tim would be out of luck, but a week could be all that was needed.

He hoped so.

He didn't bother changing out of the boxers and undershirt he wore to bed, and instead pulled on a pair of dungarees and buttoned up a flannel shirt. He'd wait until nighttime like he usually did to take a shower since he would be sweating all day working at the feed store.

Jenny was waiting in the kitchen, sipping coffee as she stared blankly out the window. When she heard him, she offered a bleak smile and got up to join him. She must've been wondering about the dream that had left him perspiring that morning, but she didn't ask him about it, probably not wanting to encourage him.

They only had one car; a nineteen-year-old Ford Mustang that Tim's parents had once owned, but gave to them when they got married. Jenny didn't need to be at work until eight, so Tim would drive her to a donut shop on the same block as the market and she'd sit and read a book until the market opened. Most days her friend Sally would drive her home from work and the days Sally couldn't he'd pick her up. The arrangement worked well enough. It wasn't like the two of them had places to be outside of work, at least not usually.

Jenny tried to shake herself out of her funk and made small talk as they drove away from their small two-bedroom home that was more shack than house. "I wonder if the town will ever pave this road," she said.

She was referring to the long, dirt road they had to drive each morning. It wasn't a private road and it should've been paved years ago, but since he and Jenny were the only ones living on it since the Hadley's abandoned their home, he doubted it would ever be paved. "It's the county's responsibility, not the town's, and they don't care one whit about us. Now if Walmart ever opened up on this road, you can bet it would be paved the next day." He forced a grin and Jenny tried to smile back. He didn't mention his missing notepad, and if she was wondering whether he had looked for it this morning, she kept the thought to herself.

Most of the drive was on that long, dirt road. Once he got off of it, it was only a five-minute ride to the town center. He parked the car and walked with Jenny to the donut shop so he could get his usual chocolate glazed and black coffee to go. After the cashier rang him up, he gave Jenny a peck on the cheek and pretended that nothing was troubling either of them.

The feed store where he worked was one town over and traffic, as it usually was on the backroads he drove, was light enough for him to be only ten minutes late. His boss grumbled over that fact, but let it go. Tim was the hardest worker at the store. He knew it and so did his boss.

Sometime around ten that morning his boss clapped him on the shoulder. "You're doing the work of two today," he said, a grin stretching over his broad face. "If you're going to work this hard, you can come in ten minutes late every morning."

It was true. Tim was working like a demon possessed. Even though he couldn't remember any of his latest dream, an uneasiness was twisting his insides and he hoped if he stayed busy enough he'd be able to ignore it. It hadn't done any good so far, though. A little after eleven, he got a call from Gannon.

"You were never in any of the hospitals in Topeka," the detective told him. "None of them have you in their records. I can't find a record of you being involved in a car crash either. I'll keep looking, but I don't believe that's what happened to you."

This didn't surprise Tim. At a gut level he must've known all along that he hadn't been in a car crash. His voice sounded dull and robotic to his own ears as he told Gannon that his parents and Jenny claimed he'd been taken to St. Mary's Medical Center.

"You were never there. I'd bet money you weren't sent to any hospital. Not in Topeka or anywhere else."

Gannon's phone call left Tim distracted, his mind racing about what he needed to do next. If his pa were still alive, Tim was sure he'd be able to get the truth out of him, but his pa had died of a heart attack five years ago at the age of forty-seven. His ma was a different story. As mean and ornery as they came. If it were up to her, he and Jenny never would've gotten that old Mustang with over a hundred thousand miles on it as a wedding present, but his pa for once put his foot down. Tim didn't see what choice he had but to try to talk to his ma. It was either that or drive himself crazy with worry. By two o'clock he was too anxious to spend another minute at the feed store and he told his boss he wasn't feeling well.

"I pay you for eight-hour days," his boss complained.

"I worked through lunch. I'll make up the hour I owe you tomorrow."

His boss folded his arms across his chest, stubborn-like. "I got a truck bringing a delivery at three thirty that needs unloading. You working through lunch isn't helping me with that."

Tim turned his back on him. "Nothing I can do to help about that," he said under his breath.

"Nothing I can do if you come in tomorrow and don't have a job."

"Do what you need to," Tim said without bothering to look back.

His ma still lived in the same house where he grew up. Two years ago she'd hurt her back at the meat packing company where she worked, and had been on disability ever since. He called her and asked if she was home.

"That's a fool question. Where else am I going to be?"

Tim didn't rise to the bait. Instead he told her he'd be over soon to see her.

"Ain't you supposed to be at work now?"

"This is important."

He disconnected the call before she could ask him any more questions. When he later knocked on her door, she didn't invite him in. Instead she stood in the doorway, a coolness in her eyes and her leathery face drawn into a belligerent scowl.

"You're not going to let me in?"

"What for? You were in such a rush to hang up on me before, I figure you're in too much of a rush for any niceties."

This was par for the course. He couldn't remember much of his life before his coma, but he was sure his ma had always been cold to him. He was also sure a good part of the reason he had wanted to go to New York with Jenny was so he could get as far away from her as he could. He reflected bitterly on the fact that if it hadn't been for his pa he wouldn't have been allowed back into the house to recuperate from the injuries that had left him in a coma.

He said, "I wasn't brought to St. Mary's after I was injured like you said I was."

Her mouth moved as if she were chewing gum or, more likely, getting ready to spit at him. "Whoever told you that is a fool. I don't misspeak. Never!"

"They don't have a record of me staying there. None of the hospitals in the area do."

Her eyes turned reptilian in their coldness and her scowl deepened. "I can't help it if that hospital made a mistake with their records. You got anything else to waste my time?"

Tim accepted there was no point in asking her anything, just as there hadn't been a point in seeing her in the first place. He had nothing left to say to her and watched as she closed the door on him. When he returned to his car, he sat confused as to what to do next. An idea eventually came to him and he called Jenny.

"Hon, everything alright?" she asked.

"Everything's good. A delivery truck is coming in later that needs unloading, and I've got a chance to pick up a few hours of overtime. Can Sally drive you home?"

"Let me check."

He heard Jenny yell out to Sally, who also worked as a cashier at the same market. Right after that he heard Sally's response.

"Yep, all set," Jenny said, her voice showing relief that he wasn't calling for another reason.

"I'll be home when I can," he promised her.

He didn't like keeping his dreams secret from Jenny, and he certainly didn't like lying to her, but he knew she'd been lying to him. He wasn't in a car accident. That wasn't how he got injured. Deep in his gut he knew that as well as he knew anything, and when he was sitting in his car after seeing his ma he thought of a way that he could prove it.

He hadn't seen a doctor since Doc Shoal died, otherwise he'd be able to see someone locally, but Topeka was only a one-hour drive and it seemed to go faster than that. He drove to the first hospital he came across and told the somewhat befuddled admitting nurse in the emergency ward that he wanted someone to check his head and see if he'd been in a car accident.

"That's not what we do here," she said. "You should call your doctor and make an appointment."

"I don't have a doctor. And I need to get this done today."

She made a hmm noise. "I guess you could go to an urgent care facility and ask for head X-rays." She wrote down the address for a nearby facility and wished him good luck.

The place she sent him to could see him right away. After the X-rays were taken a doctor with a perplexed look on his face came over to talk to him.

"Son, you've got a bullet lodged in your brain. Did you know that you'd been shot?"

That news left Tim stunned. While he was convinced that he hadn't been in a car accident, he hadn't been expecting to hear that his injuries stemmed from being shot. It made him feel queasy thinking about those vague dream fragments involving violent men and guns. It also explained why his earlier life was so fuzzy.

"I didn't know," he admitted.

The doctor seemed to believe him and the tenseness in his expression eased. He showed Tim an X-ray and explained about the part of the brain that the bullet had injured. "You were lucky that the bullet didn't penetrate any deeper than it did. I'm not sure if it can be removed. You'll have to see a specialist about that. Do you have holes in your memories, especially from when you were younger?"

"Yes, I do."

"That makes sense," the doctor said.

Tim thanked him for his help and left in a daze. He was

barely aware of driving back to his hometown, or stopping right outside the outskirts at a strip club. He didn't stop there for the naked women but because he badly needed a drink. Since coming out of the coma, he had had at most a beer every three or four months, and even that would cause Jenny to worry. As he sat at the bar, he ordered a double shot of bourbon, poured it down his throat, and ordered another one. It was while he was waiting for his second drink that he spotted a high school friend of his named Andy Banksford sitting at the other end of the bar. Andy noticed him too and picked up his drink so he could take the empty bar stool next to Tim.

"Tim Crocker," Andy exclaimed as they shook hands, "Man, it's been forever." His eyes grew thoughtful as he reminisced. "Back in high school you and Jenny Donahue were thick like thieves. You still in touch with her?"

"I'm married to her."

"No kidding? And you're still kicking and breathing?"

"What's that supposed to mean?"

Andy held up his hands in a don't-hit-me gesture. "I'm sorry Tim, that was truly uncalled for. Blame the beers I've had. Jenny was gorgeous as all hell as I'm sure she still is, and I guess jealousy reared its ugly head. After all, you got her, while I have to stop off here and make memories so I can get it up with my wife. But you have to admit Jenny was pretty wild back in high school." His eyes grew reflective and he showed a thin smile. "I guess you were too, for that matter."

Tim had a hard time imagining Jenny and himself ever like that, but he'd seen evidence of it recently. Gannon had wanted a picture of himself and Jenny from around the time they took off for New York so he could pass it along to a network of detectives. These were detectives not just in New York but in major cities all over the country, and Gannon explained that these other investigators would show the photo around and if any of them provided a tip that led to finding out what happened to Tim, the investigator would get a thousand dollars for his effort. Tim dug up a photo taken a week after he and Jenny had graduated high school, and Gannon made a similar comment about how the two of them looked like pretty wild characters back then. In the picture he was thin as a reed, but also had hard eyes and a tough, smart-alecky grin while Jenny showed a matching smirk and resembled the leather-jacketed version of Olivia Newton-John from *Grease*. It must've been a phase they were going through, and it was hard for Tim to believe that he and Jenny were ever like that.

"Did you hear about me being injured eight years ago?"

Andy looked genuinely surprised. "No, man, I didn't hear anything about you since high school. What happened?"

"A car accident," Tim lied since it was easier than telling Andy he'd been shot in the head. "I was brought back to my parents' home in a coma."

"Wow. I never even heard a whisper about it." He made a face. "You'd think I would've."

That was true. In a rural town their size someone being brought home in a coma should've been big news, but somehow Jenny, his parents, and Doc Shoal were able to keep it bottled up. Tim's drink was brought over. He drank it quickly and nodded toward Andy, telling him that he was glad they'd had this chance to catch up. The bourbon had settled his nerves, but he now found himself anxious to confront Jenny and find out why he was lied to about the nature of his injuries. Andy looked taken aback by Tim's abruptness and said something about how the two of them and their wives should get together some time, maybe for a barbecue. Tim told him that sounded swell, although he doubted that would ever happen. Twenty minutes later he pulled into his driveway and found Jenny waiting for him in the kitchen, her face flushed with anger.

"Your mom called me," she said, a harshness tightening her voice. "She told me about your visit. You think I lied to you about what happened? I'm not the liar here. You are. I called the feed store. You weren't working overtime today, and your boss would've fired you tomorrow if I didn't beg him not to. What in the world has gotten into you?"

"A bullet."

Jenny stared at him as if he were crazy. "What are you talking about?"

"I had my head X-rayed. The doctor found a bullet next to my brain. That's what caused my coma and not a car accident."

"He's wrong."

"He's not. He showed me the X-ray."

Jenny slumped in her chair. Her eyes went distant for a moment and then she looked back at Tim.

"The accident happened on a country road near the woods, and this explains why you crashed up the car," she said. "I thought it must've been because you'd drifted off, but instead a hunter or kids or someone fired off a gun and the bullet struck you. Tim, I swear I had no idea that's what happened. The car rolled a bunch of times and it was a wreck. I was hurt pretty bad myself and was out of it for weeks, and I always thought it was a car accident and nothing else."

That didn't make any sense. The doctors examining him after the accident would've found the bullet hole and known he'd been shot. But maybe they might've missed it if they thought his injuries were the result of a car crash. He decided something like that could've happened. He thought of calling Gannon and telling him what he discovered, but he put it off partly because he didn't want to risk Jenny finding out he had hired a detective and partly because he was getting sick of the whole business.

The next day when he showed up at work his boss acted as if nothing had happened the day before and he did likewise. He was beginning to think of this chapter of his life being over. His dreams of violent men with guns, at least the little he'd been able to remember, must've been his subconscious letting him know that it had been more than a car accident that had injured him. When Gannon called later that morning, Tim was going to fire him and get back what he could of the retainer, but before he had a chance Gannon told him about a potential break in the case.

"One of the detectives in the network operating out of Chicago found a witness who thinks he knows you. Do you remember being in Chicago?"

"No. I told you I don't remember anything after leaving Kansas. And not much before then either."

"Ah, hell, I was hoping that might strike a chord. This witness thinks you were named Clyde. You ever use that as a nickname?"

"Not that I remember."

"Okay, I figured as much. This witness will only talk to me face to face, so I'm flying to O'Hare this afternoon. Don't worry about the cost. There's still enough left of your retainer to cover the trip."

Gannon hung up before Tim could say anything else. The detective probably could sense that he was about to be fired. For a long minute Tim stared at his phone trying to decide whether to call Gannon back and end the investigation, but his boss distracted him by asking him to go out back and unload a delivery that had just arrived. It was the end of the day before Tim remembered about Gannon again. He figured it didn't much matter. One day wasn't going to make any difference.

That evening Jenny was more her buoyant self that Tim hadn't seen much of over the last three months. She was intuitive enough to know that things were settling back to normal and that he wasn't going to spend any more time chasing after his nightmares. Her good mood continued later into the night and the next morning. She even woke up early enough to make them both pancakes, bacon and eggs for breakfast, and she was being so sweet and nice to him that he decided to come clean. Well, that was mostly it. He also had a thought tickling the back of his mind. He told her that he had hired a private detective to find out what had happened to him, but it was over now.

She looked at him as if he had horns. Her voice didn't sound quite right when she asked if that was how he found out that he'd been shot. Her question didn't make any sense since the doctors who treated him after the crash hadn't found out about the bullet in his head, so how could anyone have known about it?

"No, he didn't find much of anything," he said, his voice catching in his throat from the way Jenny was staring at him. He tried laughing as he told her the only thing the detective uncovered was that someone in Chicago mistook him for another guy named Clyde. "He went there yesterday for all the good it's going to do him. I know I never had that nickname."

The transformation that came over Jenny was something startling to behold and it left her resembling something vicious and feral. "You killed us both," she swore at him in a voice dripping with ice. He watched in stunned amazement as she fled the table. It was only when he heard her running down the basement steps that he came out of his stupor and followed after her. He found her digging through a pile of clutter.

"What did you mean by that?" he asked.

She ignored him and continued to dig through the clutter. When he grabbed her by the wrist, fury exploded in her eyes and her free hand bent into a claw like she going to scratch his eyes out. The moment passed.

"When we were in Chicago you went by Clyde and I went by Bonnie, because we were going to be Bonnie and Clyde," she said. "Except instead of banks we were going to rob other crooks since they couldn't talk to the cops about us. Everything went to hell when we tried robbing a mob poker game. We killed people Tim, and when we were fleeing one of them made a lucky shot through a door and hit you. You kept running even with a bullet in your head." Briefly admiration shone in her eyes. "I don't know how you did it, but you didn't collapse until you got in the passenger seat."

Tim let go of her wrist and watched as she went back to rummaging through the pile of junk. She found what she was looking for. A rifle and a box of shells. He had no idea they had been down there.

"Why didn't you tell me what happened?"

"Because you were in a coma for six months and things changed with me during that time. When you woke up, I was afraid if you were still the man I once knew you'd go after them if you found out you'd been shot and I didn't want that." Her face softened as she once again resembled the person he thought he knew. "Then when you didn't remember anything, it became easier to pretend Chicago never happened."

Faint road noise from outside froze them. Jenny gave Tim a frightened look before running up the stairs. Tim felt too weak in the knees to give chase and by the time he climbed the stairs he heard Jenny slamming the back door shut.

He made his way to the front of the house and saw the two black sedans on the long dirt road leading to his house. He didn't see much point in joining Jenny. With the Hadleys gone, their nearest neighbor was over five miles away. These men would catch up to them. Besides, Tim had been chasing after the truth all these months and it was about time he let it catch up to him.

He watched as the two sedans parked in front of his house. Four men got out of each of them, all holding either rifles or pistols. All of them looked as if their faces had been grimly carved out of stone. Tim waited for them, knowing he had reached the end of the road.

THE DARK UNDERSIDE OF EDEN

Michael Mallory

Summer 1978—Springfield, Missouri—"Hell's waiting room"

Nothing masked the sound of wild, back-arching sex with a teenager like Barry Manilow's "Copacabana".

A month ago Denny was barely aware Barry Manilow existed, let alone listened to his music. But Angel liked his stuff and Denny had to admit that the guy's voice admirably covered the sounds of her moaning and gasping. And since this was her hot, stifling, fire-trap apartment and not his, he figured she had the right to play whatever she wanted.

Angel Hutson was dark blond (and Denny could attest that it was her natural color) and cute in a farm girl sort of way. She also had a body that would turn Truman Capote straight. She was nineteen and a college student; it seemed like half the people in Springfield, Missouri were college students. There were eleven colleges in town ranging from small business schools to a big state university, and a good percentage of them were religious-based. Angel attended one of those. How she squared her devotion to Jesus with her passion for getting laid long, hard, and often was something Denny did not quite understand. But neither did he complain.

Dennis Martin Venable was exactly twice Angel's age but he copped to being only thirty and got away with it thanks to a youthful face. He was morning news reporter on KTMN radio, and some in the Springfield broadcast community wondered why he didn't get a television gig where he could show off his looks. They didn't know that he already had been on television. A year ago he was the evening news anchor on KFTV in Kansas City under the air name Mart Dennis. That gig came to a sudden conclusion one night when he turned to his airhead female co-anchor and called her a stupid cunt, not realizing his mic was live.

It took quite a while for him to find any broadcast job under any name. Through a contact he learned about the KTMN gig and signed on in March, using Denny Martin as his on-air moniker. That was four months ago and he still felt like an outsider at the station. Only Angel, who interned at KTMN, had opened up to him.

In all ways.

"Do you love me?" she asked him as they lay side by side, the sweat cooling on their bodies.

"Of course I love you," he replied, knowing that to Angel love simply meant *Am I good in bed*? "Who wouldn't love you?"

"Do you want to spend the night here?"

"Sorry. Can't."

"You always say that."

"Well, I have some things to do back at my place."

"Be honest, Denny. Are you seeing someone else?"

"Like who?"

"Like Shaylene, maybe?"

Shaylene Little was KTMN's traffic manager. She was nice enough and attractive in a big-hair sort of way, but flat-chested and had an annoying, twangy voice.

"I have a hard enough time just keeping up with you," he said.

After a quick shower in an ancient tub Denny got dressed, kissed Angel goodbye, and told her he'd see her Monday. He knew tomorrow for her would be taken up with church matters.

As for Denny, Sunday was just so much wasted time. Frankly, the last quarter had been wasted time. Living and working in the Buckle of the Bible Belt, with its Sunday blue laws, its glorification of hillbilly culture, and its summer storms that erupted suddenly like violent temper tantrums was beginning to seem like a judge's sentence. Denny vowed he would not be in Springfield forever. Not even a fraction of forever.

After spending much of the evening watching shit on TV and commiserating with his only close friend, Jim Beam, Denny fell into a dreamless sleep shortly after eleven.

His four-forty-five alarm the next morning sounded like an air raid.

Despite his hangover Denny made it in to work on time (though working the early shift was also getting old; opening up the station was really the news director's job). He dutifully looked through his tickler file of leads and found nothing of interest. The teletype from the sheriff's department revealed little more than filler: another Git-N-Go convenience store holdup and a car fire on the highway—stories that couldn't be jazzed up with music and sound effects. It would once again be up to him to find something to fill up the noon newscast, the first live one of the day.

His beat consisted of morning stops at all city and county offices, usually travelling with the pack of reporters from other stations. The most promising nugget of the day came from the city attorney who announced that Springfield's star evangelist, the Reverend Tommy Lin Farris, was spearheading the crusade to keep cable television from coming to town. Obtaining a cable contract was a long-held goal of the city council, but for Farris and his minions it was the Devil's pipeline coming straight into homes.

By the time Denny got back to the station he had the story written in his head and knew which quote from his tape-recorded interview he would use to accompany it. But he wanted to flesh it out with comments from Tommy Lin Farris on the record speaking about his opposition. That would not be easy. In his experience preachers hated to be questioned as much as they loved to sermonize. Angel might be able to swing it though, seducing Farris into talking with her honey-pie voice.

Standing up to see over the top of his cubicle he called to Shaylene, asking her to send Angel to see him.

"She hasn't come in yet," Shaylene responded.

"She hasn't?"

"I know. It's not like her. I hope she's okay."

Denny didn't have much time to worry about it. He had to get his noon broadcast on the air, filling out his five minutes with chaff from the morning harvest. If his lead story lacked a comment from Farris, he would be the only one who noticed.

After the newscast he cut off his mic (which was now under his exclusive control) and stepped out of the closet-sized news booth to see Rob Thacker, the station manager, waiting for him.

"I'd like to talk to you in my office," Thacker said, who kept his tie tightly knotted and his suit coat on no matter the situation or temperature.

"Is there a problem?"

"Not with you, but...just come on in."

Once there Thacker closed the door and asked Denny to sit down, then slid his own butt onto the corner of his desk. "How well do you know Angel Hutson?" he asked.

Oh, shit, was he going to get fired for fucking the intern?

"As well as anybody here, I guess," Denny replied, hoping that was true. "I heard she hadn't come in today. Is anything wrong?"

"She's been arrested," Thacker told him.

"What? What did she do?"

"It seems a strip club was operating on the outskirts of town which the police raided last night. Angel was one of the dancers."

After a pause Denny said, "I don't believe it."

"I had a hard time accepting it, too. But I got a call from the detective in charge of the raid. I guess Angel told someone she worked here."

"I was at the cop shop this morning and there was nothing on the police blotter about a raid or an arrest."

"The detective explained that they're not releasing information on the raid pending investigation. When they're ready to say something, they'll hold a press briefing."

"I still think it's bullshit."

"Language, please," Thacker said. He ran a purely G-rated station.

"All right, you're the boss. Tell me how to handle the story."

"Denny, I called you in here to tell you not to handle the story."

"Wait a minute—"

"Hear me out. We gain nothing by running Angel's reputation through the mud until we know all the facts."

"Okay, so let me discover the facts."

"The police are investigating. Once Angel is arraigned the story will come out, but until that happens nothing about this is to be reported or even leaked."

"Rob, you're asking me to abandon my principles as a journalist."

"Not abandon them, just give them the next few days off. We need to sit on this until it's safe to report it."

"What do you mean 'safe'?"

"What I mean, Denny, is you are not to cover Angel's arrest or the reason why in any way, shape, or form. I can't make it any clearer than that. You can go now."

Denny went, leaving the office annoyed and confused. He could try to appeal to Larry Barker, the station's news director, though Barker gave precious little direction at the best of times. He was a robot whose primary function seemed to be zipping back and forth to Jefferson City to deal with state officials, leaving his small staff largely on their own.

Back at the news desk it finally hit him what Thacker had meant by waiting until it's "safe." The bastard must be worried that sponsors would flee if they found out the station employed a stripper with a police record.

Well, screw Rob Thacker. Denny thought about going to the

jail right then and there to see Angel but didn't want to get in the way of any arraignment or bail procedure. Surely they wouldn't hold her long, not for something like stripping.

Then again, this was Springfield.

But it was also Angel. He simply could not understand why she would be working in a live nude girls palace, on a Sunday, no less! Did she need money that badly?

Figuring Thacker would keep watch on his movements for the rest of the day, Denny decided to wait until tomorrow morning's rounds before pressing to see her. But Angel remained on his mind as he plodded through the rest of his shift, pulling together what stories he could to leave for the evening reporter, Pete Ashley, a kid with no news experience who'd been hired because he was the son of a big advertiser.

After stopping for an early dinner at one of the city's ubiquitous cashew chicken dispensaries Denny went to his apartment. While newer and nicer than Angel's, it was still not air conditioned. There he mapped out his strategy for the next morning, planning on breaking away from the news pack to see if he could somehow bluff his way into the jail.

Fate and Larry Barker, however, had other plans.

Upon arriving at the station the next morning Denny found a note from Barker telling him to cover the groundbreaking ceremony for a new VA facility that morning instead of morning rounds, which Barker himself would do. The groundbreaking, which would include speeches by county officials and the deputy administrator of the VA from Washington, was slated for ten-thirty and would be over by eleven-fifteen, God willing. That would give Denny just enough time to swing by the jail before homing back to write up the story. Since he wouldn't have to ditch the wolf pack that way, maybe it was even better.

Since the point of any groundbreaking ceremony is to show a bunch of people holding shovels, the VA event was covered mostly by television stations and newspaper photographers. The only other radio reporter present was Kendall Grassley from

KORZ-FM, who showed up late. It was nearly noon by the time the speechifying, digging, and posing was all over, meaning Denny would miss the first newscast. Well, tough. That was Barker's problem.

As Denny headed back toward his car, cursing the humidity, Grassley caught up with him. "I didn't see you on the rounds this morning," he told him.

"I was assigned this instead," Denny said. "My news director took the city-county beat today."

"Must be nice. I'm pretty much the entire news staff right now because we lost Carla Brenner to KY3."

KY3 was the NBC television affiliate in Springfield.

"Must be nice," Denny echoed.

"Yeah, but I'm on triple-time now. I even have to cover that four o'clock police news conference after coming in at six this morning."

"What police news conference?"

"The one about that stripper they arrested on the weekend. Angel somebody, I think."

"What about her?"

"You don't know? She's dead."

All the blood in Denny's body drained into the ground. "What?" he croaked.

"She hanged herself last night in her jail cell with a bed sheet."

After getting the details from Grassley, Denny drove off. He couldn't decide whether to race to the police station and demand to know what had happened or return to the station and confront Thacker with this news, and tell him that the story was now out, whether Thacker and his fucking advertisers liked it or not.

Instead, head swimming, he went to his apartment and tried to figure out what to do.

The Angel he knew simply was not one for suicide. So what the hell happened?

After pacing the floor and getting nowhere, Denny dropped into his thrift store armchair. The next time he looked at the clock it was a little after three. Grassley said the news conference was set for four.

Denny went to his car.

There were more local reporters milling around the police headquarters than Denny had ever seen at one time. When Larry Barker saw Denny coming he glared at him, though his face remained placid. Denny wasn't sure if Barker was capable of expression.

"What are you doing here?" Barker demanded of him.

"Why shouldn't I be here, Larry? I'm a newsman, and this is news."

"I'm covering it for the station."

"You mean you're covering it up for the station."

"What are you talking about?"

"This is horseshit, Larry, and you know it. Angel never would have killed herself."

"I have this under control, Denny, and you need to leave."

"And if I don't?"

The briefing was about to start.

"If they allow for a Q-and-A, I'll represent the station," Barker hissed. "You shut the hell up."

Walt Redfield, Springfield's police chief, stepped up to the podium. "I first want to express my condolences to the family of Angel Hutson," he began. Then he went into the basics of the case: Angel had been arrested Sunday night in an unlicensed facility housing a business that traded sex for money, which has been closed. She was taken to the city jail pending arraignment on prostitution charges.

Denny's agitation was rising by the second.

"This morning, while breakfast was being delivered to the inmates," Redfield went on, "Miss Hutson was discovered dead in her cell in the county holding facility, having hanged herself from a light fixture using a bed sheet which she knotted around her neck. This occurred sometime in the middle of the night. We do not have an exact time on that. I'm sorry to report that Miss

Hutson was a difficult inmate. She was described by jail personnel as angry, defiant, and increasingly irrational."

"Bullshit!" Denny shouted.

"Whoever said that, please control yourself," the chief cautioned.

"On whose judgment was she deemed irrational?" Denny called again, and Barker grabbed his arm. "And if she was acting as crazy as you say, why wasn't she put on suicide watch?"

A large, red-faced man in a business suit, whose lightly graying hair looked air-pumped, like a television emcee's or a bad Elvis impersonator's, stepped up to the podium. "For those of you who don't know me," the man said, looking directly at Denny, "I'm Detective Del Ollis. This was my case. If you want to know on whose judgment the characterization of Miss Hutson's behavior as irrational was made, it was mine. If you are asking why I did not call in a medical professional to examine her, let me assure you I was planning to do that today. Unfortunately Miss Hutson took matters into her own hands, proving how deeply disturbed she really was."

Denny made a move toward the podium but was prevented by Barker, who grabbed his arm and dragged him back through the crowd as Ollis continued speaking.

"Goddamnit, this is crap and you know it!" Denny spat once they were clear of the crowd. "Angel was not the suicidal type. Something's going on that they're not telling. Somebody killed her. Another inmate, a guard, somebody!"

"If you don't stop making a scene, you'll be thrown out of here."

"I'll take the chance. This stinks, Larry. This whole set-up stinks."

"You need to calm down. I am handling this."

Denny laughed.

Other reporters were starting to turn away from the podium to see what private drama was going on behind them.

"Okay, as your supervisor I am ordering you to leave right

now," Barker said in hushed tones.

"And if I don't?"

"If you don't, your job will be in jeopardy."

"Oh, will it really? Well, fuck you, Larry, I quit. You better go back and listen to the lies now so you can quote them correctly." He spun around and stormed away.

Returning to the station while his back was still up, Denny marched into Rob Thacker's office and reiterated his resignation, then went to the news cubicle and gathered the few personal belongings he kept there. On his way out he saw Pete Ashley and wished him luck, adding, "You're going to need it."

For better or worse he was on his own now. Make that for better since no one was looking over his shoulder telling him what to do. And if he were able to break the story of what was behind the mysterious death taking place in the Greene County jail on his own, major markets—maybe even national markets— would be vying for him. He'd be out of God-forsaken Springfield, and who would even remember his little television problem in Kansas City?

Before going home Denny stopped by his bank to see exactly how much money he had, since balancing his checkbook had never been of primary importance to him. His savings account had slightly over three thousand, a little less than he'd thought. But it would get him through if he was careful. He got two hundred out in cash.

While he could not bring himself to accept that Angel had killed herself, Barker had been right about one thing: he did not know everything about her. If he wanted to argue his case he would have to find out more about Angel Hutson than the color of her nipples and her taste in music.

He had to think, and he didn't want to do it at home. He needed a place with no familiarities and no distractions.

He was driving east on Sunshine Street and passed a bar called The Sunset Room. It called to him loudly enough that he turned around and pulled up across the street.

The place proved to be dark, quiet, and blessedly empty, despite a few wobbly tables and a long bar. The bartender was a rough-looking specimen, but he smiled easily as Denny walked in. A television was affixed to the wall behind the bar, and it was tuned to the five-o'clock afternoon news. On the screen a young newswoman whom Denny had noticed at a couple council meetings was reporting on the press conference held an hour ago.

"Beam," Denny told the guy behind the bar. "Double. And turn up the sound, would you?"

After pouring the drink the bartender fiddled with the volume on the TV. Then he looked back at Denny. "Am I crazy, or is that you on the box?"

Denny knocked back the drink and looked up to see himself silently shouting out a question. "Your mental state is outside my sphere of knowledge," he said. "But yeah, that's me."

"So you on TV a lot?"

"No, radio."

"What station?"

"KTMN-FM."

"Oh. I listen to KTTS."

"Good for you. Can I have another one of these?"

The bartender refilled his glass then turned back to the TV. "Too bad about that girl," he said. "But I guess those that live by the sheet die by the sheet."

"What's that supposed to mean?"

"Well, they said she was a hooker."

"They said she was a stripper. There's a difference."

"I wouldn't know. I always say there are two things I've never had to pay for. One's fighting lessons, and you can guess the other."

Denny looked at the TV and saw what must have been a high-school yearbook photo of Angel. He drained his glass and tapped on its rim.

"Take her easy on those, okay friend?" the bartender cautioned, but fulfilled Denny's request. Then he looked back to the television. "Hanging yourself must be a bad way to go."

"Is there a good way?"

"I don't know. But I had a guy in here once who talked about a fellow he knew who tried to take himself out by hanging. His woman left him, or some damn thing, and he was distraught. Anyway, he climbed up on a stool and tied the rope around something, then made a slipknot for his neck, and jumped off. But he screwed up the measurements and gave himself too much rope, so he just landed on the floor on his feet with a slack rope around his neck. He took it as a sign from God instead of his own inability to measure a length of rope, and never tried it again."

"A stool, you say?"

"Yeah. You have to stand on something or else it won't work. Look, mister, if you want another bourbon the best I can do is give you a single, but then I have to cut you off."

"Don't bother," Denny muttered, pulling out his wallet. After settling up he went back outside where he was blinded by the sunshine.

Denny sat in his car for several minutes before starting it.

Angel's frame of mind was now a moot point in his mind. Thanks to the anonymous bartender he was now convinced it wasn't possible for her to have hanged herself. But what was she doing in a goddamned strip club?

He needed to get into her apartment. Maybe there was a clue—a diary or a notebook, anything that might shed light on why she felt compelled to bare herself to strangers for cash.

He nearly sideswiped an oncoming car as he pulled away from the curb. The other driver laid on the horn and Denny honked back, flipping the guy off. Sure, he was a little tipsy, but he'd driven in worse condition. He'd just be careful.

He made his way to Angel's block without further incident, but when he got there he saw three cop cars parked in front of her building. What were they doing here?

He knew he should simply drive on and not make a scene, but he wanted answers.

Driving past the cop cars, he pulled over and parked a half-block away. When an officer standing on the porch of the apartment building saw Denny approach he came down to meet him.

"Are you a resident of this building, sir?" the policeman, whose nametag identified him as Kallman, asked.

"No." Denny fumbled his wallet out of his pocket and flashed his press card. "I have a few questions about the Angel Hutson murder."

"The what, sir?"

"You heard me. First question: since Angel was not killed here and this is not a crime scene, why are the police here?"

"Let me see that press card again," Officer Kallman asked, and then muttered, "Dennis Venable."

Because background checks were required to obtain a press card, they were issued under one's real name.

"Denny Martin to you. I'm with KTMN news." He was about to add, *At least I was*, then decided the cop didn't need to know that. "Now, for my second question: how was it physically possible for Angel Hutson to hang herself?"

Officer Kallman said nothing.

Denny continued. "She was maybe five-foot-two in shoes. The ceilings in jail cells are what, eight feet tall?"

"Yes, sir," Kallman agreed.

"So what did a five-foot girl stand on in order to reach the light fixture eight feet up and tie the bed sheet around it? Are stools or ladders now common issue in county jail cells?"

"Sir, I think you need to speak with the detective in charge."

"I think I need to prepare my next newscast."

He turned around and went back to his car.

That bit about the newscast was of course a bluff, but Officer Kallman wouldn't know that.

Once he got to his apartment he resumed his conversation with his buddy Jim Beam that they'd started in the Sunset Room. If he hadn't quit he could go back on the air and report his suspicions. Then again, if he hadn't quit he likely would not have gotten this far.

By nightfall Jim was dead and rolling across the floor. Denny would have to go to the nearest Shoot-N-Rob to find his replacement. Since the room was subtly moving when he stood up from his chair, he decided he'd better walk to the store, not drive.

Unlike the hot mother of a day he'd already endured the evening was cool and comforting, easy on his head. He was so focused on walking a straight line that he did not notice the car that started up as soon as he left his building, which was now following him.

Once inside the store he took his sweet time looking over all of the distilled offerings. He toyed with the idea of picking up two bottles, since he had money in his pocket, but reconsidered. Instead he decided to get just one, but Makers Mark, not Beam.

Sorry, Jim; life's a bitch, then you die.

With his new best friend ineffectively disguised by a paper sack, Denny headed back for his place, but he was now conscious of slow-moving headlights behind him. He stopped and turned, and watched as a car pulled up beside him and stop. Looking through the passenger window he was surprised to see Larry Barker behind the wheel.

"Jesus, Larry, I don't work for you anymore," he said through the window. "I left the tape from that stupid groundbreaking at the office. Get someone to do something with it."

"Get in the car," Larry said. "Hurry."

"It's a nice night for walking, thanks."

"If you really want to know what's going on with Angel Hutson, get in the motherfucking car!"

Denny didn't realize Barker knew words like that. He got in the car.

"How sauced are you?" Barker asked as he pulled away from the curb.

"Half-a-load, no more," Denny lied. "Mind if I ask what you're doing here?"

"I followed you from your apartment."

"Why?"

"Because you're in trouble. I was at the station an hour ago doing some last-minute stuff and I took a call from Del Ollis, the detective in charge of the strip club case, who wanted to talk to Thacker. I forwarded it to Rob, but secretly listened in on the extension. You really should have followed Thacker's instructions and stopped poking into Angel's death."

"I don't believe she killed herself."

"Of course she didn't kill herself. But thanks to you, proving that now is going to be impossible."

"What are you talking about?"

"I'm talking about the fact that you have less than no idea what you've gotten yourself into."

Barker turned a corner and sped up.

"Where are we going?" Denny asked.

"Since talking doesn't work so well with you, I'm going to show you something."

They drove in silence through the darkening city until arriving at a nondescript building in a mostly barren block at the southern edge of Springfield. Pulling around back Denny saw a large parking lot, hidden from the street, and mostly full of vehicles and motorcycles. The building looked empty until someone opened the front door to go inside and multi-colored, flashing lights bled out.

"What is this place?" Denny asked.

"What do you think?" Barker replied. "It's the strip club where Angel was working." "I thought the cops shut it down."

"Does it look shut down?"

Barker pulled into a parking spot and got out of the car. Denny blearily followed. There was no guard outside the door, but just inside stood an enormous bouncer, who nodded at them in a manner that indicated they had been seen and noted.

They did not go inside far enough to have to pay the cover charge.

The place was dark but pierced with the lights of dozens of lasers. Most of the space was taken up with a thrust stage, on which young women danced around wearing nothing but tiny sequined G-strings. Dozens of men in every mode of dress from suits to work clothes encircled the stage. Some threw money. One guy seemed to be jacking off under his bib overalls.

"There are private rooms in back where you get more than just a show," Barker told Denny. "Hard-ticket, of course."

"Did Angel...?"

Barker shook his head. "She was pressured to, but resisted."

"What's your involvement in all this?" Denny asked, but Barker remained silent.

The bouncer then appeared behind them and said, "In or out, gentlemen."

"Sorry, we've decided we're not staying," Larry said to the gorilla with a smile.

Denny had never seen him smile before. His teeth were short and square.

Once back inside the car Denny asked, "Why is this place still open?"

"The cops didn't really want it closed. Nor did they want any of the other girls arrested. They only wanted Angel."

"What the hell is this about? How come you know so much about this club and what Angel was up to?"

Larry pulled out of the lot and headed back toward town.

"She was working undercover at the club on my instructions."

"What?"

"I know you think I just sit around all day and read press releases and drive up to Jeff City every week, and do whatever else Rob Thacker tells me to. But I've been working on this story for months. And it's not simply that a quote-unquote strip club exists in Springfield, it's about who is behind it."

Denny rubbed his throbbing head and asked, "Who's behind it, then?"

"The Reverend Doctor Tommy Lin Farris is the owner of

that establishment, and others in a tri-county area."

"Farris? Mr. Devil's pipeline?"

"You really think he gets all his money from the collection plate and selling his prayer screeds? Farris is a one-man Mafia whose front business is God. I've confirmed through one source that Farris owns the joint through a dummy corporation, and that certain members of the police force are suspected of being on his payroll to make certain no one finds that out. But I have nothing on the record. So I asked Angel to apply for a job there and she was hired immediately because she had the obvious attributes for it."

"And that's all it took, your asking her? She wouldn't go see a movie on Sunday, but you ask and she gets up and dances naked for dozens of horny hillbillies?"

Barker exhaled heavily. "I might be the only one she ever told about this but Angel had been molested by men in her church throughout her adolescence," he said. "For that and other reasons she had grown to hate the way rich and powerful men used religion as a weapon, particularly against women. She decided to take control of her sexuality and used it as a way to fight back. She was happy to do it."

Had Angel considered sex with him a form of fighting back? Denny wondered.

Barker went on. "Angel Hutson had the guts of a field soldier. What I realized too late is that she was simply too inexperienced to work undercover. She asked too many questions of the others who worked there and made the questions too pointed. Even her refusal to service customers in the back might have been a tip-off to the club's management that something was wrong. Her big mistake, though, was writing down all she'd learned in a notebook and leaving it at the club. It was found. At that moment Angel became a threat to Tommy Lin Farris that had to be dealt with."

"You mean murdered," Denny said. "You got her killed, Larry."

Barker did not deny it.

They drove in silence for a few more minutes. Then Denny asked, "Just how close were you two?"

"I wasn't bedding her if that's what you're asking," Barker replied. "That kind of complication I didn't need."

As complications go it was pretty sweet, Denny thought. Then the thought that it would never happen again made for a dull ache in his chest. "Where are you taking me, anyway?" he asked.

"My place."

"Why?"

"Because it's safe. Your place isn't."

"How do you know that?"

"Because you've spent the entire day antagonizing the police, giving them every reason to think you know Angel's death wasn't suicide. They're not going to give you the opportunity to say it to anyone else."

"Aren't you getting a little carried away with all this, Larry?"

Barker slammed on the brakes and brought the car to a screeching halt in the middle of the street. "Fine, you want me to drop you off at your apartment? Let's go, because maybe I am wrong. Maybe the police aren't really there planting little bags of something nasty in your sock drawer so they can have a pretense to arrest you. Maybe they weren't really searching Angel's apartment either, and probably planting some of the same shit there as a way to support their theory that she was whacked out. Maybe I have an overactive imagination. What the hell, maybe Angel isn't really dead! You want to take the chance that I'm wrong? Fine. Just go home, and if there's no police there I'm full of shit. Feel free to point and laugh at me. If I'm right, however, you'd better have a damn good lawyer who works fast, because you might not last any longer in the county jail than Angel did. Your choice."

"Fuck," Denny moaned. "All right, you win."

"I promise you I'm not trying to save your ass because I like you. My conscience just can't bear the weight of another quote-unquote suicide."

Larry Barker's home was an old Victorian house in a quiet neighborhood not far from the civic center. "Can I bring this in with me?" Denny asked, holding the bottle of Makers Mark he'd bought.

"Go ahead," Barker sighed, getting out of the car.

The place was quaint and comfortable with a lot of wood-work, high ceilings, and not much furniture. A framed photo of a woman sat on a mantelpiece over a hearth that looked like it was never used. "Your wife?" Denny asked.

"Yes. Martha died two years ago in an auto accident. She was killed by a drunk driver who was the son of a former county commissioner. He was never charged."

"Shit," Denny said as he seated himself on an old sofa. "I'm sorry, man."

"Maybe now you understand why I get so carried away by things. I'll make some coffee." Barker went into the kitchen.

By the time he returned a couple minutes later Denny had drained two fingers of his bottle. "Since you obviously know everything that goes on around here," he said, "what's the deal with cable television and Farris's opposition to it?"

"What I've been able to glean from sources is that Farris is laying the groundwork to start his own television network which would be based here in Springfield. But if the city gets cable, that's direct competition. He was apparently shocked that the city council didn't simply kowtow to his demands, but a church-based network wouldn't generate tax revenue for the city like a commercial network would. Since the council agreed to put the matter on the ballot, Farris is running the campaign against it, and he has no shortage of followers who will be happy to go door-to-door to convince people to vote it down."

"What are you going to do with all this information?"

"When I can actually prove anything I'm going to contact the FBI," Barker said. "Until then I keep digging, quietly."

"Why not release it now? Go to the newspaper with it. Let

people know what's really going on here."

"Most people don't want to know what's going on. They don't want to be confronted with the fact that just below all the country music and revival meetings and fishing shows on television is a stratum of evil. Or, at least, humanity at its worst. Springfield doesn't have a monopoly on evil, of course. Most cities, no matter how big or small, have some kind of dark underside. But for some reason people here tend to think the town is immune to bad things. They think it's Eden. But you shouldn't be worrying about what I'm going to do. The question is what are you going to do? You have to think about getting out of the city before they find you."

"You really think Farris would try to have me killed?" Denny asked.

"I wouldn't have thought so before yesterday. I think the coffee's ready." Barker went back into the kitchen.

Denny's head was spinning, and not simply because of the booze. To hear Barker talk you'd think he had to go into witness relocation. That was not conducive to a career in broadcasting. He took another drink. Hell…Larry was simply being overdramatic. It couldn't be that dire. Maybe Denny should call the FBI himself.

His thoughts were interrupted by the sound of a dull thud coming from the other room. It was followed by a small cry and the sound of a body hitting the floor.

"Larry?" Denny said, leaping up. "You okay?"

Another man stepped out from the kitchen, a large man with Elvis hair.

Detective Del Ollis held an automatic on Denny.

"Hey, hey, what the hell?" Denny cried. "How'd you get in here?"

"Old houses are the easiest to break into," Ollis said. "Almost as easy as tailing a couple assholes in a car. Get in the kitchen."

After being forced at gunpoint into the room Denny saw the prone body of Larry Barker crumpled against the cabinets.

"He's not dead," Ollis said, "not yet." Then he pulled out a second gun and held it on Barker, while keeping the automatic trained on Denny. "You've really become a problem, Mr. Venable. You should have taken the hint when you were told to drop looking into the Hutson girl's suicide."

"Suicide my ass, you fucker," the bourbon said through Denny's mouth. "She was murdered, which you know, because you're probably the one who did it. How much did Farris pay you for the hit?"

"Not that it's any of your goddamned business, five grand. I should have gotten more. I did get a bonus, though. The Hutson girl was quite a hot little number. Do you know the slut bitch offered to blow me if I'd stop messing with her in the jail? But I couldn't do that because it would be breaking the law. Or maybe you don't know that blowjobs are illegal in this city."

Denny knew. He'd covered the city council meeting in which the outlawing of oral sex was re-ratified.

Jesus…Angel…

"Damn, you're actually crying," Ollis said, as a hot tear rolled down Denny's face. "That's a good sign because it means I've hit you where it hurts and you're too weak to fight back. So here's how it's going to work. My investigation will reveal that both you and your friend here were screwing the little chippie, but you didn't know that until she lynched herself in the cell. When you found out about each other you decided to have it out once and for all. A duel of honor. Two bodies, two guns, one dead slut, what could be simpler? And please don't waste your last breath telling me I'll never get away with it. I hate clichés. And I always get away with it."

Larry Barker started rustling on the floor and moaning. Keeping one gun trained on Denny, he prodded Barker into a sitting position with his foot.

Barker opened his eyes. "Shit," he uttered.

"Yeah, kinda sucks, doesn't it?" Ollis said.

Then he fired two shots simultaneously.

One of the bullets tore through Denny's abdomen and he went down hard, but he was not dead. At least he didn't think so. Nobody dead could be in so much pain.

He felt the flow of warm blood running out of him onto the floor. He also felt a gun being pressed into his right hand.

That was the last thing he knew...until the sound of sirens invaded his ears.

Either a few seconds or an eternity had passed by the time he heard voices and saw the movement of people, but couldn't tell if they were real. He heard someone shout, "Oh, my God!" and faintly felt someone touching his neck. "This one's still alive!" He felt other hands on his body, touching him, inspecting him. He heard another voice say, "Damn, he's lost a lot of blood. Call an ambulance, quick."

"No time!" somebody else declared. "There's only one chance for him."

Denny had often heard that the process of dying included floating upwards, and he felt himself doing so. But he stopped before reaching the ceiling. "Get him in the patrol car and drive him to the ER at Cox!"

Somehow he was able to open his eyes.

Denny was surrounded by uniformed policemen.

They were carrying him.

Then it was dark. He was outside.

"You sure we shouldn't just wait for an ambulance?" he heard someone ask.

"I'm telling you, it'll never get here in time. I know a gut shot when I see it. Get him in the car and don't spare the sirens!"

With difficulty, the cops placed him on the back seat of a police car, whose lights were flashing.

As the cop car took off, sirens wailing, a coldness overtook him.

I'm going to make it, he thought through excruciating pain. That fucker Ollis...too cocky to check...I'm alive...I'll see him burn...for Angel...I'll finish Larry's work...

A towel had been wrapped around him to catch the blood, which fell off as he forced himself to sit up, just a bit. Through the mesh barrier he could make out the silhouette of the officer in the passenger seat. "How...long...to...hospital?" Denny forced himself to say, and the effort caused so much pain he nearly passed out.

The cop removed his patrolman's cap, freeing the explosion of hair underneath, then turned around and looked at him.

"Hospital?" Del Ollis laughed. Turning to the driver, he commanded, "Kill the fucking siren."

The last thing Dennis Martin Venable heard as he floated upward was silence.

SINS OF THE FATHERS

Jaden Terrell

"Daddy, I'm afraid."

Duncan Caine's hand tightened on his phone. He didn't need her to tell him that. The tremor in her voice had said it all the moment he tapped answer on the screen. No hello, just a tearful launch into the day's events.

"I'm on my way," he said, as if she were twelve again, being picked on by the boys at school. "Are you at home?"

"A friend's. His name is Christian. You've heard me talk about him. Dad, Trey said someone told him about me. About...what I am."

It took him a moment to think of an answer. Finally, he said, "When he asked you about it, what did you tell him?"

A note of defensiveness crept into her voice. "I'm not a liar."

"You said you were living in stealth mode. A lie of omission is still a lie."

Her tone hardened. "Are you saying this is my fault? Because if you are—"

"Of course not. He hit you. You know how I feel about that." How many times had he told her—first as Mitch, from one side, then as Mikki, from the other? A man who hits a woman is no man at all.

"I know how you feel about that," she said, but now there was a sullen edge to her voice. A flash of memory came to him. His hand rising, his face contorted in anger. No son of mine...

He decided to let it go. "Are you safe now?"

"I managed to cold-cock him with a lamp and get out of the apartment. But he has resources. I'm afraid he'll find me."

"I'm coming to get you," he said. "Where does this friend of yours live?"

When she'd given him the address and signed off with a quick *Love you, Dad*, he plucked his car keys from the hook beside the door, the one she'd made in woodworking shop back when he'd had a son and not a daughter. The woodburned letters said "Dad's keys", with a heart on either side.

The hearts had bothered him at the time.

Now they were just another sign.

Mikki slipped her phone into her purse, then pulled it out again and took a couple of selfies, making sure to show the bruise on her jaw, the blood caked around her swollen nose, the eye that was beginning to blacken. She texted them to herself and then to Christian with the caption "Compliments of Trey Kilkinnen". Yes, that Trey Kilkinnen.

She put the phone away, got up and checked the windows. All locked, thank God, even though the AC was only half working and she had to fan herself with Christian's water bill. No one outside, not that she could see. The old house creaked, settling on its foundation. The pipes ticked. Old house noises. She wished Christian would come home. He'd gone out to pick up a Papa Murphy's pizza and a six pack of Bud Light.

It was too damn hot for pizza, but the Bud would taste good.

She hoped her father would hurry. She imagined him hurtling down I-40, accelerator pressed to the floor of his F-150 pickup. He'd been a Night Stalker in the army, and she could still remember sharing a bowl of popcorn in front of his big screen TV, how he chuckled when Liam Neeson said his famous line: "What I do have are a very particular set of skills." She'd feel safer if he were here.

He was a hard man, her father. After basic combat training and advanced individual training with the U.S. Army, he'd gone on to Fort Benning for Airborne School. He was good with machinery and better at tactics, and Mikki imagined the powers that be had jumped to accept his application to the Night Stalkers—more formally known as the 160th Special Ops Aviation Unit. He was training at Fort Campbell, in what they called "the Green Platoon," when Mikki was born, and she'd grown up listening to his stories about leading clandestine night missions and extracting soldiers from warzones.

"A Night Stalker never quits," he'd say when she'd wanted to give up on some sport or obligation. It was a lot to live up to. She wasn't sure she could have done it even if she'd been the boy she was supposed to be.

They hadn't spoken for three years after she'd started the hormone therapy, and if her mother hadn't gotten sick, they might have stayed estranged forever. Mom had brought them back together, and somehow they'd grown even closer after she was gone. It was funny. All she'd ever wanted was for him to be proud of her. Mikki knew she'd been a disappointment as a son, but she seemed to be a pretty good daughter.

She looked at her watch again. Jumped at a branch tapping at the window.

Hurry, Daddy. Please.

Maybe she was overreacting. Trey had gotten his punches in, and now maybe he'd just go home and sulk and nurse his headache. But she didn't think so.

She heard tires crunch on Christian's gravel drive, heard an engine rev, then die.

Christian? Her pulse thundered in her ears. It couldn't be Trey. He didn't even know where she was.

But he might have asked around. It was no secret Christian was her closest friend.

A man's voice, not Christian's, a low curse. She was off the couch and racing for the kitchen when she heard the front door splinter.

She'd been fast in high school, but she didn't have the muscle or the edge she'd had then. Even if she made it out the back door, he'd be on her before she made it down the walk. She could scream, but this wasn't the kind of neighborhood where that mattered.

She flung open the back door, then spun back and slid into the walk-in pantry. The door clicked closed moments before his footsteps pounded past. They thudded down the back steps, one, two, three, then stopped.

Shit.

Why had she put her phone away? Why hadn't she grabbed a knife?

Her hand closed around a can of baked beans. It felt solid, but not solid enough. She cupped it to her chest. Crouching in the pantry, forcing herself to take shallow, silent breaths, she prayed her father would get there in time.

Duncan turned into the driveway beside Mikki's Subaru. No other cars. Maybe her friend Christian was at work. Or out banging some dude. He pushed down a wave of disgust. None of his business. The guy had taken Mikki in. He could bang anyone he wanted.

Then he saw the splintered front door hanging by one hinge, and jammed the pickup into park. He was out of the truck before it even jolted to a stop, his mind crystal clear like it had been in the war.

Inside, also like in the war, the body of a young woman lay crumpled on the floor. One arm was bent beneath her. The other covered her face like a broken shield. Blood matted her hair and turned her white shirt red. She was wearing denim shorts and cowboy boots, like a tourist, and they were bloody too. He didn't have to touch her to know she was dead.

For a moment, like a double exposure, he saw a small head

covered in blood, crowning from his wife's loins. It's a boy. And eighteen years later, his wife's voice: we didn't lose a son; we found a daughter.

A voice cried out inside him, a sound like a wounded bull. But already, he was pushing it down into the cold, clear fire of rage.

Somewhere behind him, he heard a male voice, anxious, concerned. "Mikki?" Then, "Oh, my God, what did you do?"

While the young man, Christian, went onto the front stoop and tapped in 9-1-1 with trembling hands, Duncan verified what he already knew: Mikki's killer was gone. Then, careful to avoid the streaks and spatter on the floor and walls, he stood in the doorway between the kitchen and the living room and read the story the house had to tell. A can of baked beans, caked with blood and strands of short dark hair, said she'd fought when her killer dragged her from the pantry. A rust-colored stain above a plate-sized area of cracked plaster showed where he'd slammed her into the wall. Footprints said she'd slipped free at least twice, and each time, he'd taken her down, like a hyena on a gazelle. They'd turned over chairs. They'd broken lamps. In her battle to survive, his girl had broken most of her fingernails.

A fighter, just like her old man.

He picked his way through the crime scene, careful not to touch anything, and stepped out onto the stoop. Christian had slipped his phone into his pocket and pulled out a cigarette. He blew out a shaky stream of smoke and looked at Duncan. "They should be here in a few minutes."

"Tell me about this boyfriend. Trey, is it?"

"Trey Kilkinnen. You'll know his mom. Sara Kilkinnen."

Duncan had heard of her, a country music megastar who'd made her debut on some reality show and had since amassed a string of hits and a couple of CMA awards. "And his father?"

"He's a judge. I'm not sure what kind. I only know he's got a lot of clout."

"Money and power," Duncan said. "I don't like that combination."

Christian tapped on his phone, pulled up a series of photos, and scrolled through them for Duncan. "She sent them to me less than an hour ago. I guess she wanted a record of what Trey did, and of her calling him out." His voice broke. "She said somebody called and told him she was born a boy. What kind of person would do that?"

Duncan couldn't answer that one. Instead, he pulled his keys out of his pocket. "I've got some things to take care of before I talk to the detectives. Do me a favor, would you? Send me those pictures?"

Judge Roy Kilkinnen was one of the most influential criminal court judges in Nashville. His wife, Sara, was not only a superstar, but an icon in the community, one of the few county music stars invited to the ultra-swanky, ultra-exclusive Swan Ball. Hunched in front of his computer, Duncan found a photo of the pair, the judge in a white tie, tux and tails, his wife in a form-fitting beaded gown that had probably cost more than Duncan's truck. A news article on the city's upper crust included a photo of Trey Kilkinnen on the deck of his parents' yacht, sunglasses hanging at a sporty angle from the front of his white button-down shirt.

Duncan downloaded both photos to his phone and continued his search. Ten years ago, maybe even five, it would have taken days to build as complete a picture of the Kilkinnens as he could get from the internet in only a few hours. By then, he knew the address of their Williamson County mansion, their political leanings, Sara's tour schedule and the judge's court docket. He knew Trey had a new Maserati GranTurisimo and that he lived in an attached apartment on the family estate. And he knew the mansion had a helipad and an Airbus H130 private helicopter.

It had been a long time since Duncan had flown a helicopter, but some things you never forgot.

When he'd learned everything he could about the Kilkinnens and surveilled the estate using Google Earth, he turned off his computer and leaned back in his chair. He should probably eat something, but he wasn't hungry. Maybe a drink, but he didn't want to dull his edge. He went to the kitchen and opened the fridge. Closed it again. There was nothing there he wanted.

He felt adrift in the old farmhouse. It seemed emptier than it had ever been, but why that should be he couldn't say. His wife's hospital bed, almost two years empty, gathered dust in the spare room. He'd grown used to her absence, as used to it as you could get to such a thing. And his daughter hadn't lived there since she was in high school. The house was exactly as it had been a day ago, yet everything had changed.

He wandered from room to room, running his fingers over the photos of Mikki and her mother, straightening the afghan Mikki sat under when she came by for dinner and a movie. There were no pictures of the younger Mikki. Mitch. Those, along with Mitch's track and baseball trophies were packed away and hidden in the basement. Maybe he should pull them out, remember the boy he'd loved and failed, and the daughter he'd loved more fiercely and failed even more completely.

The doorbell broke the moment, and he was glad of it. He opened it and saw two detectives, both holding up their badges. Frank Campanella, a stocky, silver-haired veteran and Kelly Malone, a lanky red-haired woman in her thirties. He stepped aside to let them in.

"We're sorry for your loss," Campanella said.

Malone said, "But you shouldn't have left the scene before we took your statement."

Duncan cocked his head. Was this the good cop, bad cop game? Interesting casting, the pretty young woman as the bad cop.

"I..." He let his voice break, turned aside so they wouldn't see that his eyes were dry. "I couldn't stand to be there anymore."

Malone said, "The young man, Christian, said at first he

thought you'd done it."

"I suppose he would," said Duncan. "Until he saw I wasn't covered in blood."

Campanella gestured toward the couch. "Mind if we sit?"

"Suit yourself."

Campanella took the far end of the couch. Malone took Mikki's seat. Blind luck, maybe, or some lingering pheromones that said it was a woman's space. Duncan sat across from them in the recliner.

"What were you doing there?" Malone said.

"Didn't Christian tell you? Mikki called me. Told me she thought Trey was going to kill her."

"Right." Campanella shifted in his seat. "Because of the phone call. Any idea who would have wanted to out her like that?"

Duncan shrugged. "I don't know any of her friends. And as far as I know, she didn't have any enemies. Have you talked to the Kilkinnen boy? Could be he knows."

"Funny thing," Malone said. "We haven't been able to reach him."

"Maybe you should check hospitals and clinics. I think she hurt him. With the baked beans."

Campanella lifted an eyebrow. "You're an observant man."

It was an observation, not a question, so Duncan didn't see a need to answer it.

"I doubt he'd go to a public facility," Malone said. "Under the circumstances."

Duncan swung his gaze toward her. "Are you going to arrest him?"

"We'll take him in for questioning, of course. See where that goes. If his DNA is at the scene, we have a decent case."

"What does that mean, a decent case?"

Campanella said, "It means we've got enough to go to a grand jury. Between the photos she sent Christian and the forensic evidence, they'll rule there's enough to go to trial."

Duncan didn't answer. A trial meant lawyers, Trey Kilkinnen's and the state's, and Trey would have the finest defense attorneys money could buy. Duncan knew what a good lawyer would do. A good lawyer would say Trey had been traumatized at learning the woman he'd been sleeping with used to be a man. He'd say Trey was a bright young man who'd understandably snapped, a young man with a future full of promise. The jury would take one look at Trey in his thousand-dollar suit and let him go. Even if they didn't, the judge, who probably golfed with the honorable Roy Kilkinnen, would give him a slap on the hand.

Malone leaned forward in her seat. "What Frank is saying is, we've got this, Mr. Caine. What we need you to do is trust the system and let us do our jobs."

Duncan forced a smile. "Of course, detectives. I wouldn't dream of doing anything else."

Trey Kilkinnen came back on the grid on Tuesday, five days after Mikki's death. Duncan, slouched low in the F-150, Nashville Sounds ball cap pulled low over his face, watched from an alcove down the street as Trey's Maserati entered through the wrought-iron gate of the estate. A few minutes later, Campanella and Malone went in and brought him out in handcuffs. Duncan peeled off for lunch and a bathroom break, then took up his position again. He was still there when Trey climbed out of his father's Mercedes six hours later, a grin on his face and a swagger in his step.

Six hours. That was how long it took the wheels of justice to grind to a halt.

Trust the system.

Sure.

He walked back to his truck, took the Sig P226 from his glove box and holstered it, then tugged his shirt down to cover the gun. Opened the new roll of duct tape and put it back into the glove compartment, along with a package of zip ties. He checked his phone, saw that Christian had sent the photos of

Mikki's battered face.

Took a long breath.

He forced himself to scroll through them all, then put the phone back in his pocket, along with another photo he'd taken from its frame at home. He felt numb, but numb was good. It meant emotions wouldn't mess with his mind. Some people might say he was being macabre, but being macabre had nothing to do with it.

He was making himself strong.

Trey and his two-man posse, Andrew and Tyler, drove down to the Gulch for margaritas and homemade guac at their favorite cantina, then left Trey's car in valet and took a cab downtown to lower Broadway. The night was sweltering, but it felt good to be free. Or the nearest next thing to it. He'd been scared at first, but Ian Davis, Trey's new lawyer, seemed pretty sure they'd get him off, even though that lying bitch had spread his DNA all over the fucking crime scene. Diminished capacity, Davis had said. Trey didn't like the sound of that. It seemed like something that might affect his future. What law firm was going to hire a guy who beat a murder rap because of diminished capacity?

A bike bar pedaled past them, a bunch of drunk girls rocking out to country music. They were dressed in shorts and cowboy boots, T-shirts and the occasional halter top. One wore a bridal veil and a pageant sash that said Blushing Bride. Dollars to doughnuts she'd need a divorce lawyer in three to seven years. Not a bad field to go into, if you liked good money and an excuse to comfort aggrieved women. Which Trey did.

His buddy Andrew nudged him with an elbow. "I'd do the one on the end."

"The redhead? Yeah, she's not bad." She reminded him of that red-haired detective who'd hauled him in for questioning. She was too old for him, but he wouldn't mind a piece of that ass, even though she looked like she'd swallowed a persimmon when his lawyer had sprung him. He'd looked close for an Adam's apple, hadn't seen one. Better believe he'd be checking for that now.

The thought of Mikki made him mad all over again. It wasn't right, the way she'd lied to him. Basically, she'd tricked him into sleeping with a man.

They passed a couple more pedal bars—bachelorette party capital of the world, hell yeah—a few horse-drawn carriages and Cinderella coaches. Stopped to listen to a street musician, then made their way to Tootsie's for a couple of beers. The band at the front, the Dudes Terrific, was one he hadn't heard before, but they were solid, and he dropped a fifty in the bucket just because he could.

"Hey, man." Tyler said. "You ever going to tell us what happened to your face?"

"Nothing. You should see the other guy." He downed the beer, gestured for another. That was when he noticed the old guy at the next table. He was forty, maybe fifty, somewhere around Trey's father's age, with short dark hair and a chiseled face. Eyes like a shark.

Trey puffed out his chest and jabbed a finger at the old guy. "What are you lookin' at, Grandpa?"

The guy stared back, not blinking. "Nothing," he said. "I'm looking at nothing at all."

From a patch of woods on the Kilkinnen estate, Duncan kept a watch with binoculars all the next morning and into late afternoon. The judge's Mercedes pulled out shortly after 8:00 a.m. Around noon, a groundskeeper arrived and started running a mower over the expansive lawn surrounding the place. There was no sign of Mrs. Kilkinnen. According to her online itinerary, she was in Vegas for the week.

The family helicopter sat on its circular concrete pad. Duncan was studying it when Trey came out in a bathing suit, flip flops, and a loud Hawaiian shirt, a towel around his neck. He sat on the pool's edge with his legs in the water, looking hung over and morose.

Duncan waited until the groundskeeper made his way to the other side of the estate. Then he crept up behind Trey, using foliage plantings for cover. He crouched close and stuck the gun muzzle in Trey's ear. "Don't move."

Trey jolted, then slowly raised his hands.

"Put your hands down," Duncan said. "This isn't the OK corral. Now, get up, nice and slow. Stay close ahead of me. We're going inside."

Trey complied, but Duncan felt him tense as they entered the apartment. "Don't try it, Trey. You're no hero."

"Look," Trey said, "if this is a robbery—"

"Shut up and sit on the couch."

Duncan stepped away, the pistol still trained on the boy. One-handed, he used zip ties to bind Trey's wrists and ankles. Then he used more ties to secure Trey's ankles to the leg of the couch.

The boy was glaring at him. "My dad is going to—"

Duncan cut him off with a strip of duct tape over his mouth. After that, it only took five minutes to find the keys to the chopper in a garage cabinet close to an outside door. With the sound of the mower moving closer, Duncan put the keys in his pocket and came back to cut Trey's ties and remove the tape.

Rubbing his wrists, Trey said, "You're in big trouble, you son of a bitch…"

Duncan cocked his head toward the pistol in his hand. "I'm not the one in trouble, Trey."

The boy's eyes narrowed. "Wait a minute. I know you. I saw you at Tootsie's last night."

Duncan didn't bother to answer. He waited for the mower to move away again, then prodded Trey out to the helicopter. "Nice bird. How about we take it for a ride?"

They were almost to the passenger door when Trey whirled

and threw a wild punch that caught Duncan's left ear. Stunned, Duncan stumbled backward as Trey grabbed for the gun.

For a moment, Tennessee's humid heat was the dry heat of Iraq, the Kilkinnen's manicured lawn a sandblasted street in Kabul. As if it were twenty years old again, Duncan's body remembered its training. He swept Trey's legs out from under him, and as the boy went down hard, flat on his back, Duncan jerked him up in a choke hold. He kept it tight until Trey stopped thrashing and went still.

Take that, you son of a bitch.

They were at seven thousand feet over a vast forest north of Nashville, the lowering sun a bloody smear in the haze off to the left, shadows lengthening on the undulating hills below, when Trey came to and fought against the silver tape wrapping him tight to the passenger seat.

"Wha...What the hell is this? What do you think you're doing? Who the fuck are you, anyway?"

Duncan had not put headsets on either of them, but the cabin was well soundproofed, the plexiglass thick, so they only had to raise their voices a little to be heard over the engine and rotor noise. "Nice helo," he said. "I'm rusty, but this is a forgiving machine. Lots of extras. I figure it cost your father's trust about three mil, that about right?"

"You want money, is that it? Put us down and I'll make a call. My father will pay."

Of course he would. That was how you made monsters like Trey. You gave them anything they wanted and made sure they never suffered any consequences. "It's not about money, Trey. It's about what you did to my daughter. To Mikki. What we're doing here is sorting that out."

Trey stared at him. The boy was undeniably handsome, but now he looked like a cornered animal, his eyes glowing in the low sunlight. "The fuck you talking about, old man? You got any idea how much trouble you're in? My father will crucify you."

"All I want is for you to admit what you did. Then it will all be over."

"What, you recording this or something? I'm not saying anything to you."

"I'm not recording. This is just you and me. How did you know about her? Who made that call?"

"I don't know what you're talking about. Look, put us down and I'll forget all this, I swear."

The sun was lower now, a splinter of gold edging the hills. "You know, back in the day, they taught us how to do an emergency landing in a helo if you lose power. Made us practice it over and over. Let's see if we can do one in this beauty, okay?"

"Wait. No."

"First you reduce the power to idle and cut the rotor blade angle. By lowering the collective here. The thing that looks like a parking brake. Like this. Then you ease back on the cyclic stick. Puts the machine into a mush, like this. Feels like we're just floating on down, right? Getting nice and quiet. The up-rushing air is keeping the rotor blades spinning, still providing enough lift to slow the descent, but we're still falling pretty fast. Watch the altimeter there unwinding. It's tricky, because if the blades stall, we'll freefall."

"No, don't do this. I don't like it. I'll tell you whatever you want to hear. Bring the power back up. Please."

"Watch the altimeter spin down, Trey. Look outside. No ground rush yet, but there will be in just a minute or so. Why did you kill Mikki?"

"Okay, okay. I did it, okay? But I never meant to. When I...when I found out what she was, I just, I just lost it, you know? And then when I went to her queer boyfriend's place, just to like talk, she attacked me. It was only self-defense after that. Stop this dive, for chrissake."

"What you're supposed to do," Duncan said, "is flare the helo when you get down to a hundred feet or so to slow the forward speed, then, just before the ground, you haul back on the collective so it arrests the descent for a nice soft touchdown, but it's a trade-off, because you lose most of your rotor speed. You have to time it just right. Not too high, not too low."

"Okay. I've got it. Now bring the power back before we get any lower."

"Who told you about Mikki?"

"I don't know. Some girl. I think she changed her voice. It sounded weird, you know? She said she thought I had a right to know. A guy has a right to know what he's sleeping with."

The words hit Duncan like a slap. They were his words. He'd said them to Mikki not two weeks before. *If he loves you, he'll be okay with it, but he has a right to know. A man has a right to know who—or what—he's sleeping with.* Realizing how it sounded, he'd apologized for the wording but not the sentiment. She'd signed off with her usual *I love you, Dad,* but even he could hear the hurt in her voice.

She'd made the call herself. Too anxious or ashamed to tell Trey face to face, she'd tried to start the conversation by outing herself in an anonymous call. And for what? To make her stubborn, stupid old man proud.

He might as well have killed her himself.

Between clenched teeth, he said, "Remember when I told you it was just you and me? I lied. Before you came to, I called Air Traffic Control and told them who we are. Then I taped a microphone to your seat headrest, close enough so they could pick up everything we said. I taped the trigger switch on your cyclic stick so we'd be continuously transmitting. They know it all now, Trey."

"You're sick, old man. Crazy. I was just saying whatever you wanted to hear. I'll deny everything. My father...what are you doing now?"

Duncan trapped the cyclic between his knees so he could pull a photo out of his shirt pocket.

Mikki. Smiling. Proud. Full of life.

I'm putting it right, Mikki. Trey and me, we both pay.

He looked at the altimeter. Still a thousand feet above the darkening woods. Starting to get some serious ground rush now. Memories flashed behind his eyes. Every missed moment, every harsh word. But good times too. Tossing a baseball with his grinning son. Looking out across the city from the Ferris wheel at the state fair as he learned to know his daughter for the first time, her eyes bright with laughter, his mouth sweet with the taste of cotton candy.

He shut down the engine and hauled back on the collective and the rotor blades became visible fluttering overhead.

Slowing...

Slowing...

The machine abruptly abandoned the sky, heeled over, and plummeted. Duncan stared down through the expansive Plexiglass into the onrushing jumble of trees, his ears filled with the sound of Trey's high-pitched, panicked wail.

STEEL CITY BLUES

Dennis Palumbo

Pittsburgh, PA 1970

I'm sitting at my usual spot on the roof, back against one of the brick smokestacks, the revolver across my upraised knees. Chill from the river stinking of burnt oil, decaying fish and tugboat exhaust. Night black as wet ink.

There's about twenty feet of treated oak and reinforced concrete between my ass and the huge blast furnace below, here at Jones and Laughlin Steel Works, Second Avenue. Part of seventeen miles of steel mills along the Monongahela River.

Back story (i.e., home life): My mother, a bitter lapsed Catholic addicted to cigarettes and prescription meds, was little more than a shadow in her own house. Couldn't do much to stop the old man from beating me bloody on a pretty regular basis. But only when he was drunk. Which was always.

Things got worse when I went to college. Me with my long hair, head-banging music, and high draft number. He'd served in Korea and had no use for jagoff peaceniks like me.

Anyway, Mom died during my sophomore year at Pitt, so the old man stopped paying tuition. But I was determined to finish college. Maybe even go for an advanced degree. Last thing I wanted was to end up some blue-collar wage slave like my father.

So I moved out, split a crib on a side street off Forbes Avenue with three other stoners, and went job-hunting. Pitt's a state school and pretty cheap. But I still needed bread.

Which is how I ended up here in hell's sphincter, sweating my balls off in one hundred thirty-four degree heat, scarfing down salt pills. Box anneal department. Where we heat and roll steel sheets that go into the making of battleship plating for Vietnam. Or else fenders for Buicks. Nobody on the floor knows for sure.

Not that us college kids, just summer hires, are consulted on product development. We're assigned the "shit detail," so-called by the Floor Pigs. Company guys, pricks in collared shirts with pocket protectors and the signature white hard hats.

Which is to separate them from the veteran, rank-and-file steel workers—known around here as "mill hunks"—whose own hard hats are a manly gunmetal gray.

Meanwhile us newbies got outfitted with yellow hard hats. So the crane operators high overhead could ID which punks to drop trash, dead light bulbs and empty Coke cans on.

"Fuck 'em, Eddie," my buddy Gabe used to say as we dodged some half-eaten salami sandwich or bag of rivets. He's a junior at Carnegie-Mellon and knee-deep in the student protest movement. "Guys like him are toast after the revolution."

Gabe's okay—bearded, with flinty eyes behind wire-rims—except for that thing he said about Marie and me. If he didn't outweigh me by fifty or so pounds, I'd have kicked his fat ass to hell and back. Yeah, right. Total bullshit.

But I'm getting ahead of myself. Especially about Marie.

So I'm up here on the tar-papered, gravel-strewn roof. On the other side of the Mon's sluggish black water, about eye-level from where I sit, is the Duquesne Beer clock. Pretty famous around here. Big, ugly, all twelve numbers illuminated around its face.

In case I didn't mention it, I'm majoring in English Lit, so I get the obvious symbolic meaning. Time passes, relentless, indifferent, etc. It's not exactly the eyes of T.J. Eckleburg (we ended the semester reading Gatsby), but it sure as hell seems to suit the spirit of my little existential dilemma.

See, the cops think I killed a guy named Frank Harrington and they're on their way up here to bust me. And I'm trying to decide if I'm gonna let them.

I mentioned the shit detail without explaining what it is. It's the main job for non-union, smart-ass college kids like me hired for the summer. It basically involves two kinds of back-breaking work: shoveling coal to feed the insatiable blast furnaces, so expensive to shut down that they're run twenty-four seven, even on Christmas; the other fun job requires shoveling sand all around the edges of massive metal hoods placed atop train flatcars, in which stand stacks of coiled steel bound for those above-mentioned blast furnaces.

To make sure the seal is secure, we jump down into a pit-like tunnel and tamp down the sand where the bottom of the hood meets the train car flatbed. To add to the excitement, the temp hits above one-fifty, you wear thin paper masks to prevent inhaling sand dust, and there's always a Floor Pig standing up at the lip of the pit, screaming things like "Faster, you cocksuckin' spoiled brat hippie bastards!" and other such encouragements.

By the end of a work shift (mine was usually midnight-to-6:00 a.m.), you're enveloped in so much sweat, teeth-gritting dust, and embittered exhaustion that you just stand there, mute and blinking, as Head Foreman Frank Harrington reams you out about all the work that didn't get done. And all the shit he'll have to take from the White Hats about it.

Frank was in his early sixties, big and round as a beer barrel, and about as intelligent. Eyes red from drink, sweat stains decorating the underarms of his rumpled denim shirt, brow furrowed with equal parts age and disillusionment.

At the end of each shift, he'd stand with one leg slightly cocked, John Wayne-style, and gaze with obvious distaste at his crew of long-haired, stoned-out, draft-dodging Commies. During which he'd deliver his requisite speech about what a bunch of miserable losers we were.

(Frank's favorite joke, from *Hee Haw*: "What's a hippie? A Jack who looks like a Jane and smells like a john." I rest my case.)

Anyway, that was life in this hellhole. Until that one day, the day this whole thing started. Me and Gabe and a couple other miserable losers were hanging around, waiting for Harrington's usual lecture, counting the minutes till we could clock out and get high. Usually up on the mill's peaked roof.

But Harrington didn't show. Finally, bored and restless, Gabe got off his ass and peered around one of the massive weight-bearing supports that keep the roof from caving in. Motioning for us to join him, he pointed at the foreman's shack, a glass-fronted enclosure built against the near wall. The single bulb hanging from its ceiling revealed that Frank was still in there. And he wasn't alone.

He also wasn't happy. Though his huge, rounded back was blocking the view, we could see through the window his beefy body literally shaking with anger. He was obviously carving somebody a new one.

Suddenly, he was roughly pushed aside, and the object of his tirade came striding out of the shack. Heading our way, her heels clicking loudly on the mill's steel flooring.

I can't speak for the other guys, but I just gaped as the woman approached. Thirty or a little older, I figured, dark-haired, dark-eyed, and in a very dark mood. She practically quivered with a suppressed anger of her own.

Not that this registered much on me. She wasn't the prettiest girl I'd ever seen (that was Jenny Stoltz, in my freshman social studies class, perfect ass and granny glasses), but there was something about this woman.

Maybe it was the way she strode on her long, smooth legs toward us. Her body lush, full. Womanly, I guess you'd say.

Here's the thing: she wasn't like the girls I knew on campus, with their tie-dyed jeans, "Fuck the War" T-shirts and flip-flops.

This woman wore red lipstick, a low-cut jade-green dress molded to her ample curves, and black high heels. But as she stepped up to where we still stood, wide-eyed and frozen, what I mostly felt was the clarity of her anger. She could've played a female assassin in a James Bond movie.

"You're those college kids Frank's always bitching about."

She gave us each a candid look. "Well, I don't envy you guys. Your boss is a prick."

Gabe chimed in. "Hey, it's not his fault. Like all these company men, he's a tool of the capitalist state."

She smiled. "He's a tool, all right. And he wishes he was a capitalist. Instead of a big, fat loser."

Just then, Harrington's voice echoed down the cavernous walls. I turned to see him standing in the shack's doorway. Swaying slightly. Already half in the bag.

"Ya little shits, get away from her!" He waved his hand.

"Ya hear me, scumbags? Get away from my wife."

When I turned back, the woman's face had gone rigid. Eyes hard as marble chips. Also, for the first time, I noticed the slim gold band on the third finger of her left hand.

"I'll talk to anybody I want, Frank!" she shouted back. "You don't own my ass!"

He gave a hoarse laugh. "Like hell I don't! I own every rotten inch of you, Marie! You know it and I know it!"

She bristled, then snapped her teeth shut. A long pause.

"Someday, Frank…" A hiss, under her breath. "Someday…"

Abruptly, before any of us could say another word, she pushed past us and strode to the nearest exit door. When she opened it, a wedge of dull morning sun slid in. She slipped through it like a wraith and was gone.

By now, Frank had gone back inside his shack and shut the door. Hefted a half-filled whiskey bottle with a fat hand.

Meanwhile, Gabe had sidled up to me, grinning.

"I saw the way you looked at the delicious Mrs. Frank. I thought your dick was gonna pop outta your jeans."

"Fuck you, Gabe."

"Besides, she's a dozen years older than you. And way outta your league."

"In case you didn't hear me, man, I said fuck you."

"Ah, now I get it." He stroked his beard thoughtfully. "Mommy issues, eh? Very uncool, man."

By the way, this was that time I mentioned earlier, when I wanted to hit him. And didn't, of course.

One of the other guys—black, caustic, a Jimi Hendrix wannabe named Styles—spoke up then.

"Speakin' of an age gap, what's with old man Harrington and that fine piece o' ass? He's gotta be over sixty or some shit, right?" He frowned. "Christ, that's one lucky bastard."

Gabe laughed. "Maybe. Though I don't think Frank's gonna get lucky tonight."

Then he gave me a strange, knowing look. "Unless maybe you wanna look her up...?"

I didn't respond. There're only so many times you can say "Fuck you" before you start sounding like the asshole.

I admit it. First thing I did when I hit the shower back at my apartment was jerk off. I kept thinking about those epic tits straining against her bra beneath that tight, heat-dampened green dress.

Not to sound like a sexist jerk, but the girls I knew from school rarely wore bras, and most didn't need them. (Okay, that was kind of sexist.) Don't get me wrong, I'm all for women's lib and everything, but Marie...

There was just something about her. Like a cloud of steam was coming off her, and not because we were on the hot, stifling mill floor. Everybody sweats in that fucking place. Maybe I'd just stood too close to her...

Meanwhile, one of my roomies had his radio blasting across the apartment. The Stones' latest hit off their new album. "You

Can't Always Get What You Want."

Great. Irony.

Anyway, I didn't see Marie again at work, and none of us yellow hats had the guts to mention her to Frank. Though it didn't stop him from busting our balls even worse than usual.

One night, a couple hours into my shift, I'd had enough and snuck outside to the parking lot to smoke a joint. The sky was black and cloudless, a wash of moonlight glinting off the roofs of the employee cars. Endless rows of Fords and Chevys, all makes and models. One hundred percent American-made.

Every mill hunk knew enough not to show up in some dipshit foreign car. Most knew, anyway. One stupid bastard rolled up last week in his brand-new Toyota and came out to find key scratches along both its shiny sides.

I was just about to head back into the building when Lucky Stashakov ambled over. Guess he'd had the same idea I did, because I saw him flick a spent joint off into the darkness as he approached.

I'd gotten to know him slightly over the past couple weeks, since he tended to hang out with me and Gabe. Made sense. In his mid-twenties, he was closer in age to the rest of us newbies than to his fellow mill hunks. Who had no use for him, either.

By the way, his real name is Charles, but after he lost two fingers when his hand got caught between a steel coil and a grappling hook, we got to calling him "Lucky." Naturally, the more we did it, the more he hated it.

Not that he'd had a real sunny nature before that. A Vietnam vet and heroin addict (when he could score it), he was a mean son-of-a-bitch on his best days. Which was another reason the other hard-hats avoided him. And why I was surprised to see his lopsided grin in the glow of the overhead parking lot light as he stepped up to me.

"Hey, retard," he said pleasantly. "Wanna see somethin'?"

I shrugged. "Sure."

It beat going back into Dante's Inferno. Without another

word, he turned and led me past a line of cars till we arrived at his own. A beat-up '64 Ford Fairlane.

He bent and unlocked the dented-in trunk. When he pulled up the lid, he nodded at the contents inside. Still smiling.

Even in the feeble light I could make out a cache of guns. Couple rifles. Handguns. Maybe a half-dozen in all.

"What the fuck?" I said, or something along those lines.

"Never know, man. Might come in handy."

"What are you talking about, Lucky? You planning on invading some small country?"

A sour laugh. "Been there, done that. No, this is just in case. Personal protection for when the shit goes down."

"What shit?"

"Whatever. You gotta think ahead, my man. Be prepared. Like the Boy Scouts say."

"Yeah, maybe. Meanwhile, you better shut the damn trunk before someone sees us. And I don't even want to know where you got all this stuff."

"Good. 'Cause I wasn't gonna tell ya."

With a last longing look at his private armory, he slammed the trunk lid down. Then we walked briskly—or as briskly as a couple of stoners can manage—back toward the mill entrance. The last thing we needed was more bullshit from Frank Harrington if he caught us sneaking back in.

Across the street from the mill's front entrance stood The Steel Keg, a weary, run-down bar. Typical Pittsburgh watering hole: outside, dark wood and chipped red brick, buzzing neon Iron City beer signs in the windows. Inside, equally dark walls and the smell of cigs, stale beer and sweat. Place had been here forever, and conveniently open at 6:00 a.m., to serve those of us hearty workmen coming off the midnight shift.

It was a couple days later, and Gabe and I were sitting on stools a good bit away from the regular mill hunks, drinking our morning beers. Avoiding the baleful, suspicious stares of the long-timers in their "Love It or Leave It" caps.

"Christ, they hate our guts." Gabe took a big pull from his mug. "That's 'cause we're here instead of gettin' our brains blown out over in Nam. Like real Americans."

I leaned toward him. "Keep it down, will ya, man? I'd like to make it through the summer in one piece."

"Don't be such a pussy." Gabe pushed awkwardly off his stool. "Anyway, I gotta roll. I'm meetin' a guy about some choice weed. Righteous dude offers a student discount."

With a mock wave to the rest of the barflies, he headed out the door, his every step registered by the scowling mill hunks.

I figured I'd better polish off my beer and get my own ass out of there before something seriously fucked went down. I hurriedly threw some bills on the bar, walked out into a blindingly bright sun, and nearly ran into Marie Harrington.

Waiting right outside the door. In denim shorts, casual sandals, and a man's work shirt tied up under her breasts. Beads of moisture dotted her deep, sun-bronzed cleavage.

"Hey, Eddie." A sly smile. "It's Eddie, right?"

I managed a nod. Suddenly aware of the foamy beer mustache on my upper lip. Real smooth.

As I reached up with my sleeve to wipe it off, her hand gripped my wrist to stop me. Eyes boring into mine.

"Here," she said softly. "Let me."

Then she leaned over and licked the foam from my lip.

By now, my heart was clanging in my chest. The warmth of her breath against my face, the way her breasts lightly brushed me as she moved forward. How she savored the beer foam on the tip of her tongue before swallowing it.

"Better?" Her gaze knowing, self-assured.

Another dumb nod. Finally, I dug up some actual words from the back of my brain.

"Look, Mrs. Harrington, I don't think—I mean, we're on the sidewalk here, in broad daylight, and if—"

"Call me Marie, okay? Since we're going to be friends. But you're right about our...exposure..."

With that, she gripped my wrist again and pulled us around the corner of the weathered building. There, in a deserted alley whose shadows hid us from the sun's glare—and the eyes of passers-by—Marie shoved me up against a rough-bricked wall.

"C'mon, Mrs. Har—I mean, Marie...what the hell are you doing to me?"

"Nothing, so far. But the day is young."

Now my confusion turned to a mounting fear.

"Shit, if Frank finds out about this..."

"You mean my old, broken-down husband? He'll huff and puff, all right, but he won't do a thing. Not to me."

"I'm not talking about you." I tried on a smile.

She considered this, her sensuous gaze slowly making its way up and down me like a searchlight.

"You've seen *The Graduate*, haven't you, Eddie?"

"Marie, please...I mean, this is crazy..."

"You're right. We should go find a hotel room."

I walked her back a step, willing myself to breathe normally. Stared into those dark, fathomless eyes.

"Listen, I don't know what you're doing..." Trying to sound firm. Resolute. "Maybe you just want to fuck with Frank's head. I don't know and I don't care, but—"

Unfortunately, my raging boner was doing a lot of damage to my credibility. She moved in, pressed herself against it. Her voice cool and measured.

"Jesus, Eddie, it's not that complicated. I just want to get laid. I noticed you the other day, hanging with your college friends, and...well, you seem like a nice kid...smart, good-looking...a bit innocent, maybe..."

I sniffed, offended. "I'm not a virgin, lady."

An indulgent smile. "Of course, you are."

She put her hand in my jeans pocket, slowly stroking my stiff cock, at the same time whispering in my ear.

"See, Eddie, it's like this: until they've been with me, all men are virgins."

With that, she turned, strode quickly out of the alley and disappeared around the corner.

It wasn't till I got back to the apartment that I realized she'd left a slip of paper in my pocket when she'd slid her hand inside.

There was a phone number written on it.

The next day, I called it.

I know what you're thinking. Same thing I was thinking. Getting mixed up with Marie Harrington was crazy. Hell, she was probably crazy. But so fucking hot I didn't care.

Then there was her husband Frank, the less-than-incredible Hulk. If he ever got wind of it, I'd end up in one of those goddam blast furnaces.

But like I said, there was just something about Marie...

Turned out, the number belonged to a friend of hers.

"From the old days," she'd explained later. This "old friend" told me over the phone to meet Marie at The Swan, a low-rent motel in Wilkinsburg, that night at nine. I did.

And that's how it all started.

Every other night we'd meet at nine, three hours before the start of my shift at the mill, and fuck our brains out.

I'll never forget the first time. I'm standing there, mute, death-grip on the tumbler of whiskey she'd insisted on pouring me. Watching her strip out of a black miniskirt, languorously sliding her panties down over her taut thighs. Then, turning, she had me unhook her bra. Some webbed, lacy thing. Given her full breasts, a marvel of construction.

Turning again to face me, she said one word. "Well?"

I have to admit, she was right about me back in that alley. Despite my real (though limited) experience, I might as well have been a virgin. When I was a senior at Penn Hills High, a girl complained that I came too quickly. Then my first girlfriend at Pitt said I was clumsy. That one hurt.

But Marie Harrington was unlike any woman I'd ever known. For one thing, she took her time, devouring me slowly. Making every moment, every touch of her manicured fingers, every flick of her tongue count.

She also loved to trip me out. Once she surprised me by wearing fishnet stockings, which she let me slowly peel off her stunning legs. I nearly popped my load halfway through. Another time, when she was on top and wearing only a silk blouse, she'd make me answer some stupid question about the news or some shit. Every time I got one right, she'd unbutton another button on the blouse. It was excruciating. And fucking great.

Afterwards, she said she liked my brains as much as my cock. Really turned her on. That didn't suck, either.

Still, I'll always remember that first night, and not just for the explosive sex. Lying naked in my arms, she took a quick, hesitant breath and filled me in on her marital situation. I'd rolled her a joint and I guess it made her feel like talking.

"The old story. I'd been hanging with a scummy crowd. Lotta partying, sex and drugs. Usual break-your-mother's-heart stuff. Then it was dealing, and petty theft. Truth is, Frank's right when he says he dragged me out of the gutter. He was no prize, but as they say, any port in a storm…"

I stirred. "And you married him?…"

"He made a lot of promises he didn't keep. Truth is, he's nothing but some loser mill hunk who somehow slithered up the ladder to foreman. His brothers are complete mooks, too. One works as a morgue attendant. Another drives a cab. Not exactly ambitious, the Harrington boys."

"Tell me about it. All Frank does is chew our asses out. I've never seen him do a lick of work on the floor."

"Yeah. Lazy as well as stupid. Plus he can't get it up anymore. And he was a lousy fuck when he could."

"Why don't you just divorce the bastard?"

"I can't. Like he said back there, he owns me. Has evidence

of some of the shit I was into before. Especially the dealing. He'd see my ass thrown in jail before he'd ever let me go."

A shadow darted across her luminous eyes, and then just as quickly departed.

"Speaking of ass…" A slow, curling smile. "How do you feel about being a real back door man…?"

As she turned away and pressed herself against me…

We were three weeks into whatever the hell we were doing, and every time I saw Marie's husband my guts did a twist. Throughout my shift, I found myself constantly glancing his way, looking for telltale clues on his fat, unshaven face. Any hint that he knew—or even suspected—something was going on between me and Marie.

But he seemed no different than before—sweating like a pig as he walked the mill floor, cursing at us at full volume, even over the roar of the machinery. Or else camped out in his dingy office, leaning back in his desk chair, engrossed in some beaver mag.

Then one day, to my surprise, Marie sauntered across the mill, carrying a lunch pail and heading for Frank's sanctum. It was the same day that one of the light bulbs in the overhead crane's cab went out, and the whole floor had to shut down for ninety minutes while we waited for a guy from the electrician's union to climb up there and change it. Union rules forbade the crane operator from changing the bulb himself, so we all just parked ourselves near the vending machines and talked shit.

But my attention kept being diverted to that office. Having taken the lunch pail from her, Frank stood with Marie in the doorway, a thick arm wrapped protectively around her waist. She wore some kind of summery dress, almost translucent, and those same flirty sandals.

Other eyes were equally drawn to her. I was hanging that day with Styles and Lucky. Gabe had called in sick, though we all knew he was really on campus, leading a protest of Nixon's continued bombing of Cambodia.

In the real world. A million miles away.

"She's wearin' red toenail polish." Styles squinted across the floor. "And sandals. Sexy, but stupid. Fuckin' steel floor plates got no give. Feet gotta be killin' her."

Lucky grunted. "Don't think she'll be stayin' long."

He was right. By now, Marie had slipped out of Frank's grasp, but not before he could give her departing rear end a vigorous slap.

As she hurried off, not even glancing in our direction, Frank offered us a leering smirk. I didn't return the look. Instead I just imagined his reaction if he knew who else was on intimate terms with that enticing ass.

I didn't see Marie for the next couple nights. Her idea, not mine. She had plans, she said, and they didn't concern me.

That really bugged me. Not that I had any claim on her. In fact, I kept telling myself it was just lust. But that word doesn't do justice to the gnawing hunger I felt for her. How impossible it was to think of anything else. Her touch, her tongue, her fingers. She gloried in how much I wanted her.

It was stupid. Crazy. Dangerous. But I was hers and we both knew it. And I was going to ride that high as long as I could.

"Fuck, man!" It was Gabe, yelling over at me. "Ya wanna get yourself killed?"

I snapped out of my reverie, making a big show of adjusting my safety goggles. Styles, Gabe and I had been pulled off the shit detail to help guide the overhead crane's grappling hooks as it swung a load of steel over our heads. The temp was a balmy one hundred forty-five degrees and dank sweat poured from us like piss down a leg. My goggles steamed up as we struggled to position the hot steel sheets onto the floor-length conveyor belt, to be pressed flat between the giant rollers at its cavernous mouth.

Styles tapped the searing stack with both gloved hands. It

swayed erratically. "Keep your shit together, motherfucker!"

I did, finally, and we three watched the steel sheets rumble down the length of the conveyor. The roar as the virgin steel was flattened between the great, grinding rollers was ear-splitting. A thunderous, mechanized death rattle.

When I turned around, head pounding from the noise, I spotted Frank Harrington lounging in his office doorway, looking suspiciously at us. Or was it just at me?

I hooked up with Marie again the following night and, after our usual round of mind-blowing sex, I totally lost my cool. I told her I loved her.

"Love?" She leaned up, naked breasts sheened with sweat. "Honey, what do you know? You're barely twenty. Besides, love is shit. You'll figure that out when you're older."

"But I'm not just some horny kid. I know what I want, Marie, and it's you."

"So what? Does that mean we're just supposed to run off together? With Frank having the goods on me? You don't think he'd track us down? And you without a pot to piss in? We wouldn't last a week."

There was something in her voice. Something soft, hesitant.

"But you think about it, don't you? I know you do."

She said nothing, but just began kissing my chest, slowly working her way down. Until soon my brain lost the ability to hold a coherent thought.

Finally, after the greatest blowjob in the history of Western Civ, she looked up at me. Eyes gone feral in a way I'd never seen before.

"Do me a favor, will ya, Eddie? Get me a gun."

Again, I know what you're thinking.

Besides, Marie promised me she only wanted to use the gun

to scare Frank. Get him to cough up the evidence he had about her past. Fix things so that she could get a divorce.

When I asked what that meant for us afterwards, she said she couldn't promise anything. But that I was growing on her.

Good enough for me.

The next step was easy. One of my roomies back at the apartment knew a guy who knew a guy, so I was able to score some high-grade heroin. Took practically every penny I had, but I figured it was the only way to get Lucky to part with one of his precious guns. Hell, I was only borrowing it, anyway.

The exchange took place out in the parking lot the next night, Lucky and I peering in the dim light down at the weapons in the trunk of his car. He pocketed the horse, I pocketed a revolver. Deal was done.

I gave Marie the gun two nights later in our usual room at the roach motel. Then I asked when she planned to confront her husband with it.

"Soon." She couldn't stop staring at it. "I want to time it just right. But I'll let you know."

The following night, right at the beginning of the midnight shift, Gabe, Styles and I were ankle-deep in the train car pit, shoveling sand. Between the face masks and the clouds of dust, we weren't saying much. Just gasping and sweating. A lot.

Suddenly, Frank Harrington lumbered up to the edge of the pit. Half-hidden in shadow, he scowled down at us.

"Eddie! Yeah, you, dumbfuck. Get your ass up here!"

I felt that familiar twisting in my gut.

Frank pointed at Gabe and Styles. "Not you two scumbags. You keep workin' the pit. I just want Eddie."

I swear, my knees had literally started buckling, but somehow I managed to climb out of the pit. Frank just glared at me for a moment, then let out a grunt of a laugh.

"C'mon, college boy. I got a special job lined up for you."

My legs felt encased in concrete as I forced myself to walk beside him. Looked like we were heading for the east wall, along which ran the conveyor belt. As we approached, I could hear those massive rollers turning. The scrape of metal on metal.

I was barely breathing. He knew. The words screamed in my brain. He knew about me and Marie.

When we reached the conveyor bay, a large, dimly-lit area flanked by heavy machinery, I said my first words since leaving the sand pit. With the ceaseless roar of the rollers pounding my ears, I had to shout to be heard.

"Hey, boss! Where's the rest of the night crew?"

Frank's own voice was a bellow. "I sent 'em all over to the loading dock. Got a big Teamsters truck comin' in."

He took a deliberate step toward me.

"Besides, this way you and me can have a little chat. All nice n' private."

It took everything I had not to lose my shit then and there. Willing myself to move, I backed away from him.

Another strained laugh, a low rumble against the fierce rattling of the conveyor belt. "Jesus, Eddie, you look scared as a fuckin' rabbit."

Sweat dotted my forehead, but not from the heat.

"Look, Frank...Mr. Harrington...I—"

Suddenly, another voice rose up over the din. Marie.

"Leave him alone, you fat fuck!"

Still rooted to the spot, I could only stare as Marie Harrington came striding toward us from a shadowed corner.

Hair pulled back, in jeans and boots. And pointing the gun.

Frank whirled as she approached.

"Marie, goddam it!"

"I mean it, Frank!"

He just laughed. "Listen, you fuckin' whore—"

Without hesitating a step, Marie fired. She missed. The bullet must have hit a pipe on one of the steam conduits to our right. The mammoth machine screeched as if mortally wounded, and within seconds the whole bay began filling with steam.

"Holy shit!" I didn't even recognize my own voice as it died behind the relentless roar of the conveyor and the rising hiss of the steam. I felt its billowing heat bee-stinging my exposed skin. Scalding my face and hands.

Panic crowded my chest. Disoriented, I stumbled a few steps forward, visibility practically zero. All I saw in front of me were swirling clouds of nearly opaque steam, beyond which two blurred figures seemed to be heading toward each other.

Then, another gunshot. I squinted so hard my face hurt. Barely making out what was happening. The bigger of the two figures, staggering back. Toward the conveyor.

At the same time, a powerful overhead fan came on and the steam began to dissipate. The blurred images in my field of vision started to clear. Become distinct. Vivid.

I almost cried out. Because seeing was worse.

Frank Harrington was sprawled on his back on the massive conveyor belt, his bulky frame being carried toward the waiting rollers. In a heartbeat, the motionless body was pulled between them, crushed, flattened...

A terrible, sickening sound. Swallowed instantly by the grating, remorseless howl of the room's machines.

I turned away, gasping. Unable to look.

By now, the steam was a low mist, swirling at my feet.

And then I heard those numbing, gut-churning words.

"Dad!" Marie. Shouting. "It's done!"

I looked past the eddies of steam slithering across the floor to see Marie and Frank Harrington, the latter very much alive. Smiling as he approached her. His fucking daughter.

Before I could react, the revolver came sailing across the room. Instinctively, I caught it. Gripped the handle.

Then, as though it were a live, writhing thing, I let it drop to the floor.

Even as I tried to grasp what was happening, Frank put his arm around Marie in that gross, familiar manner.

"Good job, baby girl."

My words were a babble. "But...I saw your body..."

Marie's voice was sharp and clear. "What you saw was a corpse that Frank's brother got for us out of the county morgue. Some dead transient. Though now he's got a nice round bullet hole in what's left of his remains. Poor bastard's pretty much egg custard by now. Impossible to identify."

I stared at Frank. "Your...your brother...?"

"Blood's thicker than water, kid. Especially once I gave him a couple grand for his trouble. Dave's always short of cash. We carried the stiff in tonight and hid it till we needed it."

Suddenly, as though it had just occurred to him, he very deliberately threw a switch attached to the wall beside him. In less than a minute, the screeching conveyor belt ground to a halt. The rollers slowly rotated and became still.

Frank let out a gale-like sigh. "So fuckin' tired of that noise. Been poundin' my head to jelly for twenty goddam years. That's enough for any man."

Marie stroked his cheek. "That's all over now, Dad. From now on, we get everything we've dreamed of. You get to lie on some beach half-way around the world and I get to start my own new life. Destination undecided."

Her father looked longingly at her. "But we'll always stay in touch, right, baby? Just like we talked about."

"Sure, Dad." Her voice cool, even. "Just like we talked about." Her hand fell away from his face.

My ears still ringing in the abrupt silence, I'd recovered enough to move closer to the pair. Though my gaze was aimed squarely at Marie.

"But...but why?..."

"Another old story, lover. Like the one I told you. We took out a million-dollar life insurance policy on my old man here, and now we're going to collect."

Frank nodded. "All I had to do was get any witnesses out of the way, rig the steam conduit, and let Marie do her thing. She happens to be a pretty good shot."

Ignoring him, I shook my head at his daughter.

"That's not what I mean, Marie. I mean, why me?..."

She shrugged. "You were perfect, Eddie. Horny, lonely, and just cocky enough to think you could get away with fucking the boss' wife."

Before I could respond, another sound seeped into the leaden silence of the conveyor bay. Coming from maybe a couple miles away. A police siren, getting louder and louder as the squad car approached.

"Forgot to tell you, Eddie. Before I came in, gun blazing, I called 9-1-1. Told them I just saw you shoot my father."

At the same time, I could hear the running footsteps and muffled voices of the other mill workers. Drawn by the gunshots from the other side of the building. Heading our way, too.

Marie patted her father's shoulder. "Better get going, okay? Time for me to play the grieving daughter."

As Frank lumbered away as fast as his awkward bulk would allow, I found myself staring down at the revolver at my feet. Then, unthinking, I scooped it up.

Aimed it at her.

Marie's voice was a taunt. "What are you going to do now, Eddie? Shoot me?"

Believe it or not, it wasn't until that very moment that I realized Marie was wearing a glove on her right hand. The hand that had fired the gun.

Which meant that the only prints on it would be mine.

The siren grew louder, and I heard tires screeching as the cop car pulled into the mill lot.

I found my voice. "What are you gonna tell them?"

"Whatever works. Won't be hard. Maybe the cops'll figure you killed Frank because you had the hots for me and I rejected you. So you wanted him out of the way. Or maybe he confronted you about hitting on me and you shot him. Doesn't matter. I'm an eyewitness. Your prints are on the gun. They'll make it stick."

Marie's eyes narrowed. "Now answer the question, college boy. Think you have the balls to shoot me?"

I guess by then we did know each other pretty well, because we also both knew I wasn't going to do it.

So I did something else. Something as stupid as everything else I'd done up till then.

Still clutching the revolver, I turned around and ran.

I'm still holding it, resting on my upraised knees, here on the roof. From the sound of footsteps pounding up the stairs just below, I know it's only a matter of minutes before the access door opens and a pair of cops will be aiming their own guns at me.

Then there's Marie. Even now, I can't stop thinking about her. The siren song of her body. The taste of her lips on mine. Wondering if, moments after I took off, she suddenly felt badly for me. Or felt anything at all.

I guess I'll never know. I guess—

Shit, I just heard the access door open.

So what am I going to do? Shoot it out with the boys in blue and get my head blown off? Or surrender and get sent to prison for life for a murder I didn't commit?

Tell you the truth, at this exact moment I have no idea. But I do know one thing for sure, and it kind of pisses me off.

Either way, I'm never going to finish college.

WHERE I BELONG

Alison Gaylin

Some cars, you stay away from: Full-sized vans with sliding doors. Town cars with tinted windows. Anything you can't see into thoroughly. I was told this by Larry, an old junkie I met on the FDR a few days after I ran away from home. There's a reason, he told me, why they don't want you to see inside.

Larry could have been anywhere from fifty to one hundred years old and he smelled like ass, but I did trust him on the car thing. "I've hit up probably five thousand drivers so I know what I'm talking about," he told me. "I've been on the street for ten years."

Ten years. I mean, come on. Ten years ago, I was eight.

Anyway, a traffic jam is a captive audience, and the FDR (aka Fuck Dis Road) is a non-stop traffic jam. So, for a couple of days there, Larry and I had a pretty good thing going. We'd split up, knock on windows and show them our signs: *Need Food. Will Work for $$. Jesus Loves You.* The soft-hearted types would throw cash at Larry because he looked so pathetic, and I'd get the scared ones because I'm a big dude—six foot three, two hundred thirty pounds. At the end of the day, we'd pool our earnings, split everything fifty-fifty and go our separate ways. It was working until Larry decided to go his separate way and never come back, taking all the money with him, along with my duffel bag and iPhone. That was a week ago. Fucking junkie.

It's a hot day. That type of New York summer heat when the air feels solid and weepy and when you take a deep breath, it's almost like drowning. I'm moving down the center of the FDR with my old sign in my hand, but at this point I think I'm probably both scary and pathetic, so I'm not getting any takers. Everything stinks of exhaust fumes and the car windshields shimmer at me. I'm pretty sure I'm going to die soon.

I don't know how long I've been out here, but it's long enough to start thinking that it was a stupid idea to run away, that I should go back home to Staten Island and apologize to my mom and stepdad for making them nervous, because they have to be nervous, right? I've been gone for so long. And if they've tried calling, they've gotten crazy-ass junkie Larry, or whoever he sold my iPhone to, probably telling them I died or something. If I were to go home now, they'd think I was a ghost.

I picture myself banging on the front door and them opening it. My mom hugging me and crying and jumbling her words together, the way moms on TV do when their missing kids come home unharmed. "ThankGodyou'reback—wherewereyou—weweresoworried—isitreallyyou—it'samiracle…" But then I remember. It was my mom who kicked me out of the house, not the other way around. I think about all the shitty names she called me, how she told me to never come back and she hopes I drop dead, and I let go of my sign and fall to my knees, right in the middle of the FDR. You don't belong in this home. You don't belong here. I'm sobbing like a girl now, my stomach churning, the pavement hot on my hands and arms, then my lips, then my forehead. Horns blare. I taste blood in my mouth.

This is it. This is how I'm going to go. Face down on the FDR, crushed under the wheels of some pissed-off Tesla driver. And no one is going to miss me. No one at all.

* * *

"Hey." It's a woman's voice. My mom's voice.

But when I push myself up from the macadam to look at her, I can see even through tears and bright sun that she's not my mom. I can also see that she's driving a white, full-sized van with sliding doors.

"Get in," she says. Or "Get him." I'm not sure which. The van's door slides open and some big guy spills out of it and yanks me up to my knees and shoves me in.

Any other time, I would have yelled and kicked and thrown punches. But not now. I just let him do it. There are seats inside the van and I collapse onto one, the air conditioning washing over me. I figure he's going to slug me or shoot me in the head or worse, but I'm too tired to fight back or even care. What he does, though, is this: He pulls the seatbelt over me and buckles me in, as though I were a little kid. Then he slips into the front passengers' seat. I close my eyes, fuzzy images of long-ago road trips with my parents, my real parents. My dad singing along with corny country songs on the radio. My mom laughing. The leather seat hugs me.

"Are you all right?" The woman says it like she knows it's a stupid question.

"Yes, ma'am."

"Are you sure? Do you need to see a doctor?"

"No, ma'am."

The man says, "We're driving home, but we live far from here. The Hudson Valley."

I'm not sure how I'm supposed to answer. "Oh?"

He turns around in his seat and looks at me. He has a shaved head that seems as though it was carved out of granite. His fist sits on the chair, the size of a catcher's mitt. He's old—forty at least—but there's no question he could beat the crap out of me.

"Would you like to stay with us?" he says. "We live upstate. Just outside of Woodstock."

There are times in your life when you're forced to weigh options. Either one feels doable, and the best choice keeps shifting back and forth to the point where you feel like you can't trust your own instincts and you wind up paralyzed.

But when your skin is raw and peeling and your stomach is sucking in on itself and your throat feels as though someone rubbed it with sandpaper, options aren't a thing—especially when you're in a moving vehicle, strapped to a chair. "Sure," I tell the man.

There's a small cooler between the two front seats. He flips open the top, hands me a cold bottle of water. He smiles, and it's like a fissure in the earth. "Bet you're thirsty," he says.

I drink three bottles of water, then pass out for most of the ride. When I wake up, it's dark, and my ears are clicking. We're driving up a mountain, a twisting road shrouded with trees. The front windows of the van are rolled down and the air is warm and alive with crickets. It's like nothing I've ever seen or felt, but it brings back memories: Summer camp, toasting marshmallows, having a home to miss. It isn't 'til I'm fully awake that I notice that the man and woman are whispering furiously to each other.

"I don't know," the woman says. "I just don't know."

I clear my throat.

The man says, "You awake, son?"

"Yes, sir."

"Well then. Welcome to our home."

The woman huffs out a sigh.

We're pulling up a driveway now, so steep it's almost perpendicular to the road below. She parks the van, gets out, slams the door without saying anything. I watch her through the windshield. She is tall and slim and wears a tight skirt, and as she heads for the door, she doesn't turn around. Not even once. All these hours, and I still don't fully know what her face looks like.

As I unlock my seatbelt, the man gets out of the van and opens my door from the outside. "Is she mad?" I ask him.

He shakes his head. "No, Kurt."

I blink at him. "You know my name?"

"Yep."

"How?"

"The video."

"Video?"

He just looks at me.

"Oh…I…There's a video?"

"Viral."

"Oh…Oh God."

"We're not big internet people, though. We saw it on local news."

"Look. Look. I can explain…"

"No explanations necessary, man." He smiles again, teeth gleaming. "I get it. I get angry too."

The house is built into the side of the mountain—all glass and sleek lines like a rich person's house from some nineties' movie. By the time the man and I are inside, she's already in the bedroom, the door slammed behind her. He leans in close, speaks in a whisper. "My wife didn't recognize you 'til you were sleeping. She wanted to throw you out of the car, but I wouldn't let her."

It's like I've been dropped into deep water, and I have to start treading. "I…I didn't mean to hurt him. I swear."

He puts a finger to his lips. "Like I said. I get it."

"No sir, no. With all due respect I don't think…"

He hands me his phone. The video's rolling. Two guys yelling at each other on a square patch of lawn, the taller one slugging the other in the head, then knocking him to the grass and kicking him—a much older man, his hands covering his face… Monster, I want to say. Because even though I know it happened, it's hard for me to believe that the tall guy was me, just two or three weeks ago. The older guy was my stepfather.

"What made you so angry, son?"

"I...I don't know."

"I think you do." The man takes the phone back. Claps me on the shoulder. I almost fall to the ground. "Videos like that. They only tell one side of the story."

I try and think back on it, but I come up with nothing. Everything's such a blur since she kicked me out. The nights under the overpass by the side of the FDR, Larry shooting up beside me. The hot sun and the cheap beers and bags of fast food scraps, slipped through the windows of cars. Like a dream you never wake up from, the kind caterpillars must have when they're in the chrysalis, their body parts rearranging. Here in his sleek living room, the big, bald man looks older, kinder. He feels like a second chance, and so I can't lie to him. "I'm sorry," I say. "I really don't remember."

He nods. "Okay. Well...help yourself to whatever you can find in the kitchen," he says. "The guest room's over there to your left. It's got a bathroom, with clean towels in it. Take a shower. Catch a few hours of sleep."

"Thank you."

"I gotta get you out of here in the morning though, okay? I promised my wife."

"Yes, sir." I look around the living room—there's a big comfy couch and a glass-topped coffee table with photographs all over it. The bald guy and the woman wearing leis on white sand. Another of her blowing out candles, the man beaming next to her. Still another of the two of them, toasting each other with champagne. She has blond highlights, high cheekbones, the type of smooth, shiny skin that only rich women have. She's probably my mom's age, and I have to say, she doesn't look younger than her; just better taken care of. "I'm sorry if I made her upset," I tell the man.

He shrugs it off. "Women."

"Yeah."

"Listen though, can I offer you one bit of advice?"

I look at him.

"You're practically unrecognizable with that beard." He says it with a smile. "I wouldn't shave it off if I were you."

The guest room is all white—walls, bedding, dresser, draperies—all of it spotless, the way my house never was. There's a white terry cloth robe hanging on a hook in the guest bathroom. After I shower, I put it on and get under the white comforter. It feels like I'm in the middle of a cloud, or in heaven.

As I drift off, my mind clears for a few seconds and I remember three weeks ago—the fight on the front lawn, my stepfather's bloody face, the neighbors screaming, my mother calling the police and shielding him. Coughing blood. His teeth on the lawn. My mother's voice: "That's right, run, you little piece of shit. Get out of here and never come back. If I see you again, I'll have you arrested. You don't belong in this home. You belong in jail."

I remember running until my lungs ached, 'til the muscles in my legs felt like broken rubber bands, my fists clenched so tight, it was as though they'd never come undone.

I want to believe I had a reason. I want to believe I was justified in what I did to him—a man forty years older than me and fifty pounds lighter. I want to say I snapped after months of cruelty and verbal and physical abuse. But it wouldn't be true.

The truth is, I have a bad temper. I beat the crap out of my stepfather because he cut off my allowance. "You're eighteen. You have to get a job," he had said. "Money doesn't come easy. You need to learn that."

The truth is, I'm an asshole. It's the last thought I have before falling asleep.

"Okay, Kurt, up and at 'em," says the bald man, whose name I still haven't learned. He's standing over the bed, light pouring in through the white draperies and haloing all around him. "Gotta get you outta here before the wife gets up."

I rub sleep out of my eyes. My clothes are neatly folded at the foot of the bed, a stack of twenty-dollar bills resting on top of them.

"Washed your clothes," the man says.

I sit up in bed. My throat tightens. I have to swallow hard to keep from crying. I don't deserve this. I don't deserve any of this.

"I wish I could pay you back."

He smiles in such a way, it's hard to tell what he's thinking. "Get yourself changed, buddy."

He leaves the room. I dress quickly, count the money out. It's a hundred bucks—less than I'd hoped. I pocket it, hoping Woodstock isn't as expensive as NYC.

We drive down the mountain in silence. The clock in his car reads 6:00 a.m., and the sky is still pink from the sunrise. He makes a few turns, until we're on a narrow street with a few restaurants, some art galleries and hippy-type gift stores, the windows packed with tie dye and bongs. Everything is clean and colorful and, except for a Cumberland Farms, everything's closed. "We're here," he says, pulling into the Cumby's.

I gaze up and down the street. I see a health food store. A bank. "Where's the rest of the town?"

He smiles. "This is it, pal," he says. "Greater metropolitan Woodstock. Home of peace and love." He says goodbye, and I get out of the van. Take in the clean morning air, the chirping birds. My new home, I think. It doesn't make me very happy.

At Cumberland Farms, I buy a breakfast sandwich, a couple of bags of Funyons, a big bottle of water, four ready-made sandwiches and some gum. I try to buy a six-pack, but the frizzy haired woman behind the counter cards me and I remember I have no ID—fake or otherwise—thanks to Larry. I figure I look older with the beard, though, so I give it a shot. "I left my driver's license at home," I tell her. "I'm twenty-four, I swear."

"Uh huh."

"Come on. It's just beer."

"You gotta be twenty-one," she says. See the sign?" She gestures with her head at a sign behind her: YOU MUST BE 21 TO BUY ALCOHOL.

I feel anger bubbling up inside me. "That sucks."

"I don't write the laws."

"I know, but..."

"No ID, no beer. That's how we roll."

I hate Woodstock. I hate it more than the underpass next to the FDR. Hate it more than my mother or my stepfather or Larry, who at least bought me beers. "Fine." I say it between clenched teeth. I want to break everything in the place. Instead, I buy a Juul starter pack and some extra pods. My bill is close to eighty bucks.

"Fucking great," I whisper.

She glares at me as I dole out the cash. "You look familiar," she says.

I aim my eyes at the floor. "We've never met."

"No, but you're...I've seen you somewhere. Recently."

"I've never been in this town before," I say. "Can I just buy my stuff, please?"

"Wait a minute... Aren't you..."

"No."

"You're Kurt Campbell. From Staten Island."

"I don't know who that is."

"Don't bullshit me, Kurt Campbell. I have a photographic memory."

"I swear I'm not..."

"You're even wearing the same clothes. Jesus. The same clothes as in the video. Oh my God. It's you."

"Can I have my change, please?"

"You're sick, you know that? What you did to that man.

Your own stepfather. There's something wrong with you."

"I'm not him," I say. "I'm not Kurt…"

"What are you even doing here?"

"I…I…"

"You should be in jail. There's a warrant out on you. I'm calling the police."

"No, please."

She picks up her phone, and I get out of there fast, running down the silent street, sweat pouring down my back. Last night, I emptied that couple's refrigerator before I took a shower and went to bed, and I'm regretting it now—the leftover spaghetti and the pint of Ben and Jerry's and the entire box of Hot Pockets. It's slowing me down now, all that food. I've got a stitch in my side.

I see a police car ambling up the road about three blocks away, and I pivot up a side street, past a real estate office and a clothing place and an art gallery with a flower on the sign, and I keep it up, this wheezing, painful run, up a sloping hill and through some open gates and onto a field.

I run until I can't run anymore, and I'm bent over, grasping my knees, struggling for air. Finally, once I've caught my breath, I look around. I'm in a cemetery. Perfect.

I sit down on the damp grass, thinking about that bitch in Cumby's, how I'd run out of there without taking my food or my money or even the damn Juul. I want to cry again, but I won't. I'm never going to cry again. I lean up against a headstone and stare up at the sky.

Back when my real dad was alive and my mom still loved me, she used to take me to church every Sunday. I'd fuss about the starched collar she made me wear, the stupid clip-on tie and the uncomfortable shoes. But deep down, I liked it. The smell of the candles and the priest's soothing voice and my mom's hand on my shoulder—it all made me feel… This is going to sound weird, but it made me feel safe. Listened to. Understood. I used to pray there, too. I didn't just pretend. "God always answers your prayers," Mom used to say. "It just may not be the answer you expect."

A cemetery may not be a church, but it's as good a place to pray as any. So, I close my eyes and I pray for something, anything, anybody, to get me out of this town. "Please," I whisper, again and again, "Take me to where I belong."

It has to be an hour later, maybe even two, when the bald guy shows up at the cemetery gates. He's behind the wheel of the white van, and when he calls out to me, I get up and jog over to him, thinking about prayers and unexpected answers.

"What?"

"You heard me."

"You want me to—"

"Kill me."

The bald guy and I are sitting in his van. It's started to rain—one of those crazy summer downpours, big drops splashing on the windshield, gusts of wind bending the trees. The perfect backdrop for this conversation, which had started with, "Remember back at the house, when you said you wish you could pay me back?" and ended with what he just said. Kill me. Is everybody in this town freakin' nuts?

"Why would you want me to kill you?"

He draws a deep breath, then lets it out slowly. "I'm dying, Kurt."

"What?"

"Pancreatic cancer. I haven't told the wife because she'll want me to get treatment, but the doc says I'm far gone. It'll be a waste of time. And you know what? I don't like pain."

"How long have you known about it?"

"Weeks. I knew it when I picked you up. It's part of the reason why I did."

"What?"

"Look. If I kill myself, the wife won't get my insurance. You break into the house, shoot me, she gets the money, I get off this earth. It's win-win."

"Not exactly."

"What do you mean?"

"Well...what do I get?"

"How does ten grand sound?"

I stare at him. "You're serious."

"As a funeral. Pardon the pun."

"I don't know...what if I get arrested?"

"You won't. I've got it all worked out, starting with the ten grand."

I turn to him. "Really?"

"I pick you up in the van, drop you in the woods behind my house. You wait there, 'til it starts getting dark, and you hear the wife's car, driving away. She's got her book club tonight."

"Okay."

"Okay. So, you go through the screened-in porch at the back of the house. The door will be open. Unlocked. There's a big basket out there with a cover on it. It's where we keep firewood, but if you look inside, you'll find a leather wallet with ten thousand dollars in it. Count it if you want, but I promise it'll all be there, along with a loaded gun."

"Then what do I do."

"You go into living room. You wait behind the couch 'til you hear my car pull up. I'll come in through the front door. You shoot me. I die. It's that easy."

"But..."

"I guarantee you'll get out of there before anybody calls the cops. I'll leave the key in the van and you can just take it. Drive up to Canada or wherever you want to go."

The rain starts to let up, the wind dying down, the sun peeking through the clouds. I turn to him. "One question."

"Yeah?"

"How do you know I won't just take the money and run?"

He shrugs. "There's only one way out of there, and that's down the mountain. You try that, I'll have you arrested before you get to the bottom."

"Oh. Uh. Okay."

"But I'll tell you what else, I know you won't do that. I know it because I know you, Kurt. I know you have integrity."

"I've never killed anybody before. I don't know if I can."

"I know you can do it." The man says it like a coach, or a dad. "It's why I picked you up, Kurt. It's why I took you here."

The storm is over now, everything bright and clean, and I know there's a rainbow somewhere, too, that Bible sign of hope. "I know you can do it." He says again, and I want to do it for him, more than anything. I want to help him with his problem of being alive. "When I come through that door," he says, "just imagine I'm someone you hate."

I turn to look at him, and we both smile.

"Imagine I'm your stepdad, coming back for more."

An hour later, he picks me up in the van, and leaves me in the woods behind the house with a bag of food—turkey sandwich, ice cold Snapple, a bag of those gourmet chips. I eat what I can, which isn't very much, then I stay there waiting. It feels like hours.

Finally, I hear her heels clicking on the driveway, her car leaving. Ready, set...

The door to the back porch swings open. I lift the lid off the basket, and there's the wallet and the gun, just like he said. The wallet is packed with bills I don't bother counting before I slip it into my pants pocket. The gun is heavy, but it fits my hands well. My fingers wrapped around the grip, I feel like a movie hit man. James Bond, even. Back in the van, he'd told me the safety would be released, so I make sure to handle it very carefully, just like he said, as I slip into the living room. It's pitch black in here, and with my free hand, I feel around for the couch and slip behind it, the gun cradled in my hands like some fragile living thing.

More time passes. With the dark and the quiet, I almost fall asleep. I tell myself it's not going to happen, that this is all some sick joke and the gun isn't even real. And then, finally, I hear the van pulling into the driveway, the door slamming. Go time, I think. Like a movie hit man.

I don't want to kill him, but the way I see it, he's giving me a gift. When you pull the trigger, he had said, think of freedom.

The key slips into the lock of the front door, catching slightly. Freedom. The door swings open and I can see the outline of him, backlit by his dying headlights. I raise the gun without thinking about it. I pull the trigger and it explodes in my ears. I've never heard anything so loud. When I was a kid, I went deer hunting with my real dad a few times. We used shotguns, but they were nothing like this. My ears ring. My shoulders ache from the recoil. You did it, I tell myself. You did it, Killer.

It isn't until he falls to the floor, moaning, that I realize that when he opened the door, he was carrying a suitcase. And he had hair.

I find the light switch. Flip it on. The first thing I see are the pictures on the coffee table. A couple side by side at a fancy dinner. Atop a mountain in matching backpacks. The two of them at their wedding, much younger, feeding each other cake.

The same woman. A different man.

That man, the man from these new pictures, is on the floor now, whispering cuss words through his own blood. I move over to him and kneel beside him. His shirt is covered in blood. He's on his way out. I don't know what to say or do. "You're her real husband," I whisper. "Not the bald man."

His eyes go big and glassy. "You're the...the asshole...from that video," he says. Or maybe I just imagine him saying it, as the life eases out of him and the sirens come.

It's a month later, when I'm watching TV with a few of the guys at the county jail, that I finally learn the bald man's name: Wallace Perry. "He doesn't look like a Wallace," I tell Jimbo, the big dude sitting next to me.

Jimbo says, "I'm not sure what a Wallace is supposed to look like."

"Yeah, me neither I guess."

Wallace Perry is on the screen next to his sister-in-law Denise. They're being interviewed by a morning anchor all the guys here think is hot—all cleavage and bottle blond hair and big, sympathetic eyes. She's just given us the refresher on the poor Perrys— Denise returning home from book club to find her beloved husband, famed financier Henry Perry, dead at the hands of fugitive Kurt Campbell, already wanted for assault after a brutal, videotaped attack on his own stepfather. "He was just coming back from L.A." Denise says through tears. Denise, the sole heir to Henry's twenty-five-million-dollar fortune. "He'd been gone for weeks. I couldn't wait to see him."

The hot anchor turns her attention to Wallace. "You've been a tremendous source of comfort to Denise," she says.

And he nods slowly. "We both loved Henry. We both lost him. It's a blessing we're able to be here for each other."

The anchor turns to the camera. "There's one silver lining here," she says.

"What's that, baby?" shouts my cellmate, Little Stan.

And she looks straight out at us, with those sweet blue eyes, as though she's answering Little Stan and Little Stan alone. "The silver lining is that Kurt Campbell is behind bars. He won't be able to hurt anybody else, ever again."

The guys all erupt in whoops and cheers. Jimbo claps me on the back. "You hear that, Mad Dog?" he says. My prison nickname. "Nadia said your name! You're a superstar!"

I don't mind it here. That's the truth of it. I get three square meals, I can work out in the gym. Nobody hassles me. In fact, I have more friends here than I ever had on the outside. My trial's in a few weeks, but my lawyer wants me to go for a plea deal, and I think I might do it. I don't feel like standing in front of people, answering questions. And anyway, I did kill the guy.

I'm not mad at Wallace Perry. I'm not mad at Larry or my

stepdad or my mom or anybody. Not anymore. It's as though, when I pulled the trigger, all the meanness slipped out of me, and I could see the world for what it is: A bunch of fucked-up people. All of us trying to get through the day.

"You're a hero, Mad Dog."

Remember that thing my mom said, about prayers being answered? I believe it. I really do.

NASHUA RIVER FLOATER

Tom MacDonald

The 7:00 a.m. phone call surprised me and so did the man calling, a New Hampshire state trooper named Captain Leo Raymond. He asked me if I was Dermot Sparhawk of Louis & Sparhawk Investigations in Charlestown, and I told him I was. He said he wanted me to look into a matter, an important matter that he, because of his position, couldn't look into himself. I asked him what it was about, and he said he'd rather tell me in person. I was between cases at the moment and had plenty of time on my hands, so I told Captain Raymond I could drive up to Nashua to meet him today.

"Not Nashua," he said.

"Where then?"

We agreed to meet halfway, in Lowell, at McDermott's Green. He asked me if I knew where it was, and I said I did. I knew the story behind it, too. Red McDermott, a Lowell bookie, was murdered in a neighborhood called the Acre. Red was my father's friend. They served together in Vietnam. I remember the dreary day when my father took me to Red's funeral mass. I was thirteen at the time and got to skip school. I remember Red's widow scattering the ashes on what is now McDermott's Green. Things went from dreary to dreadful. The next day my father fell to his death, washing windows on a downtown highrise, a thirty-story drop to Boylston Street.

"McDermott's Green, at the stone church," I said.

"Right, St. Patrick's, I'll see you there at twelve."

At twelve noon I parked on the corner of Cork and Cross and walked to McDermott's Green. The man I presumed to be Captain Raymond was waiting in his state trooper uniform. His getup included shined boots and a Smokey the Bear hat. He was older than I expected, but he was fit and erect, which made him look younger than he probably was. We shook hands as if we were friends, and he thanked me for coming up.

"I got your name from Superintendent Hanson in Boston," Raymond told me, and then for some reason he said, "You played football."

"A long time ago at Boston College," I said.

"Not that long ago I followed your career. You were an All-American and won the Butkus Award." He said this like an athletic department press secretary. "You were also slated to go high in the first round, until you busted a knee." He removed the khaki hat and finger combed his silver hair. "Before you think I'm a weirdo, I love college football, and I follow all the college stars."

I enjoyed the accolades, but I've grown jaded. I wondered if he was working an angle. We stepped onto McDermott's Green, a grassy patch with a footpath running up the middle. Raymond refitted the hat on his head.

"We found a body in the Nashua River, a man named Vincent Dunn from Charlestown. He was shot in the mouth, shot in the head. Did you know him?"

The Vincent Dunn I knew beat a man to death with a hammer in a poker game. No witnesses came forward to testify, thanks to the Charlestown code of silence. He was never charged. "I knew him but I haven't seen him around."

"Dunn did ten years in a federal pen for armed robbery. He got out last month, early release." Raymond spread his arms wide. "I got to know him. Dunn was trying to do the right thing. He deserves justice."

A cop who thinks a crook deserves justice? We stood on the fading grass of McDermott's Green. The oaks and elms were bare of leaves. The exposed branches were knobby and gray.

"Where do I come in?" I asked.

"Nashua is handling the case," he said. "I want you to investigate the killing on your own and report to me."

"A shadow investigation?" I laughed. "You're kidding, right?"

"I never kid about homicide," he said, sounding a little too principled for my liking. "So will you take the case?"

Interfering with a Nashua police investigation didn't seem smart, but the idea of looking into a townie's killing intrigued me, and I needed a challenge. I told Raymond I'd take the case.

"You'll need this." He handed me an envelope. "It's a temporary New Hampshire investigator's license, valid for a month. Take this, too." He gave me a manila folder. "The initial crime report—forensics, photos, witness statements—everything you need to get started."

"I guess you were pretty confident I'd take the case, Captain." I tucked the packet under my arm and waited for him to look at me. "Why did you want to meet at McDermott's Green?"

"Today is the twentieth anniversary of Red McDermott's murder."

"Did you know him?"

"Here's my card," he said. "Call me if you need anything. There's a thousand bucks in the envelope, a retainer to get you started. Any questions?"

"No questions," I said. Not that he would have answered them.

I watched him walk back to his car. Measured and poised, he marched like a military man who'd just won a battle.

From McDermott's Green I drove to Athenian Corner and ordered chicken kabobs with lentil soup and a Greek salad. After

I ate I started perusing the police report. The tedium of reading was eased when the waitress brought me baklava with vanilla ice cream and that gooey sauce, and a cup of coffee with cream and sugar. A sugar high—the best medicine for a recovering alcoholic.

I flipped a page. On October 23rd at three o'clock in the afternoon, a woman named Clair Corneau, while walking on Canal Street, called 9-1-1 when she saw a body floating in the Nashua River. The next witness, a man named Len Rancourt, also saw the body, and he too called 9-1-1. I wrote their addresses in my notepad. The Nashua Police responded to the calls and fished Dunn out of the water. Detective Paul Vachon of the Nashua Police Department signed the report. I looked at the crime-scene photos of Vincent Dunn, with his face shot and bruised. I never would have recognized him. I closed the folder and called Buckley Louis, my partner in Louis & Sparhawk, and told him about my meeting with Captain Leo Raymond.

"He hired you to investigate Vincent Dunn's murder?" Buck said. "I don't like it, Dermot. Cops don't hire private investigators to solve murder cases, especially when there's an ongoing investigation. Do you think he's setting you up?"

"I don't think so," I said. "My gut tells me he's okay, but he's definitely holding something back. It was a flag that he wanted to meet in Lowell instead of Nashua."

"Hmm." Buckley always says hmm when he's mulling a situation. "I'd feel better if Harraseeket Kid was working with you. When is he back from Nova Scotia?"

"Don't know, I'll call him."

That night I booked a room at Henri's Motor Lodge near Route 3 in Nashua. I rested on the bed and closed my eyes. The whir of cars and trucks reminded me of the Tobin Bridge, and I soon fell asleep. In the morning someone knocked. I opened the door and Harraseeket Kid came in, dressed in denim jeans and a denim jacket, and carrying two cups of coffee. Kid is a full-blooded

Micmac Indian from Antigonish, Nova Scotia, and he is also my first cousin. Kid honors Micmac tradition by wearing his long black hair in a ponytail. Tough and smart, nobody messes with Kid, which comes in handy in my line of work. He sat in a chair and plunked his work boots on the coffee table.

"Buck told me the story," Kid said. "What's the plan?"

We divided the tasks. Kid would follow Detective Vachon. I would investigate Vincent Dunn. We agreed to meet back at Henri's Motor Lodge at seven. Outside in the parking lot on a crisp October morning that seemed colder than it should have been, Kid opened the door to his Ford Super Duty F-450 and stepped on the running board to vault in.

"Let's switch vehicles," I said to him. "A police detective might catch on that you're following him in that tank."

"And I'm stuck with your sissy car?" He tossed me the keys. "Don't dent it. I just waxed her."

I drove out of the lot in Kid's shiny pickup, which handled better than my sissy car. When I got to East Dunstable Road, I called Captain Leo Raymond to get pointed in the right direction. He told me that Dunn drank at McNally's Tap on Canal Street.

"Canal Street?" I said. "They fished Dunn out of the river on Canal Street."

"They did," Raymond said without elaborating.

At one o'clock I went into McNally's Tap. The place was so dark I had to wait for my eyes to adjust. The brightest light in the joint came from a Wurlitzer jukebox, which was so old and junky it flickered like a strobe on Quaaludes. The barman stared at me with his arms crossed, giving his tough guy best. It's the same in every neighborhood taproom when an outsider comes in. Drinkers, like dogs, are territorial. But even in the gloom of the bar, I could see his face was red and raw, a drinker's face.

I put a fifty on the counter and asked for a Coke. He poured it, looked at the fifty, and said, "Got anything smaller?"

"Keep it." I slid the bill into the bar gutter. "My friend used to drink here. He said he enjoyed the atmosphere."

"Atmosphere?" The barman laughed. "We're right up there with Studio 54."

"My friend liked it."

"No kidding." He pocketed the bill and folded a damp bar towel. "What's your friend's name?"

"Vincent Dunn," I said.

His face flushed and his Adam's apple bobbed. He re-crossed his arms and said, "What do you want?"

"I don't want any trouble," I said, "just information."

He walked away, leaving me alone. I sipped my Coke. Bars are usually quiet in the afternoon and McNally's was no exception. The few patrons in the place sat on stools, with plenty of stools between them. The barman poured a draft for a client and made his way back to me. He said, "Dunn came in once and again for a drink, that's all I can tell you."

"You know he got murdered," I said.

"Everyone knows. It was on the news."

"The police found him in the river out back." I peeled off a hundred and placed it on the bar. "Can you think of anyone who will talk to me about Dunn?"

"Maybe." He looked at the bill. "Robbie was friendly with Dunn. He comes in at three." The barman pointed across the room. "Robbie sits in the last booth, the one in the corner."

"Thanks." I took my finger off the bill.

"You didn't get it from me," he said.

"No sweat," I said.

He tucked the bill in his shirt pocket and said, "Wait 'til five o'clock. Robbie's more talkative after he's had a few."

"Aren't we all," I said.

From McNally's Tap I drove to an Alcoholics Anonymous meeting at Immaculate Conception Church. The hall was bright with sunshine and cheerful with fellowship. The homey smell of brewing coffee added to the warmth of the room, unlike

McNally's, which reeked of stale beer. I found a seat in the first row in front of the podium.

The chairwoman asked if there were any visitors attending for the first time. I raised my hand and said I was Dermot from Charlestown. The group said welcome. The meeting commenced. After the Lord's Prayer I stayed for coffee. A tall woman with iron-gray hair came up to me and said, "I grew up in Charlestown. My husband and I moved up here twenty years ago. We wanted to get away from the city, the whole hectic scene of it—the nutty pace, the crazy drivers, the drugs and crime."

"It's quieter up here in New Hampshire," I admitted. "Which part of Charlestown are you from?"

"North Mead Street, next to St. Francis De Sales."

"I'm friends with the pastor."

"We lived on the corner of Bunker Hill Street," she said. "I can still smell the bus fumes coming into the kitchen." The memory of bus fumes knocked the sentiment from her voice. "So what brings you all the way up to Nashua, not that it's very far?"

"I'm looking into the murder of Vincent Dunn."

My answer prompted a second moment of silence. The topic of Vincent Dunn's murder was a conversation ender, both at McNally's and A.A.

"Vincent Dunn." She drank coffee and contemplated how to respond. "I read about his murder in the paper, about the armored-car heist, too. He probably figured New Hampshire for an easy score. Typical townie." She tossed her cup in the trashcan. "Are you a cop?"

"Private."

"Did the Dunn family hire you?"

With her rapid-fire questioning, she'd make a good detective herself. I said, "A friend of Dunn's hired me."

"Why did he hire you? Is something shady going on, something not on the up and up? A crooked cop? A corrupt judge? Tainted evidence?"

I should hire her as an adjunct.

"I don't know yet." I handed her a card, my ticket to the exit. I wanted to get out of there before she solved the case for me. "Call me if anything comes to you."

"Will do." She put the card in her purse. "I'll ask my husband. He's a Teamster. Teamsters know everything."

At five o'clock I walked into McNally's Tap and waited the requisite three seconds for my eyes to adjust. I looked at the corner booth and saw a man sitting alone, a man I hoped was Robbie. At the bar a curvy woman with black hair was working behind the stick. She wore a Bruins throwback jersey, number 12, with the name Cashman embossed on the back. My father loved Wayne Cashman. Now I can see why.

The talk at the bar was all Red Sox, who were on the verge of another World Series title, their fourth in the 2000s. I ordered a Coke and went to the corner booth.

"Robbie?" I said.

He looked up from his beer. "Who wants to know?"

"Dermot Sparhawk," I said. "I'd like to talk to you about Vincent Dunn."

"Not today." He dipped his head to the mug, and his floppy brown hair fell into his sad brown eyes. "Not tomorrow, either. Vincent is dead."

"Can I at least buy you a drink?"

He didn't respond, which I took to be a yes. I went to the bar and asked Cashman, the curvaceous bartender, what Robbie was drinking.

"Molson Canadian," she said. "How do you know Robbie?"

"I don't know him. I'm investigating Vincent Dunn's murder, and I heard Robbie was friends with him."

She put a mug of Molson on the bar. I took a coaster off the stack and said, "Did you know Dunn?"

"No, I didn't." She sounded defensive. "Robbie might appreciate a whiskey to go with it."

"Pour it."

I carried the drinks to the booth, placed them on the table and sat across from him. He muttered thanks but didn't look up. I drank a mouthful of Coke. Cashman made a phone call on her cell and glanced in my direction. I said to Robbie, "A friend of Vincent Dunn hired me to look into the murder."

He reached for the jigger of whiskey and took a small sip, just enough to tease the taste buds. I'd have gulped it in a swallow. Robbie took the jigger and did it right, draining it empty. I ordered another one at the bar. Cashman poured it, not looking at me. I put the whiskey on the table. Robbie gathered it in.

"What can you tell me about Vincent Dunn?" I said.

He drank beer and sipped whiskey.

"Vinny got himself into something," Robbie said. "I don't know what he got into, but it made him nervous. The day before they killed him, he was jumpy, like he knew they were coming. He kept looking behind him and he flinched every time the door opened. Vinny was shitting his pants."

"Any idea why?"

"None." He moved the jigger in circles on the tabletop. "A couple of days before the murder, a guy in a fancy suit came in. He talked to Vinny over there, at the end of the bar."

"Tell me more about the guy in the suit," I said. "What did they talk about?"

"Vinny never said."

"Can you describe him? Height, weight, hair?"

"He was tall and lean, strong-looking, like he worked out, blond hair almost white. He was obsessed with his shoes. He kept wiping them with a cloth."

Robbie stopped for a beer break and gazed at the TV. His eyes were getting glassy. I'd better get what I needed before he zonked out, but I was too late. He was gonzo. I sat back and pondered my next move. A GQ-dressed man came in and went to the bar. He stood out like a limo in the projects. Cashman went up to him and leaned close and whispered in his ear. GQ tried to be discreet when he glanced at me. I pretended not to notice him. He put money on the bar and went out the door.

I put my card in Robbie's jacket pocket and left McNally's Tap. I was walking to my car on Canal when a black sedan sped by with the windows down. Two shots rang out, shattering the rear window of Kid's truck. They could have easily hit me if they wanted to.

After I picked myself up off the sidewalk, I looked at the damage. Kid would be furious. I wish they'd hit me instead. Just then my phone rang. The man on the other end said, "Next time we won't miss." He had a Boston accent.

The next day Kid continued to follow Detective Vachon, and I drove to the crime scene. My phone rang. A woman named Dottie was on the other end. She must have heard the confusion in my voice because she said again, "Dottie. We spoke yesterday." Was it Cashman from McNally's Tap? My hopes were dashed when she said, "At the A.A. meeting, I'm Dottie, from Charlestown."

"I apologize, Dottie. I was distracted."

"I told my husband you were investigating the murder, and he called Vincent's brother Eddie. Eddie wants to talk to you."

"Is he in Nashua?"

"He's still in Charlestown. Eddie's a Teamster, Local 25. That's how my husband knows him, through the union."

Dottie gave me Eddie's phone number.

I called Eddie and we arranged to meet in Lowell in two hours. What was it with Lowell as a meeting place? At least he didn't say McDermott's Green. That would have spooked me.

I parked in the lot of the Lowell YMCA and waited for Eddie Dunn. Ten minutes later an eighteen-wheeler rolled down YMCA Drive and pulled over at the curb. The airbrakes hissed and the diesel gurgled and died. The driver got out wearing a Local 25 jacket. We met on the sidewalk next to the truck.

"Eddie?" I said.

"Eddie Dunn, Vin's brother. Thanks for meeting me here. I have a run up to Portsmouth and this is on the way."

We stood like two townies at an outdoor wake, talking about Vincent's murder. Eddie told me about the Dunn family, saying it was just he and Vin, no other siblings, his parents had passed on. The talk was preamble and we both knew it.

"You're friends with Dottie's husband," I said to get things going.

"We're in the same union." He looked down the road and said, "Why are you looking into Vin's murder?" Overtones of suspicion tinged his voice. "What's going on?"

"A man hired me to investigate, but I can't give you his name." I paused, giving him a chance to respond. When he didn't, I continued. "He liked Vincent. He wants to make sure he gets justice."

"The man who hired you doesn't trust the police?"

It was a fair question, one I'd been wrestling with myself.

"Maybe," I said.

We stood on the sidewalk. A block away the traffic on the Lowell Connector roared. Traffic is louder in the fall and winter, when the leaves have fallen, with nothing to muffle the sound.

"I asked around town," Eddie said. "People I trust, friends with good judgment, they tell me you're reliable. Dogged, too. You won't stop until you get the truth."

"Your friends are too kind."

"Not really." Eddie blew on his hands. "Do you trust the man who hired you?"

"Yeah, I do," I said.

We went silent amid the echoing traffic. A jogger bundled in sweats ran past us toward the Y. The frayed hood was drawn tightly around his head. No fancy sweat suits in Lowell.

"Vin went away, Lewisburg," Eddie said. "They let him out

175

early, because he made a deal. Vin became an informer." I should have guessed it. Vincent gets out, Vincent gets dead—it smacked of the FBI. Eddie continued. "I struggled with my brother being a snitch. We don't do that in Charlestown. We don't talk to cops." He looked at me. "This is between us, right?"

"Yes, us," I said.

"And then he goes and gets himself murdered, and you wanna know what I thought? He got what he deserved." He looked away. "But I wanna kill the bastard who shot Vin twice in the head."

Being a townie is complicated business. We're expected to balance family loyalty with neighborhood norms, and the balancing act is always fuzzy, never in synch. The responsibility is burdensome at best and deadly at worst. People get killed when they violate the code.

"You're no rat," I said. "I'll do my best to nail his killer."

A tear ran down his cheek. He wiped it away and took out his keys. "I gotta get to Portsmouth." He stood next to his truck, not moving. "I have to be careful what I say. I have a wife and two boys."

"Don't put your family in danger, Eddie." I gave him my card. "Call me if you want to talk."

"Tony Cedrone, out of Somerville, and a townie named Duffer Barry," he said.

Tony Cedrone and Duffer Barry? Maybe I should walk away while I can.

I went back to Kid's truck and thought about Vincent Dunn. Two in the head eliminated the possibility of suicide. Two in the head meant murder, Tony Cedrone's calling card.

From the Lowell YMCA I drove to McDermott's Green. I don't know why I went there, but it had something to do with Captain Raymond. I reconsidered the talk we had the day he hired me, but nothing came. Maybe it wasn't about Captain Raymond at all. Maybe it was about Red McDermott's funeral. My father took me to the funeral, and the next day he was dead. The scattering of Red's ashes is the last memory I have of my father. My phone rang. The man on the other end was talking before I could say hello. He talked so fast I couldn't understand him.

"Slow down," I said. "Who is this?"

"Louis Robinette," he answered. I recognized the voice but not the name. He said, "I saw the guy."

"What guy?"

"The guy from the bar with the shiny shoes."

Robbie from McNally's Tap. "Where did you see him?" I asked.

"At a coffee shop in Concord," he said. "I followed him to the James C. Cleveland Federal Building, got a photo of him, too."

"Nice work."

I'd underestimated Robbie. My phone pinged with the photo.

I drove back to Henri's Motor Lodge and went in. Kid was honing a Bowie knife on a whetstone. He sheathed it and put it under his pillow. He told me about his day tailing Detective Paul Vachon of the Nashua Police Department.

"I followed him to a cop bar on Main Street called Bressoud's. You're going to love this one, Dermot." He leaned forward. "The FBI took the case away from Nashua. I had to spend a thousand to find out. That eats up the retainer."

"Money well spent, Kid."

I brought up my contact list and found Emma Hague, an FBI agent I met when working on another case. We got close, too close, and then we got intimate. I thought I fell in love with her. She thought I was a good resource.

I dialed and she answered.

"Emma, it's Dermot. I need your help."

* * *

Three days later I drove to the Acre and parked in front of St. Patrick's. Captain Leo Raymond was waiting for me on McDermott's Green. He was dressed in civilian clothes this time, not the state trooper uniform. The clothing disarmed him, making him look older and smaller. I joined him on the gravel walkway. He turned to me and said, "I heard you solved the Dunn case."

"Yeah." It was noontime on a cloudy day. The Angelus bells chimed Immaculate Mary. I removed my Red Sox cap until it ended. "I went to Boston police headquarters and talked to Superintendent Hanson. You said he recommended me. Hanson said he never heard of you. So I asked myself, why did Captain Raymond mislead me about Hanson? Why did he hire me for the Dunn case?" I didn't wait for an answer. "It wasn't about Vincent Dunn, was it? It was about the FBI. Dunn was a means to draw me in. I did some homework. It wasn't about the FBI, either, was it, Captain? It was about my father. You thought his fall wasn't an accident."

Captain Raymond looked up at the church steeple. A lone seagull preened on the cross. The white feathers stood in contrast to the gray spire and leaden skies.

"Your father could walk an I-beam like he was walking on a sidewalk. No way he lost his balance and fell."

"He was murdered," I said. "My contact in the Boston FBI office gave me Red McDermott's case file. Red was an informer. Tony Cedrone tried to muscle in on Red's bookie business in Lowell. Red didn't like it, and he reached out to the FBI. He called O'Dwyer."

"O'Dwyer, the Boston director?"

"Cedrone was a snitch, too. O'Dwyer was his handler. O'Dwyer told Cedrone about Red contacting the FBI. Cedrone and O'Dwyer were worried what Red might've told my father, so Cedrone threatened a window washer to drug my father's thermos. Doped, my father fell off the scaffolding."

Raymond turned gray. He bent forward and when he came back up he looked ten years older. "You're as smart as they say."

"Why did you hire me to investigate Vincent Dunn?"

"You already answered the question."

"Is there more?" I asked.

Raymond nodded. "The FBI took the Dunn case from Nashua. When they did, a faint bell rang in my head, a bell from twenty years ago, when the FBI took Red McDermott's case from Lowell. I saw parallels between Red McDermott and Vincent Dunn, and then I thought about your father's death. The investigations happened twenty years apart, but I saw similarities."

"The similarity was Tony Cedrone. He killed Red and he killed Dunn, and as it turned out, he killed my father, or had him killed." The lone seagull alighted from the steeple and soared toward the river, flying past smokestacks and mill buildings long since closed. "You wanted me to find out if my father was murdered, and if he was, you wanted me to solve the case, didn't you?"

"Yes."

"I asked myself, why did Captain Raymond want me to solve the case? What motivated him?" I gestured to a granite bench and we sat on it. "I dug out my mother's papers last night. I found family photos, report cards, little league pictures. I also found my baptism certificate. I had two godfathers, Timothy McDermott and Leo Raymond. My given name is Dermot Raymond. I was named for you and Red."

He nodded but didn't reply.

"I finally remembered where I saw you before. It was at Red's funeral Mass. You were wearing a suit, and you were with a beautiful woman."

"My wife."

"My father died the next day," I said. "Why didn't you contact me? Red had an excuse—he was dead—but you didn't."

"It's complicated."

"Try me."

He got up from the granite slab and walked to the path, where he stopped.

"I respected your father. Our time in Vietnam was a big part of it." He took a step and crunched in the gravel. "You father's drinking cost him his job with the ironworkers, and then he disappeared. Nobody knew where he went. We thought he went to Nova Scotia. You were just a kid at the time. Your mother called me. She didn't have any food in the house, so I brought her some groceries. The next week I brought more."

"I don't remember seeing you," I said.

"I came by late at night, after my shift ended." He looked at the ground. "She was proud and she didn't want you to know. Soon I developed feelings for her, and I sensed she had feelings for me. It was all unspoken, neither of us acted on it." His eyes welled. "I never pursued her, and she never encouraged me, but the feelings were there. My love for her grew so strong I couldn't bear it any longer. I had to walk away."

I thought about my mother and the cirrhosis of the liver and the daily drinking that destroyed her life.

"She died young," I said.

"She did, and then your father died a few years later, and then my wife died shortly after that, cancer. I've been alone since." He paused for a beat and said, "I should have contacted you. All I can say is I'm sorry."

"You walked away from my mother out of respect for my father." I considered the decency of his act, the difficulty of it. "You don't have to apologize for anything."

I pondered my love for Cheyenne Starr, who left me after she got hit by a car meant for me—collateral damage they called it. It's not collateral when you love the woman who got damaged.

"You're a better man than I am," I said.

The wind kicked up and bent the trees surrounding the church grounds. A coatless boy rolled by on a skateboard with condensation spewing from his mouth. He didn't notice the cold. I zipped my jacket and shove my hands in the pockets. My ears were frosty and my nose was runny. I wanted to get warm.

"I'm going to Athenian Corner for a bite to eat," I said. "Do you want to join me?"

DETOUR TO DOLMADES

Stephen D. Rogers

Diana Hamartia, crisp in her whites despite the hours she'd just spent in the kitchen, stared across her desk at Ginger, whose red hair added a plume of color to her all-black, long-sleeve, long-pants uniform. "Ginger, I'm told four parties asked for you by name."

The server grinned, "I made more in tips tonight than I did all week in my day job."

"That's right." Diana sniffed. "Working here is just a lark for you, isn't it?"

Ginger flared. "I bust my hump out there. Ask any of my parties."

"Dolmades is the finest Greek restaurant in Providence because I've made it one of the top restaurants in Providence period. I'm the chef-owner. The first half of that means, without me, nobody comes through the doors to leave you a tip. The second half of that means, without me, nobody signs your check."

"Excuse me, but is there a problem?"

Diana cleared her throat. "Do you know why parties ask for you by name?"

"Because I'm good."

"Because you like to think you're special. You crave the attention. You preen. Out there on the floor, swirling between your tables, you think it's all about you."

"I don't—"

Diana raised a hand. "You're wrong. It's never about the server. It's about the food, and the chef that prepares that food. When you're out front, you're nothing more than an extension of me."

"Did someone complain about my service? Those two guys from Cranston? Because they—"

"Stop. I told you what the problem was: your ego."

Ginger crossed her arms. "Not for nothing, if it seems like I'm full of myself, and I'm not, it's only because I'm the best server you've got."

"Then you'll have no trouble finding another job." Diana smiled.

"What?"

"You heard me. You're fired."

"You can't just fire me."

"Actually, as chef-owner, I can do anything I want." Diana flashed her teeth. "After you change, leave your uniform in the basket and empty your locker. I never want to see you in this restaurant ever again."

"I wouldn't eat here if you paid me."

"No worries there." Diana opened her middle drawer and tossed her planner on the desk.

"You're making a terrible mistake." Ginger jumped out of her chair. "You're going to regret this."

"Close the door on your way out."

Diana thumbed through the planner.

After catching her breath, Diana scooted up against the head-board and arranged the covers.

Ray sighed. "We got hammered tonight."

"I've told you before, I don't want to hear how well my competition is doing."

"Your idea. I was happy working at Dolmades."

"We're not having this discussion again." Diana yawned.

"Long shift?"

"I had to let someone go."

"Yeah, I heard that."

Diana turned to face him. "You heard that? How?"

"If that decker we rented on Chalkstone was Providence, the restaurant business is what passed for our bathroom."

"Step out of the shower and into the toilet. That's why I brought us here to Chestnut Street." She blew him a kiss.

"Providence used to be the costume jewelry capital of the world. What are we now?"

"Home to the best Greek restaurant on the east coast."

"Is it? Is it still? I wouldn't know. It's been so long since I was there."

Diana clenched her teeth. Forced them apart. "You were a distraction."

Ray swung his legs off the side of the bed, turning away from her. "You say that with such warmth."

"You know what I mean. I couldn't be involved with an employee. It's my restaurant."

"Your restaurant, your rules. Sleep with whomever you want."

She placed a palm against his bare back. "They'd use it against me."

"Who, the other bartenders? The Guatemalans on dish?"

"What's bothering you?"

Ray took several deep breaths. "I'm just tired is all."

"So go to sleep. You earned it."

Ray stood, leaving her hand hanging in midair. "I think I'll get something to eat."

Diana entwined her fingers over her belly. "Stay away from spicy foods. They'll keep you up."

"Thanks, Maw." Ray padded out of the bedroom without looking back.

Diana rubbed her face.

That Ray, sometimes he just... Why couldn't he be happy with what he had? Why did he have to keep asking, keep pushing? It's not like it changed anything. They were having a nice time here tonight until he started up again.

She heard him slamming cabinets.

Ray was one of those people who couldn't leave well enough alone. Well enough? Things were great.

This apartment was fantastic. Things were good between them, the sex at least. Dolmades was struggling, but she was going to take care of that. She had a plan. The restaurant would emerge from the other side of this irksome business stronger than ever, her reputation intact.

Ray just needed to chill, give her some room to maneuver.

Tomorrow morning, she'd take him to Olga's. Coffees in the courtyard. If that didn't clear his head, she'd bring him back here and climb on top.

She'd make him see sense.

Diana slid down under the covers.

She moved the pan of shrimp and artichoke hearts to a dark burner, and shifted the pan with tomatoes and garlic onto the flame.

"Diana?"

"Hmm?" The chef painted with the wooden spoon, adding layers of oil and lemon to the tomatoes as they cooked down.

Sylvia licked her lips. "Table four wants to see you."

"I'm in the middle of dinner."

"I explained that, but he's insistent. He said to tell you his name was Mr. Villanova."

Damn. "Gary! Take over." Diana didn't think Villanova would come here in person, especially as so far none of the people she'd talked to had even mentioned his name.

When Gary finally arrived at her side, Diana explained the active slips. "I'll be back as soon as I can."

She left her apron on the hook before leaving the kitchen, smoothing her whites as she entered the restaurant.

Table four. Mr. Villanova looked younger than she expected, but maybe it was just the thick dark hair, the sunglasses that masked a third of his face.

She stood before him, her hands crossed. "I hope everything is to your satisfaction."

"Good, yeah. This is a nice wine." He motioned towards the bottle on the table, a bottle of their finest. "I'm going to have the lamb."

"The lamb is especially good this evening."

"You decide how to prepare it. Surprise me."

"Did you already give your order to Sylvia?"

"I'm giving it to you."

"Of course. I'll make something special." She dipped. "Dinner's on the house."

"You say that as if it's a gift."

"No, I—" Diana quickly rejected every response that came to mind.

"I wanted to come in, see for myself what you're putting up for collateral." He glanced around the dining room, nodded in approval. "You design this place yourself?"

"Nothing happens here without my approval."

He turned his dark glasses on her. "That thing we discussed, it's on the desk in your office."

"My office is locked."

"That's good. You don't want somebody wandering off with my money." Mr. Villanova examined the room, counting tables.

Diana rubbed sleep from her eyes as she answered the phone, "Yeah?"

"Justin Silva. What are you trying to do to me?"

"I—" Diana smacked her lips. "I don't know what you're talking about."

"Did I wake you up? Seriously?"

"Seems that way." Diana stared at the nightstand clock, the

time three hours past when the alarm should have shrieked. Did Ray leave without waking her?

She hadn't slept this late since college.

"I have a hundred-plate wedding reception, and lover boy is my primary. You think I think his no show is no accident?"

Diana scissored her legs under the twisted sheets. "Justin, honestly, I'm just trying to get the blood flowing."

"I know you're in trouble, Diana. We all know you're in trouble. But sabotaging my business? Sabotaging the wedding of this beautiful young couple who now have to deal with their wedding guests only half in the bag? That's not like you."

"What do you mean I'm in trouble? I'm not in trouble."

Justin laughed. "What do you think we do at these association meetings? Compare menu fonts? For months, you've been the refrain, everybody betting on whether Dolmades will survive the rent hike."

"I'll be fine." The money she borrowed from Mr. Villanova would get her over the hump, and once the restaurant rebounded, she'd pay him back no problem.

"You should pull your head down out of the clouds, querida, and join the rest of us mere mortals. I did you a favor, taking in lover boy."

"He's a good bartender." Ray never missed a shift.

"Right. You don't want him sleeping with your waitresses, so you send him to A Cozinha so he sleeps with mine. And today he doesn't show."

Diana shook her head. "Ray wasn't sleeping with my servers."

Again Justin laughed. "Ah, querida. Let me share with you I something learned from my grandmother. Gossip: it's good for the soul."

It wasn't like Ray to ignore her texts, to send her calls to voicemail. What was going on with him? Did he actually forget he was scheduled to work?

Diana's car shot out of the parking lot.

And where did Justin get off making insinuations? Nobody cheated on Diana Hamartia. Certainly not Ray. He wouldn't dare.

He probably wouldn't even know how.

She slowed to turn right onto Weybosset, the narrow road channeling her northeast towards the river, towards Dolmades.

And the association? They had no right to discuss her business as if she were some character on a reality series. Truth was, they should spend less time gossiping and more time on running their own restaurants. They should focus on working with the chamber to make Providence a destination city.

Road closure.

Gritting her teeth, Diana nodded at the officer detouring her onto Delta Street.

As if it wasn't bad enough she overslept today, the city had to decide to decorate with sawhorses and orange barrels as if the one ways didn't frustrate tourists enough.

Where was Ray if not at A Cozinha? What was so important he couldn't reply to her texts?

It wasn't her birthday. Could today be an anniversary, Ray afraid he'd spoil the surprise if he interacted with her? First date? No. Moving in together? No. That languid afternoon at the hotel she would have just passed if not for the detour?

Diana smiled at the memory.

Unfortunately, that tryst being the anniversary didn't make sense either.

Delta ended at Pine Street, which forced her right, away from Dolmades.

Of course this was Ray she was talking about. Just because Diana knew today wasn't an anniversary didn't mean Ray hadn't confused a date or miscalculated the range.

Have some pity on the guy. Play dumb and act surprised.

She could always correct him later.

Diana made a series of lefts to exit the maze of one-way

roads: Pine to Hay to Friendship to 44.

A red Corvette went flashing by, the driver and passenger paying too much attention to each other to notice Diana.

Ray. Ray and Ginger. What was Ray doing with Ginger when he was supposed to be at work? What was Ginger doing with Diana's man?

Diana glanced at the rearview, and discovered too much time had already passed, too much distance had opened between them. Even if she flipped around, she'd never catch up, and she couldn't imagine where they might be going.

What the heck, Ray?

Diana took in the dining room as she strode through Dolmades, through the kitchen, until she reached the sanctity of the line where she said to Gary, "It looks like you have things well in hand."

"That's why you pay me the big bucks." Gary drizzled ladolemono over a poached salmon. "Ray said you'd be late, the two of you celebrating into the wee plus hours."

"Yes." She'd shared her plan to save the restaurant, and the two had indeed celebrated until the sky began to lighten.

Which hadn't been enough to keep Ray from getting up early. Or to cruise around town with Ginger sitting beside him as if he didn't care who noticed.

Gary continued, "I assume he found what you sent him for."

"You let Ray into my office." Ray who only last night learned about Villanova's money.

"No, he said he had his own key."

That's why he silenced her alarm this morning.

Why he slipped out the door making sure not to disturb her.

Diana studied the plate that Gary lifted up onto the shelf. "I want to introduce a new garnish, roasted fig with feta."

"Sounds good."

"You have this under control. I'll be in my office."

* * *

The money was gone.

The bag of money wasn't on the floor.
It wasn't in the safe.
It wasn't anywhere else.
Diana dropped into her chair and covered her eyes.
The money was gone.

Sitting behind a mahogany desk, Mr. Villanova looked crisp, alert, everything that Diana wasn't.

After closing the restaurant, Diana had stepped outside the building to find a dark car waiting for her, muscle in a suit holding open the back door. She'd actually paused, wanting nothing more than to go home and collapse onto her bed.

"Sit, sit." Mr. Villanova motioned at one of the chairs between them, leather with brass nails.

She sat. His desk...it was the size of a prep table. He could build two hundred salads on that surface easily, especially as there was nothing on it.

Nothing on the walls, either. Except the man standing against the wall to Villanova's left, staring straight ahead, his hands hanging at his sides. Meat on a hook.

"I heard what happened."

Diana refocused. "With what?"

"With my money. With your boyfriend. Don't look so surprised. When things happen in my city, I know."

"I'm not even sure I know what happened, and I was there."

Mr. Villanova chuckled. "Human nature happened. It's a biological imperative to improve our situation, to leave behind a better world for our children."

A flash of Ginger, young and free. "To be quite frank, I'm

sure Ray's thinking about something else entirely."

"Children. Sex. I'm sure you see the connection."

Diana grunted. "Maybe if—"

"I didn't bring you here to discuss that knucklehead. You and I, we have business."

"You'll get your money back. Maybe it will take me longer than I expected, but I'll pay you every dime I owe you."

A bartender and a waitress. They could go anywhere, work anywhere, work for straight tips under the table. She would never find them, never find her money. Mr. Villanova's money.

"Diana, you came to me because your expenses were outstripping your income. That's not going to change." Mr. Villanova paused. "I stand corrected. It is going to change. It's going to change right now, now that we're partners."

"Partners?"

"We had an understanding, you and I. Your boyfriend...his actions mean you can't keep up your end of the deal."

Diana leaned forward. "You'll get your money."

"You let your boyfriend steal my money. I can't trust you to look out for my interests. Sorry."

Diana shuffled through possible explanations, excuses, promises. Nothing seemed capable of getting past Villanova's dark eyes.

"Look, Diana, this is going to be good for you. Good for Dolmades. First thing, I'm going to save the restaurant money on the back end. I've got a linen company, a liquor distributor, and access to fresh meat, fish, and produce. Reducing costs, that's a good thing, right? Business 101."

She nodded, unable to speak, unable to bear the idea that she'd lost everything.

"I'll bring in my accountant, take that burden off your shoulders, let you focus on what you do best. The name of the restaurant is Dolmades, but it might as well be called Diana's, right? Tell me if I don't have that correct."

"I'm accustomed to running everything myself. Gary's a

help, of course—"

"Diana, I'm not asking. You lost my money. This is how you stay alive." He frowned. "If you could have gone to a bank, you would have gone to a bank, walked out with a free lollipop. You came to me."

"I just—"

"I've also reduced operating expenses. To wit, rent is half of what it used to be before your landlord jacked the rate."

"I don't understand."

"We're business partners, you and I. This is what I bring to the business. What you bring to the business is you keep people coming in the door spending their money. You stop doing that, you're done."

"I'm not sure I understand."

"You're mine. You—and Dolmades—belong to me."

"I—"

Mr. Villanova raised a hand. "It's late, and I've said what needs to be said. You should go home, toss a few of his belongings out the window, torch something else of his in the kitchen sink, and claim both sides of the bed."

"I can fix this."

Mr. Villanova turned his head to speak to the man against the wall. "It's almost cute, the way she thinks she's still in charge."

He faced Diana and frowned. "Some people say I speak too plainly. Maybe I'll use this conversation as an example of a time I apparently didn't speak plainly enough."

"Mr. Villanova—"

"Diana, if I tell you tomorrow to fire every single one of your employees, that's what you're going to do. If I tell you to torch Dolmades for the insurance…" He chuckled. "Well that wouldn't actually make sense because at the moment you don't own the building. My point is, you're no longer in charge, Diana. I am. I'm in charge of Dolmades. I'm in charge of you."

Mr. Villanova stood. "Go home. Get some sleep. We'll talk more tomorrow."

THE DARK SIDE OF THE RIVER

Brendan DuBois

I got home that night two hours later than expected, shoulders aching, but it had been for a good cause. My boss at the supermarket had needed more pallets of groceries unloaded and those extra hours of income would be nice when it showed up in my paycheck in two weeks. I had called Mom and she said she could fend for herself for dinner, so for the next one hundred-twenty minutes, I had maneuvered the heavy pallets of plastic shrink-wrapped groceries from the cold interior of a tractor trailer truck, out to the rear storage area of the supermarket. Mindless, repetitive, grunting work, which suited me just fine.

At home I washed up in the kitchen sink, noted the time. If I ate quick and if Mom wasn't particularly talkative, then I could have a solid hour of studying wrapped up before going to bed and getting up at 4:00 a.m. for my other job, delivering copies of the state-wide newspaper, the *Union Leader*, to a hundred or so sleeping customers in this part of the state. After wiping my hands on a length of paper towel—the store brand, which I bought not out of any loyalty to the store, but because it's twenty-two cents cheaper per roll—I went out to check on Mom. She was stretched out in a reclining chair, a knitted afghan spread out over her, her eyes closed, gently snoring, glasses sliding down her nose. I took a breath, my fingers tingling. One of my other jobs, as well. Taking care of Mom. Not the kind of job I had imagined four or so years ago, but one that was dumped in my lap and one I was doing the best I could.

Our home was a prefab double-wide, ditched in a series of other pre-fabs in something grandly called Louisiana Estates, and which most of the people around here called Lousy Estates. In a wonderful example of small-town graft, it was built over the objections of some of the brighter residents of Thebes along the banks of the Pawtucket River, which floods out every spring and dumps about a foot of water on the expanses of grassy mud that passes for lawns. Even though Dad has been dead for more than five years, the room still smelled of stale tobacco and bad memories. On the cheap paneled walls were equally cheap photographs, taken at a local department store years ago, showing our family in yellow-tinged colors: me, Dad, Mom, and my brother. And it was like me seeing those photos woke up Mom, for she coughed and said, "Eddie?"

"Yeah, Mom."

"You get home just now?"

"Just a couple of minutes ago. You eat all right?"

"Yep." She shifted in her seat, winced. Her right hip is nothing more than two bare bones, rubbing against each other, and one of these days, she should have hip replacement surgery. Yeah, one of these days. She looked up at me and said, "Frank's coming over."

"Oh."

She motioned with her right hand. "Don't sound so angry. He's still your brother."

"Yes, but..."

"But what?" she asked.

But everything, I angrily thought. Frank was the reason why I was here, staying home with my mother, working two jobs and studying in fits and starts, trying to finally get my high school GED certificate, when I should have been doing almost anything else, anything and everything.

Frank. Who had doomed me here, to this life.

"Nothing, Mom," I said. "Did he say what he wants?"

A smile from Mom, who I think still liked to believe that

everything was going to turn out all right, that her husband hadn't died nearly broke, and that her two sons really did get along, despite everything that had gone on between the two of us.

"No, but he said he'd like to talk to you for a bit."

"Oh." One of my more favorite words to answer Mom whenever she brings up Frank's name.

"There's still some of the tuna casserole left in the fridge, if you're hungry."

"Thanks, Mom." I bent down to give her a peck on the cheek, and went back to the kitchen, fists clenched.

In the small kitchen I sat and waited for a while, then got up, went to the refrigerator. Out came the small bowl with plastic wrap covering it, and after taking the cover off, I plopped it in the microwave. I heated the small bowl three times, and after each heating session, I opened the microwave door and rotated the bowl a bit. The microwave is small and old and doesn't have a turntable.

Heating the tuna casserole this way meant portions of the meal were hot enough to burn my tongue, while other portions were still lumped together in a cold, congealed mess that didn't go down easy. I ate from the bowl over the countertop, drinking tap water. There were bottles of Budweiser in the refrigerator. I let them be, waiting for my brother.

After I cleaned up the dishes and put them away, Mom limped into the kitchen, an embarrassed smile on her face. "Looks like I slept through my shows," she said. "Did I miss Frank?"

"No, Ma," I said. "He hasn't come by yet. Are you sure he said tonight?"

She nodded, holding onto the edge of the kitchen counter for balance. "I'm sure."

"Maybe he forgot."

"Oh, no," she said. "He'd never forget. I'm sure he'll be by. Make sure you wake me, all right?"

"Sure, Mom," I said, fibbing with ease. "I'll do just that."

Mom turned and went back down the hallway, and I listened carefully to her progress, as she limped down to the other side of the double wide. There was the briefest sound of glass moving, and I knew she had just used a tiny display case of ceramic bunnies—one of her proudest collections—to balance her again as she made her way to her bedroom.

I sat at the empty kitchen table, hands folded in front of me, and waited. Down the hall was my bedroom and my English textbook and an hour's worth of studying to be done, but my focus and concentration were all off. So I waited.

The time I usually go to bed came and went, and about seventy-three minutes later, I decided that my dear older brother had in fact forgotten whatever it was he had promised our mother, so I decided to pack it in. Maybe I could squeeze ten or fifteen minutes of studying in, try to remember what the hell a gerund was. As I got up from the table, headlights from outside flashed through the kitchen window, and I heard the crunch of gravel as a car rolled into the driveway.

I went to the door and opened it up, the cold air forcing its way in, and there was Frank, coming up the wooden steps, grinning. I could smell the beer before anything else.

"Well, Eddie," he said. "Glad to see you got the message."

"Yeah, some message. Mom waited up for you, waited until she couldn't stay awake anymore."

He shrugged, held out his hands in a whaddya-gonna-do gesture, and said, "I got tied up. Sorry. I'll take her out to lunch this week or something. That'll make her happy."

I stood there in the doorway. Frank looked up at me, his face now a bit more set. "Hey, you gonna let me in, or what?"

"I don't know, Frank. You tell me what the what is, and maybe I'll let you in."

He forced a smile. "Still my home."

"Doubt that. Look, it's late. Mom's sleeping and I don't want to wake her up, and I've got to be up in a few hours and start delivering newspapers. So why don't we—"

"Eddie, please," he said. "I'll be here, just for a few minutes, that's all. And I'll keep my voice down, promise. All right? Just let me in and we'll talk. That's it."

I suppose I could have closed the door on him, and that might have been smart. But I never knew with Frank. After the door closed, he might have gone back into his car and gone back to one of the pubs on this side of the river, or he might start screaming at me from the doorsteps, about what a lousy brother I was, keeping him from coming home, and that'd wake up Mom and the neighbors, and who needed crap like that?

I gave up and backed in, and Frank came in, too, rubbing his hands, heading over to the refrigerator. He's four years older than me and packs at least forty pounds more, mostly around his belly and thighs. He opened the refrigerator and pulled out two beers—and put one back when I shook my head—and came over, twisting the top off. Poor dumb Frank. Mom makes sure that there's always beer in the refrigerator, and he still likes to think that Mom buys it for herself—her taste is for cheap sherry, every now and then, just before bed—and that he's just "borrowing" a brew or two every week.

He sprawled out in the chair, took a long swallow, and said, "Still delivering those papers."

"Yeah."

"And working at the Pricemart?"

"Unless I got fired and they didn't tell me," I said.

He smiled, his face now pudgy and worn, like he had spent way too many nights of his life in one of the town's pubs, drinking and smoking and listening to loud music and dumb conversations. I said, "Still at the mill?"

Another swallow of the beer. "Sure enough. But that might change."

A muscle memory, of feeling something in the air change, a

little buzz, a little adjustment in the situation. The back of my neck got cold and crawly, and I felt like I should scratch my hands. I cleared my throat. "What's going to change?"

He held the beer in his hand, and then leaned over to talk to me more quietly.

"I've got a plan," he said, with confidence.

Oh, God, I thought, not again.

Frank waited to hear from me, and I was too busy right then, remembering everything that had happened more than four years ago, when I was younger, dumber, and didn't quite appreciate the depths of the flaws in my older brother's character. I had been in high school, barely hanging on with Cs and Ds, and my older brother just seemed to be a funny guy, in complete control of anything and everything. He was at the leather mill, working in the shipping department, laughing and joking, secure that he had "A Job" and was going to go far in Thebes. But he was never quite satisfied with what he was doing, with how much money he made. Dad had said something like that before passing on, and I remember hearing him tell Mom, "That boy, if he's making two hundred a week, he spends three hundred. And if he makes three hundred, he spends four hundred. What in hell is wrong with him?"

I was young. I didn't think anything was wrong with him. I thought he was the best older brother a guy could want, a guy who bought you beers on the sly, passed along porn magazines when he was done with them, and introduced me to the so-called joys of nicotine and cannabis.

Yeah, some brother.

And one night, Christ, almost like this, he had come to me with a scheme. He and a couple of guys, they were fixing on breaking in at one of the summer places, up on the upper reaches of the Pawtucket River, where it was wider and some rich knuckleheads from Massachusetts or Vermont came during the summer, to fish and run their speedboats and basically look at us like we were employees at a summer theme park or something. This place was one of the bigger ones, and it had good locks on the windows and doors, except a pal of Frank's, a guy named Pete Cloutier, who delivered firewood, he said the garage wasn't that tough to break into. And last fall, Pete had piled up some split pieces of oak in the garage—a three-car obscene piece of work that was bigger than most people's houses in Thebes—and found out there was a key under the mat to the door leading into the kitchen from the garage.. All you had to do was jigger a window in the garage—send somebody in nice and small and slim, like me—and in just a few minutes, the place would belong to Frank, Pete, and me.

That was the plan. And for a while, it had worked, right up to the point where I got into the house, and was going through the huge living room, past the big-screen TV set and stereo equipment and nice silverware display on a shelf, and I got belted down from behind. See, what Pete and Frank didn't know was that some other enterprising morons, next town over, had already hit the place twice. And a college-age guy from this rich family from Vermont, he had been spending the nights on his spring break at the place, ready to catch whoever came in next.

Which had been me.

And after he got me on the floor, he had started whaling on me, and I smelled how clean he was, that this guy actually used an aftershave or cologne or something, and I started whaling back. And cocked him good. I was so pissed I worked him over with a golf club, until he was crying like a boy who had lost his toy soldiers, and the cops came 'cause somebody had heard the screaming, and bang, it was done. The college guy I whaled on barely made it, I was tried as an adult, and now, four years later, I came back to Thebes from Concord—the state capitol, and home to a prison and mental hospital, how nice the planning, to put such three important institutions in one city—with a felony record, no high school diploma, and a smiling brother who was about to screw me over again.

"Well?" Frank said. "You want to hear it?"

"No, I don't."

"C'mon, look, it's a plan that'll—"

"Shut up, shut up, shut up," I said, trying to keep my voice level, knowing Mom was sleeping, just yards away. "The last time I listened to you, I was sent down to Concord for four long years. You did me over so well that I still can't sleep well at night. Forget it."

"It's a good score, Eddie, a really good score," he said. "It'll set me up, it'll set you up, and even straighten things out with me and Cheryl."

"Cherry? You're still dogging after her?"

He frowned. "Name's Cheryl, and you know it."

Sure. Cherry. Rough nickname for a girl from the other side of the river, whose real name was Cheryl but most called her Cherry, since she always claimed, with every boy, that whenever he rounded third base and got home, that he had been the first. Sure. A nice well-off girl who had sunk her claws into Frank some years ago, got married and divorced from some other well-off clown from across the river, and still strung Frank along, like a pet ferret or something. Whenever her toilet backed up, or the roof leaked, or the driveway needed shoveling, Frank was there with a hopeful smile to do whatever she wanted.

"What the hell does she have to do with this?"

"She's pissed at me, for what I did to her, couple of months ago. This score will help set us straight, give you and me a piece, too."

"You pissed her off? How?"

He looked embarrassed, which is a stretch for Frank, since most times being embarrassed is something not in his vocabulary. He said, "Couple of months ago, I was tapped out. Seriously tapped out. I was about a day away from being evicted from my place. And Cheryl had a party and I went over and had some fun...got a good buzz on, danced with her a bit, and she was showing off this new stereo system she got. Tiny little thing that can blow sound through a room, like it had speakers ten feet high. Pricey little piece of work."

I shook my head. "You stole it? From her?"

He took another long swallow. "Well, it's not like she can't afford it, you know? Plus, I don't know, I got kinda mad at her later that night, she wouldn't dance with me again, and when people were passing out or puking or leaving, I grabbed it. Stuck it in my truck, took it down to Manchester and hocked it for a couple of hundred bucks at a pawnshop."

"How did she find out?"

The embarrassed look on his face remained, which was a time record of sorts for him. "Some guy out in the woods, taking a leak. Saw me take it. Cheryl got ugly over me and said I needed to pay her back. Which I can't. But she turned me on to this deal."

I should have told him to leave. I should have told him to shut up and go away. I should have done a lot of things. But right then, Mom came in, still shuffling along, grimacing at the pain in her hip, and smiled a bright one when she saw her two boys sitting there, passing the time.

"I thought I heard you," she said, kissing the top of Frank's head, while he grinned. "Can I get you anything? Another beer?"

"No, Ma, I'm fine...look, it's late, why don't you go back to bed," he said, using that same soothing voice that he had used against me four years ago, the same soothing voice that worked, so that Mom did smile and turn away, confident in her belief that her boys were hanging out together, still friends after all these years, and as she went down the hallway, I heard the slightest gasp of pain from her, as she bumped her hip into something.

Her hip.

The pain.

I looked back at Frank and God help me, I think he knew

what I was thinking, and if he were to give me a smile of triumph, I was going to clock him.

But he kept quiet. Lucky for him.

I took a breath. "All right. What's the plan?"

Frank looked at me and said, "Okay, but before I go on, I gotta know, are you going to help me, or what?"

I just nodded, feeling quite tired. "Yeah, I'll help you. Talk to me."

Frank's mood seemed to improve with me rolling over on my back and showing him my belly and exposed throat, so he got right into it.

"Here's the deal. I've got a setup later on with this character named Pelletier."

"Who's he?"

"Some guy Cheryl knows, lives up at Grayson's place, on Mast Road. On the other side of the river."

"And what does he do?"

Frank smirked. "Import-export work."

"Marvelous," I said. "And what's the deal?"

"Cheryl set me up with it," he said. "He's bringing in some crank from Montreal, but he's too well known, further south. State cops and DEA know him real well. So I'm gonna meet him tonight, take it off his hands, and turn around and mule it to some contacts in Boston that Cheryl knows. Get five percent of the profit, right off the top. We'll make two, maybe three grand at least tonight. And then off we go, again and again, month after month. Stuff gets shipped in, I play the courier, and there you go."

"Why?"

"Why, what?"

"Why did Cherry set you up with this Pelletier guy? Because she still likes you, even though you ripped off her radio?"

He said, "Yeah, something like that." Frank turned, like he was trying to see if Mom was still up or something, and he said, more quietly, "Cheryl just wants to help me out, that's all. As a friend. She knows I was tapped out when I scarfed her radio."

"And you believed her?"

"Sure," he said, taking another swallow from the beer. "Why not?"

I didn't feel like debating the point, so I went on. "Okay, then why me?"

He grinned. "Cheryl told me Pelletier, he's a guy who likes to think he's big time. He's a bit of a show-off, and he always has this muscle around him. I figured I needed the same thing, to show him that he could trust me with muling this stuff, and who better than my convict brother?"

If I had not seen my mother limping not more than ten minutes ago with a hip that needed surgery, I would have punched my brother in the face and tossed him out of the house. Even then, I had to take a couple of deep breaths before I could go on.

"All right, when do we start?"

He slapped his hands together. "Right now. Guy's at Grayson's place, waiting for us."

I got up. "You were pretty confident I'd say yes."

"You need confidence, going into business like this. Oh, you can do me one thing, Eddie?"

"What's that?"

A pitying smile. "Can you change your workshirt, Eddie? I don't want this guy to think we don't got class, you coming in with a sweaty shirt that says Pricemart."

"Sure, Frank," I said. "I'm all yours tonight."

"Good enough."

So after I changed, we went.

And in a matter of seconds, we didn't go anywhere. Frank's truck refused to start, the ignition grinding and grinding, like the gears inside of the damn thing were rubbing each other into a spark-filled shower of metal parts. I looked around at the darkened homes of Lousy Estates and said, "Come on, we'll take my car."

"Thanks. Can I drive?"

"Sure, just don't hit anything."

We went around to the other side of the driveway, and I tossed my keys over to Frank, who was carrying a small leather knapsack, which he threw in the rear. My car is a dark blue Ford Escort with standard shift, nothing fancy but it runs, and in a manner of minutes, we were out on the state road, heading to the other side of Thebes. To get to the richer part of town meant going through the James E. Chamberlain Memorial Tunnel, which passes underneath the Pawtucket River, and which was a prime example of Congressional pork and corruption. James E. Chamberlain was a congressman from Massachusetts, who had a vacation camp on the upper part of the river, back in the early 1950s, during a time when the river was spanned by a metal-and-wood bridge that usually was damaged when the ice floes broke up every spring. Upset at having to drive a long detour to get to his favorite retreat, he gave us a tunnel, whether we wanted it or not.

It's narrow and not too long, but in those scores of yards, you travel from one side of the river to the next, and from one universe to the next. I don't know how it was planned, or even if it had been planned, but the side of the river me and Frank and Mom lived on had places like Lousy Estates, had the mills, had the shops, while the other side had homes with nice lawns and fences and a few restaurants, and, of course, the summer places. All of us kids growing up on this side of the river would say, "yeah, watch me, I'll make some big bucks, slide on through the tunnel and to the other side. Just you wait!" And for most of us, my brother and I included, the wait was still going on, and I always thought about those old boasts, each time I drove through.

Frank drove my car with ease, and smiled over at me as we

emerged on the other side. "Funny thing was, just the other day, before Cheryl came to me with this deal, I was gonna hit you up for a few bucks. Lucky this thing came together, huh?"

I folded my arms, just looked at the nice homes as we drove by, knowing that Cherry lived in one just like these, up near the border with Canton. "Yeah, real lucky. Look, how long do you think this'll take?"

"Not too long, little brother, not too long. And you can get your share and I'll bring you right back home."

I didn't say anything, just watched him drive. Soon enough the homes started becoming sparser, and then we entered a long stretch where there was nothing but trees on each side, with the occasional dirt road that led off to the left, heading down to the river. Frank kept quiet, too, until he spotted a place that had two pie tins nailed to a pine tree, and he said, "Here we go."

I had to give him credit, he drove nice and slow down the dirt road, which was so narrow that branches were scraping the side windows. Up ahead I noted lights, and I also noted the tightening in my chest. This seemed crazy, so damn crazy, and I couldn't help but think what kind of power this guy next to me had over me, to do this. And as we slowed and he parked the car, leaving the keys in the ignition—"just in case we have to leave quick," he said with a grin—I knew it wasn't him that had the power over me. It was the thought of the money, and what I could do with it.

"All right, there's one more thing," he said. "Oh...make that two more things."

"Yeah?"

Frank said, "This guy, he's the real thing, all right? Let me do all the talking. We gotta stay cool, 'cause I'm sure this is going to be our only chance. I really need this, Eddie, honest to God, I really need it. Okay?"

I just nodded, tired of saying yes, yes, yes, to my older brother. He said, "Good. There's one more thing." He reached into the rear of the car, retrieved the small leather knapsack. He unzipped it and with his free hand, took something out and dumped it in my lap.

A pistol.

Mother of God.

"Take it back," I said. "Take this damn thing back."

"Look, I know—

"You know shit, and you've always known shit," I shot back at him. "I'm still on parole, you moron, and I can't be in the possession of a pistol. Anybody sees me with this tonight, the word gets back, and I'm heading off to Concord. Not going to happen, Frank."

Frank said, "Quiet down, Eddie, quiet down. You don't have to do anything with it, anything at all. Just put it in your pocket or waistband, make the guys in there know you're carrying. They see you're carrying a friend like that around, then we'll be all set. Okay? Just a few minutes, that's all, and you can give it back to me and it's over."

I closed my eyes, wished the whole damn thing was over, and I picked up the heavy piece of metal and stuck it in my right-hand coat pocket. "Christ, let's get it done, okay?"

"Great."

We stepped out in the cold night air, and I thought about what had gone through my older brother's head earlier to have brought both of us here, through the tunnel and on this side of the river. Any other world, I should have been at home, sleeping, my head still whirring with the intricacies of English grammar, and slumbering with just a few hours to spare before getting up to deliver newspapers. I shouldn't be here, I shouldn't be doing this, but there I was. My coat sagged where the pistol was, and I looked in front of us. There was a two-story home, lights on, and a long stairway leading up to the front door. Towards the rear the land fell away to the river, and from the light of the house, I could make out a couple of docks and moored power-boats. Parked to the side were two of those large pickup trucks with extended cabs and big tires, for people who hate to get their feet dirty. Both pickup trucks had Quebec license plates, blue and white. Music was coming from the house and Frank grabbed my arm, started propelling me up the stairs.

"Come on," he said. "Let's get a move on."

I went with him up the stairs, the pistol still weighing heavily at my side. Frank rapped a couple of times on the door, the music was lowered, and somebody yelled something out that Frank seemed to understand. He turned to me, smiled. "See? They were expecting us."

Frank opened the door and I followed him in, and right from the start, I was scared to death.

It was all wrong.

The door opened up into a large living room, with a large-screen television set on the far wall. The television was showing a porn film of sorts, with the sound off. The air was hazy with smoke, and there were three guys and a woman, sitting on couches and easy chairs, looking over at us. Drinks and empty bottles of beer and bags of snacks were spread on coffee tables and the floor, and as we came in, two of the guys and the woman looked to the largest guy in the room, as if paying instant obedience. The large guy was sitting by himself in a chair, cigar in his thick fingers, staring up at us, smiling wide, but his eyes were hard and shiny. His head was cut to a black stubble, but he had thick, Elvis-style sideburns, and he looked at me and I looked at him, and flashed back to my first week in prison. He was sizing me up, and I was sizing him up, just like a guy named Cooper, down in Concord. The only resemblance they had with each other was the hardness of the look from their eyes, and Cooper that day came up to me in the yard, offered to protect me for a pack of smokes a week, and I nodded and punched him in the throat. I got the crap kicked out me before the guards came, but the message had been sent. I had been left alone for the rest of my time there.

I knew what was going on with the Elvis guy, but I didn't think Frank did. He gave a big smile and said, "Jacques! Told you I'd make it!"

Jacques took a puff from his cigar, kept on looking at me. "So you have," he said, in French-accented English. "So you have."

The two other guys—muscular, wearing black jeans and snug black turtlenecks—whispered to each other in French. The woman, young, blond, wearing a short leather skirt and sleeveless white blouse, watched the porn on the television, seemingly bored. She smoked a cigarette and had long red fingernails.

Jacques said, "And this your criminal brother, eh? Here to help?"

"Here to do whatever it takes," Frank said, still sounding too damn eager. Damn it Frank, I thought, slow down, you fool. You wouldn't have lasted a day in Concord.

Jacques stood up and said, "Bien. We'll see that you're all taken care of. Hold, please." He rattled off something in French and the two guys suddenly stood up. My hand was now inside my coat pocket, around the cold metal. One guy went into an adjoining room, while the other walked to the other side of the room and stopped, arms folded, looking at me. I knew what was going on. I was now covered.

The porn film kept on flickering. The blond woman was still smoking. My legs were beginning to quiver, and I whispered, "Frank..."

"Shut up, all right?" he whispered back. "Just shut up."

The other guy came back, carrying a dark green gym bag, which he handed over to Jacques. The older guy said something else again in French, and the guy was still standing up. Jacques unzipped the top of the bag, bent it over some. There were bundles of green bills in there, sitting on top of some plastic-wrapped packages. He made sure that it was seen, and after zipping the bag closed, lifted it up and down a couple of times, and said, "You want, Frank?"

"Yeah, you know I do. Look, it's been settled with Cheryl and—"

"Ah, Cheryl, yes it has all been set up. Payment for her,

drugs for you to mule. Look. Show me how much you want this bag. Come over here and fetch it, all right, then?"

I tried to grab Frank's arm but he shrugged me off and walked over, and Jacques laughed and held the bag away from Frank, and Frank tried to laugh along, like he knew what the joke was and how he could play along like anybody else, and then Jacques, with his free hand, slapped my older brother hard across the face. Frank stumbled back, face red, and like it moved on its own, my hand was still firm around the pistol butt, inside the coat pocket.

Frank said, "Hey, what's the beef, what's the problem, what is—"

"What, what, what," Jacques said in reply, mimicking my brother's voice. "You sound like you have a pinecone up your ass. Talk to me, talk to me before I give you this bag. All right?"

Frank raised a hand to his face, like he was going to touch where he had been struck, and then he lowered his hand, like he was afraid it would be a sign of weakness. He said, "What do you want me to talk about?"

"Talk about where this bag is going, where it is going in Boston."

"You know...contacts that Cheryl's set up, that's where."

Jacques hefted the bag again. "Name and address. Right now. Or you leave right now."

Frank looked over at me, terrified, and I had a flash of quick and horrible understanding of what happened, and Frank stammered and said, "Uh, there's a guy...Samuel Jones. Ah, Fourteen Main Street...uh, Boston, ah, I mean, Roxbury..."

Another slap to his face, and Frank closed his eyes. Jacques said sharply, "You see, my friend, I no longer believe what you say. What I do believe is that there are no contacts in Boston, nothing like that at all, and Cheryl and you, you are here to steal my money, steal my product, and for that—"

Both guys on either side of the room started going towards objects underneath their turtlenecks, and I couldn't believe it, but I beat them, but not by much, and I got the pistol out, fired a shot over one head and another shot over the other guy's head, and give Frank credit, he ducked but managed to grab a hold of the gym bag, now screaming, "Eddie, run, Eddie, damn it, run!"

But there was still movement, guys diving behind the furniture, smoke in the air, Jacques yelling, and Frank barreled by me, and I backed up, pistol still out, still looking at the two guys, and from out of the corner of my eye, I saw the blonde on the couch calmly drop her cigarette on the floor, reach into the couch cushions, and bring up a sawed-off shotgun. It made an impressive flash of light and hollow boom when she shot at us.

Somehow we got down the stairs and to the car. I got into the driver's side and started up the engine and threw it in reverse, as Frank got himself in, one leg in, one leg out, I backed madly up the dirt driveway, eyeballing where I was going by the rear backup lights, more gunshots coming from the cabin, Frank finally getting the damn door closed so the dome interior light wasn't spotlighting us, and we scraped bottom as we reached the paved road, and only then, did I bother to turn on the headlights. Frank was yelling something but I ignored him, pounding the accelerator down, going right up through the four speeds—first, second, third and fourth—in record time. I looked over at Frank and the gym bag was in his lap, and he was panting.

"Idiot," I said. "This was a setup, right? Cheryl sent you here to rip this guy off, right?"

Frank nodded, still panting. "She used to date him some. Then he got drunk one night and knocked her around. Black eye and some dental work. You know Cheryl. She never forgets. So that was the deal. You're right."

I pounded the steering wheel. "And you didn't bother to tell me? Your own brother?"

We sped down the road in the darkness, the headlights

catching the bright eyes of a frightened animal on the side of the road, huddled in the tall grass.

No answer.

"Frank?"

He coughed. I turned and he was looking over at me, holding up a hand, dripping onto the gym bag.

"Eddie," he said quietly. "I'm hurt."

It took some time but later that morning, I eventually found the house I was looking for, on the other side of the river, a nice two-story colonial type, with a dark wood stain and an attached two-car garage. A small pond was in the front lawn and after I parked the car, I went up to the open farmer's porch and rang the doorbell, again and again, until she answered. Cheryl stood there sullenly, cigarette smoldering between her fingers, wearing stone-washed jeans and a red tanktop, her brown hair down to her shoulders.

"Cherry," I said.

She just stared at me, brought the cigarette up to her mouth, the hand slowing because it was shaking as it approached her lips. I looked at her and went back to my car, and returned with a gym bag in my hand. She looked at the stains on the top of the bag and I said, "Yeah, that belongs to Frank. It's his blood."

"How...how is he?"

"He was airlifted to Maine Medical in Portland. Still not sure what's going to happen to him. I'm going to drive over there, bring our mom, to...to be with him. But I wanted to get this over with first."

I unzipped the bag, showed her the money and the plastic-wrapped drugs inside. She glanced inside the bag and said, "I don't know what you're talking about."

"Sure you do, but you won't admit it to me, you won't admit it to the cops, and you won't admit it to any lawyer you hire in the next few days to straighten this out. But I'll tell you, as a public service or some damn thing. It's an old story. A story about those who got it and those who don't, and how those who got it think those who don't are here on this earth to serve them and their damn whims."

I held the bag up to her eye level. "So some clown from Canada hurts you, and you decide to pay him back. And you don't do it personally. Oh, lord no, you can't get your hands dirty or break a fingernail. But what you do is to sucker some dumb sap who's been following you for years, hoping for a touch or a smile or anything, and you get him to do your job for you. Why not? He's dumb and from the wrong side of the river, and he stole your fancy radio. What did you do, flash your tits at Frank or something?"

She dropped her cigarette and said, "Leave."

"You bet." I turned the bag over and dumped the cash on the porch. "That should cover the radio, Cherry."

And then I took out the drugs, held them for a moment, and tossed them into the little pond in her front yard. "And there's your damn drugs, if you want them."

She went back inside and I went back to my car, knowing eventually I would have to face the cops, but not right now. I drove away from her house, and even though the hospital and my brother awaited me, I couldn't do it. I couldn't go through that damn tunnel, so I drove home the long way, to get my mom.

It was the only thing I could do.

ON AN EYEBALL

Andrew McAleer

No man could kill her spirit. Not today. After years of psychological torture and months of secretive, clever scheming, Correction Officer Jenny Boyle felt good things looming. Something deep in her bone marrow informed her that her plan would manifest soon—maybe today. The mere thought of success made her momentarily forget the hideous aspects of her job—four months of close observation of one of the commonwealth's most brutal killers and rapists, endless sexually charged ribbing from her largely male coworkers, the way her immediate superior constantly leered at her, and little possibility that she'd get an easier assignment any time soon. Years of burning hatred begged for release.

Waiting in a scrum of COs for the 6:45 a.m. shift change at the Massachusetts Correctional Institute Sawmill Junction, the Bay State's maximum-security prison, Jenny noticed for the hundreth time that the sole desirable aspect of the correctional facility was its location in the southern most point of Suffolk County, and therefore, generously insulated from "proper" Boston. The prison had been constructed in the nineteenth century, when Boston's elite insisted on a safety net to protect them from the flood of Irish and Italian immigrants they feared would destroy their tranquility. If you couldn't stem the tide or control them, lock them up somewhere we can't see them. Oddly enough, over the years, the surrounding areas of

Sawmill became an attractive location for Victorian mansions, with yards as spacious as public parks, replete with gardens and duck ponds, making the prison look and feel like the dank pit it had become inside. The irony didn't escape Jenny. Things are often darker on the inside.

The young CO drew in a breath as she contemplated yet another day in segregation where Sergeant Sparacio loved to sentence her to an eight-hour eyeball watch, observing, up-close-and-way-too-personal, Sawmill's worst inmate. As a newly minted CO, Jenny had no seniority and had committed the unpardonable sin of being a female to boot. The sergeant became weirdly obsessed with her from her first day, stared so hard at her whenever she walked into a room that it felt like his eyes were burning through her dark-blue uniform. He did his best to get a rise out of her and thought he had succeeded in pushing her buttons, but she'd shielded herself from his creepy desires and never let him get to her. She'd just act rattled until she could give him what he really deserved. Men could be so stupid, and so easy to fool. She also knew the pedestrian-trap officer would target her out of the hundreds of entrants for his "search of the day." Like most men, he got a thrill from wielding what little power he had and used his metal detector and grasping hands to try to humiliate her on a daily basis. She hated him with a steely passion, but never let him see one sign of her disdain. Besides, the only contraband she harbored would never be detected by the pedestrian-trap officer's wand or the pat search that always included pushing his grimy hand into her privates and repeatedly groping her breasts. In any other setting, it'd be sexual assault, but at Sawmill her male superiors considered it "breaking in the rookie," even though she'd now been going through this humiliation for four exasperating months. Today she took pleasure in knowing that the only dangerous object she was secreting past inspection was coiled in the darkest corner of her mind. They all thought the thick concrete walls and all the entry and exit gates and procedures would protect them from danger, but they didn't know Jenny Boyle's mind, or what she could do with it on the inside. While waiting for her turn through the security gate leading into the confines of the jail, Jenny watched the four outer control officers acting busy, when, in truth, they had the best gig at Sawmill. They didn't have to enter the dark entrails of Sawmill. They controlled things from the outside—who got in and who got out, what got in and what got out. They spent their shifts greeting the public, shooting the breeze with management, buying ice-cold Cokes from the lobby, and once in a while, pressing a button that opened the pedestrian-trap, otherwise known as the "P-trap." Jenny knew they'd put in their time inside, doing exactly what she had to do, but she couldn't help envying them, wondering if she'd *ever* get assigned to Outer Control. "Keep dreaming, Boyle," Sergeant Sparacio said, pushing through a pack of blue shirts and bumping against her before nodding at Outer Control. "It'll take more than your spit-polished boots to get you outside the wall. Be twenty years before you score a bid inside the Bubble."

Jenny bristled. She could smell the strong body odor that wafted around him, and still felt bruised by his brutish strength as he'd pressed his body against hers for longer than necessary. He was always brushing against her, touching her hands, arms, and shoulders for no reason, always trying to engage her eyes. She longed to flip her finger behind his back but turned around and spotted Lieutenant Vitória Paredes a few feet behind her and thought better. Play the game. Just play the game.

The only other female on the crew didn't like her and she knew it. Paredes had not been blessed with long, thick naturally blond hair, a shapely figure, or a pretty face, and from the looks of her, she was far older, probably approaching fifty. Where Jenny attracted too much attention, Paredes faded into the background like nondescript wallpaper—and the jaded lieutenant may have acted like she didn't care, but the young CO knew she did. "Good morning, Sergeant," Jenny said, smiling broadly, so a small dimple would form just under her left eye.

Men were suckers for that dimple.

Her superior turned to look at her. "Ready for another exciting day of corrections?" he asked. Jenny glanced briefly into his eyes, avoiding the bad stitch jobs, lopsided jaw, and his thrice-busted nose. She'd heard the stories about how he acquired his busted jaw and the multiple times various Sawmill inmates punched him hard in the face or sliced at his face with hidden toothbrushes they'd filed into shanks. He wore the scars, lumps, permanently swollen knuckles, and bumps like they were prized possessions, his Purple Heart for being a bad-ass CO who now ran the show, but Jenny found them hideous—though she'd never let him know that.

"Roger that, Sergeant," she said.

"Excellent attitude, Boyle, because you're on an eyeball again in the DDU. That all good with you?"

"All good, Sergeant," Jenny said, smiling again, and halfheartedly pumping her fist. "Gotta do my time." It was true that all new COs served their time in the departmental disciplinary unit, where the prison's worst criminals were housed and observed one-on-one, but Sparacio seemed to take cruel pleasure in assigning his youngest, prettiest CO to the most vile prisoner in the block.

"Should I post you up with your boyfriend?" he asked.

She ignored his implication that the prisoner was someone she'd admire. In a practiced motion, keeping the dimple working and her eyes on the sergeant, Jenny gathered her long, blond hair back and twisted it into a tight bun that she tucked under her collar. "Oh, you know I don't have a boyfriend, Sergeant." She used her most innocent voice, knowing full well he liked thinking of her that way. Innocent women were pushovers, after all. Someone an animal like him could manipulate and lure into his web.

Sparacio pointed at Boyle playfully as the P-trap gate began to slide open. "Okay, Boyle," he said, walking backwards towards the entry, "but I know Cutter's got a thing for you, so you can count on me to keep my eyes on you two." The big sergeant drifted into the sea of blue uniforms spilling into the P-trap, which could only process twelve COs at a time. Boyle didn't make the first cut, so turned around to see if Paredes had overheard the sergeant and saw Officer Ronnie Cutter heading towards her. An all-American type—neatly-cropped reddish-blond hair, blue eyes, a charming smile, and a frame so lean and taut one might have assumed he invented the push-up—Cutter was a man used to getting his way. Everyone knew he was crushing on Jenny, and lately she'd been playing along—all part of her master plan.

"What did Spar want?" Cutter said.

Boyle smiled and lightly touched Cutter's arm. "Oh, just letting me know I'll be on an eyeball in the DDU."

"Phillips again?"

"I'd put big money on that bet."

"Damn. I can't believe he keeps sticking you with that sick bastard. I'm rolling the food cart through the DDU today. Maybe we can swap? Want me to hit Sarge up for the eyeball?"

Jenny shook her head. "I appreciate it, Ronnie, but Sparacio thinks it's the best way to teach me the ropes, so there's nothing to do but take it. Eventually he'll boost me up the ladder."

"Yeah, well, if I were you, I'd file a grievance, learn the ropes somewhere else. As a union steward I'll handle the grievance for you."

Jenny flashed her most winning smile, shrugged, and brushed her fingers lightly over his broad shoulder, as if she were brushing off a piece of lint. "Nah. It'd be the same circus just different clowns."

Cutter returned her smile and winked. "Okay, rookie, but like I said, I'll be on food cart duty so I'll come around and check up on you. You've officially hooked up with Sawmill's most dedicated steward."

"I can handle Phillips," she said, narrowing her eyes only slightly before remembering that she never wanted to let him— or anyone in this pit—see her real feelings.

"Of course you can," Cutter replied. "I just want to make sure you're not nodding off on the job." He grinned, reached over to lightly punch her shoulder in jest.

Jenny lifted her eyes slowly and engaged his. "You'll never see me sleeping, Ronnie...not here anyway." She knew she'd hit the ball over the fence when she literally saw his entire frame quiver. Her pointed flirting was paying off. He wanted her—bad.

Boyle, Cutter, and Paredes all made it into the next P-trap round and heard the outer-lobby gate release a wail as it clang shut, meaning they were locked in until they passed muster and were allowed into the confines of the facility. As expected, the P-trap officer signaled Jenny. "Boyle, search of the day," he said, waving his metal detector toward her.

Jenny stepped into position and ignored the obnoxious catcalls from the throng of male COs. "Take it all off," and "Glad I brought a wad of one-dollar bills," echoed through the P-trap chamber. She didn't have to look to know that Ronnie Cutter had cupped his hands around his mouth to form a megaphone and joined in what the predominant males saw as their rightful fraternal game. "Sorry, gents," Jenny shouted over the hubbub, "but I don't see a pole in here long enough for me to dance with."

Jeers and loud challenges to her claim exploded as the P-trap officer used his wand and his hairy hand to slowly trace the curves hidden under Boyle's freshly starched uniform. Just as he forced her legs open and slid his hand between them, Jenny looked up to see Lieutenant Paredes watching her closely. The young CO wondered if the sour-faced Paredes had once endured all this unwanted attention—and if she did, how did she react? Did her clear weariness come from the repeated humiliations, or because a younger, prettier CO had taken her place? Maybe Paredes hated the fact that Jenny knew how to control her emotions and never let those bastards get to her. No matter, Jenny ignored her, like everyone else.

* * *

Once they cleared muster, the P-trap gate was raised and the COs were released into No-Man's Land, a scrubby patch of ground surrounding the main facility. What the COs called "No-Man's" for short. One asphalt path led to the entrance of the main facility and another to the DDU. Before anyone could enter the main facility they had to pass through yet another P-trap secured with inter-locking gates. Like Outer Control, the occupants of Inner Control enjoyed an environment secured with steel gates, concrete, and plate-glass separating them from block officers and inmates. Here, they controlled the gates. Prison staff called it "the Bubble" since plate-glass windows wrapped around Inner Control, providing staff with a full view of Sawmill Junction's main hallway. The DDU was a different animal than the main facility, more like the red-headed, bastard child of the Massachusetts correctional system. Located about three hundred yards from the main facility, the DDU's concrete structure had been poured into the hill. Only a sliver of gray slab remained visible from ground level. To Jenny, she saw it as a shark's fin, and she often felt like she'd been thrown into the shark's mouth for lunch while there. Everyone knew madness and danger lurked below its surface. This segregated unit housed the worst-of-the-worst of the Commonwealth's inmate population. Their crimes so heinous and vile they would be murdered by fellow inmates if ever fed into general population. The DDU was permanent residency to vicious sexual predators, serial rapists, serial murderers, and deviants whose insatiable appetite for human cruelty meant they had to be segregated and constantly monitored and controlled. As a direct result, the DDU correctional staff were also segregated. As Jenny and Cutter walked towards the DDU, they enjoyed the last moments of what was a delightfully sunny, crisp autumn morning. Once posted-up inside the facility, they'd be forbidden to leave until shift's end. Cell phones had to be left in their cars, which meant no involvement with the outside world for the next eight hours. Countries and governments could topple and the COs wouldn't learn about it until they got in their cars at the end of their shift and turned on their cell phones.

Just before they entered the DDU, Jenny paused on No-Man's and sighed. "Eight hours a day for life," she said. Her companion laughed. "You're sounding like an old pro already."

Jenny looked up and smiled. "Thanks for being such a good friend, Ronnie."

Cutter seemed to study her face. "Are you sure we've never met?"

Jenny laughed. "No way, I'd remember you."

Cutter smiled, nodded. "It's because I'm a stud, right? I mean most ladies will at least give me a whirl."

"I'll bet they give you a lot more than that," Jenny said, suppressing a smile. She didn't want to over-feed his ego—just enough to get what she wanted.

"You do know that I'd like to be more than your friend," he said, squinting in a way he must have thought was seductive.

Jenny drew in a breath to tamp down her revulsion. "Right now, I'm just glad to have such a special friend inside these walls," she said.

"Would you two stop flirting?" Paredes said, brushing past them.

Jenny looked at Cutter and laughed. Just before leaving him at the door to the DDU, she turned around and waited for him to pause too. "Of course, an *inside friend* on the outside might not be so bad either," she said, smiling, winking, and squeezing his bicep before releasing him to spend his day fantasizing about her.

Because inmate Phillips was a problem child, even for the DDU, the Commonwealth had arranged a special cell for him, as well as special care and custody instructions. Instead of being housed behind a steel door, his door consisted of three-inch, shatter-proof plate glass, with a dozen holes an inch in diameter for air and ventilation. At least one CO had to sit just outside his cell, observe him twenty-four seven, and keep detailed activity logs to track every single, minute thing he did. He was considered highly dangerous and not without good cause. Phillips stood six foot four and was all concrete block. The COs considered him a rabid animal who'd stalked, raped, tortured, and brutally murdered young couples, taking particular and deviant pleasure in the torture and mutilation aspect. Like many inmates, Phillips possessed a high intellect and could be exceptionally cunning. Even when correctional staff were fully briefed on his history, some could still find Phillips charming or convince themselves that they had earned his respect, which made their post more dangerous. Too dangerous and smart to be housed in a closed-door setting where he could brew up any kind of mischief, including fake suicide attempts that would require the opening of his cell. The DDU, however, was prepared. A Special Response Team—the SRT, consisting of six specially-trained COs—were always ready for full battle-rattle and could spring into action, to move or control Phillips. In fact, strict DDU policy dictated that under no circumstances could Phillips's cell be opened until the properly armed SRT had arrived at his cell—which they could do in about two minutes. Even in cases of inmate suicide attempts or other emergencies, COs were forbidden, for safety reasons, from entering inmate cells alone. In Phillips' case, it was mandatory that the SRT be there before *anyone* in the DDU Bubble pushed the control button that would open his cell door.

Still, even in a constantly monitored, open-view setting, with countless safety controls in place, Phillips found ways to temporarily escape the confines of Cell 23. He was known to fling his feces or smear himself with them just to get him out of the cell and into the showers. As Jenny assumed her usual post, just outside Phillips' cell, she cast a glance up to the DDU Bubble located behind her on the second tier. As usual, Sergeant Sparacio was *eyeballing* her. Even without looking, she knew he'd be focused on her. Everyone knew his career had been his entire life. The man had never even married. Jenny thought he was too selfish to share his salary, or his pension; others just assumed he was *that dedicated* to his career. All she knew for sure was that Sergeant Sparacio had a sexual obsession with her and likely spent a lot of his waking hours fantasizing about her finally surrendering to his forceful seduction. It was all about control and power for men like Sparacio. He thought he controlled everything—in Sawmill's DDU and at home. He didn't love her; he just wanted to possess her—and she'd be damned if anything remotely like that ever happened. Looking up, she met his eyes briefly and nodded. He nodded back and pointed from his eyes to her. While she typically hated the way he watched her every move, today it might well play right into her plan.

Just as she'd done for the last four months, Jenny settled onto the high stool positioned about ten feet in front of Phillips' cell and wrote in the activity log.

Inmate Phillips appears to be sleeping, snoring deeply in a normal fashion.

…awakened and is taking efforts to make sure I know he is masturbating.

…has begun moving around his cell, swinging his arms, apparently exercising.

…is now jumping up and down, shouting about being hungry, claiming someone put something weird in his applesauce yesterday and it better not happen again.

…is now saying he has to defecate, asked for ten sheets of toilet paper, which were delivered through his cell's wicket in the usual manner. He appeared to use them all, and flushed his toilet.

The activity log would eventually make its long journey up Sawmill's chain-of-command. First to Sergeant Sparacio, then to Lieutenant Paredes, then up the line to the operations captain, director of security, the deputy superintendent, and finally the superintendent. It would be reviewed by everyone, but closely read by no one—unless things got jacked up. Which rarely happened under Sparacio's control.

Thus far, today's eyeball proceeded the same as it had from

day one. The hair on the back of Jenny's neck rose as she watched Phillips run from one end of his cell to the other, naked, slamming himself against the wall. The first day she witnessed it, she wondered what the hell this murderous psychopath was trying to achieve, but now it was just another day on the block. For a brief moment she worried that she was becoming as desensitized as Phillips. Then she realized that this mental state would serve her well as her plans unfolded. God she hoped it happened today. To keep her sanity, Jenny thought about how safely guarded everyone at Sawmill assumed they were. A thirty-foot concrete wall surrounded the facility, fortified by a dozen guard towers, housing officers armed with M-16s, evenly distributed to provide full view of the confines. Concertina wire had been wound tightly and placed on top of the exterior walls. To get behind the walls, you had to get through the two Outer Control P-trap doors. To access the DDU, you first had to get buzzed in past the chain-link gate, the main gate, go downstairs, get buzzed though a grill door into the DDU lobby, by its outer control officer, then go through its P-trap, then get buzzed into the DDU cell block by the DDU Inner Control, a.k.a. the Bubble. Each inmate was secured behind a steel door—or a thick plexiglass door and extra protections—to secure his eight-by-ten cell. Jenny loved thinking about how all these protections gave staff a sense of security. This lulled some into complacency. The very thing the academy warned recruits against again and again.

Jenny Boyle had attended the academy training camp in Shirley, Massachusetts, where she had a particularly tough drill sergeant. He wasn't the first man to torment her, but when it started on her first day, she felt like a target had been tattooed on her back.

"Bring your A-game every shift," Drill Sergeant Juan Martinez had screamed in Recruit Jenny Boyle's face the first day of training. She was standing in formation, beside all the new recruits in the training academy's drill compound. She tried not to look at

Martinez, or his starched uniform, its creases as sharp and long as rapier swords. He angled over her like a swaying length of rebar as he held a slate board, containing a roster of sixty-five recruits, pressed against his left thigh. Supposedly, he'd just *happened* to choose her name for this little game of intimidation. She shouldn't have been surprised; she always seemed to get selected in these situations. Martinez's spit sprayed over her right check, as he leaned even closer. "A-game! *Every* minute of *every* shift. Every *second* of every shift. Do you understand, Recruit Boyle?" And when she didn't instantly reply, "Do you understand, Recruit Boyle?"

"Sir, yes, Sir."

Martinez's Smokey-the-Bear hat angled over her face; its rim as sharp and hard as a diamond-edged circular saw blade. Making it worse, he head-butted her as he raised his voice even louder. "I'm sorry...am I interrupting important plans, Recruit Boyle?"

"Sir, no, Sir."

"Then why are you answering me like you don't give a rat's ass? Were you supposed to get your va-jay-jay waxed today? Is va-jay-jay waxing more important to you than this drill?"

"Sir, no, Sir."

He laughed, turned to look at the other recruits. "I think *you think* it is."

Jenny did her best not to grimace. He may have been a hard ass, but he had no idea what she'd gone through as a teenager. If he thought she was a powder puff that he could make an example of he'd picked the wrong girl. "Sir, no, Sir!"

He shoved that pointed hat into her forehead so hard she could feel it piercing her skin. "Are you calling me liar, Recruit Boyle?"

Still, she refused to flinch.

"Sir, no, Sir."

"When is it game on, Recruit Boyle?"

Jenny hesitated.

"When is it game on, Recruit Boyle?" he shouted.

She'd forgotten the question, and, truth was, he'd pissed her off.

"I'm waiting." He tapped his spit-polished boot in an effort to make her laugh. Some recruits around her snickered, and Martinez shot them harsh glares before shoving his hat into Jenny's forehead again. This time he lowered his voice just slightly. "It's a simple question, Recruit Boyle. So maybe, when you have time, you could tell me your answer?" He straightened up, looked towards the heavens, and then shouted, "What's your answer Recruit Boyle?"

"Sir, I don't know, Sir."

Martinez twisted his body to the left and flung his slate board, sending it skittering across the drill compound. "Pathetic, Recruit Boyle. Get the *hell* out of my formation. You sicken me, Recruit Boyle. You're gross. Come back when you have command presence and can sound off like a correction officer who actually gives a rat's ass!"

Jenny tilted her chin up. She broke out of line but hesitated because she didn't know where she was supposed to go.

Drill Sergeant Juan Martinez jabbed his finger towards a side area. "Over to the Hole and start pushing. Move, move!"

The "Hole" consisted of a giant mud puddle at the edge of the training field that had somehow become Martinez's pride and joy. Every afternoon, at the end of training, he would use a garden hose he kept meticulously coiled up to keep the Hole moist and mucky. He made the recruit formation dutifully watch his watering routine before dismissal, offering a foretaste of what awaited them at first formation. Jenny had been the first one to suffer the Hole's punishing conditions. Heeding her drill sergeant's instructions, she assumed pushup position, her hands sinking into the mud as she poised her body inches above the puddle. At first she did the push-ups slowly, as if this would somehow reduce the effects of her pressed uniform sucking up the muck each time her torso sank beneath the surface. "Twenty-five more pushups, and really get down there, Recruit Boyle,"

Sergeant Martinez ordered. "Touch your nose to the floor."

Jenny bucked up and did as ordered, cringing only slightly when her face first submerged into the sludge soup and brown water splashed into her mouth, nose, and eyes. She spit out what she could, but dirt seeped into every pore. As she pushed through each repetition, biceps burning, her fury turned into adrenaline and she pushed harder and faster, almost relishing each plunge into wet Mother Earth. All the other recruits had been dismissed to watch and Sergeant Martinez had moved closer to harass her. Still, even as he taunted that she couldn't complete another repetition, she did…another, and another, and another…faster and faster and faster, until at last he ordered everyone—including Recruit Boyle—back into formation. As she stood among her fellow recruits, a soggy, haggard mess, with mud dripping from her hair and face, the irony didn't escape her. Clearly contrary to his desires to humiliate her, dipping into that mud puddle both fortified and began to cleanse her body, her mind, her soul, and her spirit. It somehow diminished the dark spirit that often dragged her down.

Jenny glanced at her analog wristwatch—the only personal "technological" device COs could possess in the facility. Cutter was due with the food cart any minute, which would give her another chance to rattle Sergeant Sparacio's chain. He was so jealous it didn't take more than a gesture or two to make him furious that she preferred Cutter to him. When she returned to staring at Phillips, she saw him with two pieces of toilet paper in his hand and watched as he balled them up and threw them against the wall above his bunk. She recorded this in the activity log, including that he then picked up the small tissue "ball" and flushed it down his toilet.

Or at least she thought he did. Just as she'd thought he'd used all ten pieces earlier and flushed them down the toilet.

When she looked up again, Phillips stood square against the

plate glass staring at her. This didn't faze her. He did it all the time, as if he, too, could intimidate her by leering at her.

"What're you writing about me, Boyle?" He said, grabbing his scrotum. "You writing about my balls? You like them, don't you?" He picked up one, and then the other, waggling them at her. "Write about them all you want."

Boyle stared back. She had learned to make her dimple appear even without smiling. It flashed for a split second, enough for Phillips to notice.

He closed his eyes and lifted his nose to the air holes. "I can smell your body wash, Boyle. It's fruity and sweet, almost like an alluring perfume, but you're not supposed to wear perfume, are you Boyle? Sawmill policy and procedures. Rules and regulations governing all employees. The man with the fuzzy nuts got more rules for you than me. I know all about 'em. They'll kill you, Boyle." She wasn't wearing perfume, but Jenny tried to ignore whatever he said to her, as she was supposed to do. If he thought he could charm her, he was wrong. She had an inner strength that few could dismantle. She wasn't anyone's sucker anymore— not Cutter's, not Sparacio's, and certainly not Phillips's.

"You want some of William Phillips, don't you, girl? I know you do, cuz you are loving what you see." He lifted his limp penis and shook it while also sticking out his tongue. Jenny ignored him, though she did record all of his actions in the activity log.

Phillips headed towards the back of his cell, but she could still hear him clearly. "You'll get what you deserve, little Miss Boyle. You'll become what you hate just like the rest of them. This block'll take the shine right off your boots." He turned his face toward the glass and looked up at the Bubble. "Just remember, Boyle while you're sitting there on your stool all day...your mind can only absorb what your ass can endure." He spread his arms and looked around his cell. His chin canted as he admired his enclosed world. "We both know this is the real Bubble around here. You can see through glass. But I can see through you. I can see through bubbles."

* * *

After Phillips drifted off to sleep again, Jenny flashed back to the last day of academy training, and a feeling of warmth and pride washed over her. Drill Sergeant Martinez's methods had toughened her, kept her adrenaline in constant overdrive. She'd lost fifteen pounds and could bang out forty-seven push-ups a minute—even in goopy mud puddles.

She remembered being so proud that last day and could still see Drill Sergeant Martinez gliding up to her in his starched uniform and gleaming boots, angling his ramrod frame over her, and whispering, "First Squad Leader Boyle."

"Sir, yes, Sir."

"When is it game on?"

"Sir, *every* second of *every* shift, Sir."

Martinez squared off in front of her and saluted. "First Squad Leader Boyle..."

"Sir, yes, Sir!"

"...move my platoon to the training room for final instructions."

He'd been hard on her—and everyone—in the beginning, but he'd never had bad intentions. Not like her current sergeant, who longed to use his power over her to weaken her into submission. She could feel Sparacio's vile sexual desires perking below his surface. He wanted her the way a rapist wants a victim—and she hated him for it. Yet, there was one person she hated more.

At 11:30 a.m. on the nose, Ronnie Cutter pushed the food cart up to Cell 23. Boyle hopped off her stool, angled herself toward the Bubble, and smiled at Cutter, knowing Sergeant Sparacio would be fuming.

"Our favorite inmate behaving today?" Cutter said, pulling a cardboard lunch tray from the cart.

"Like a choir boy."

Cutter spun his head around to look at her. "Careful. Don't fall for his charm. If he got out of that cell, and you didn't have the SRT on deck, he'd kill the first CO he saw. And that means you, lovely lady."

Even though she employed plenty of sarcasm, Boyle rewarded Cutter with her brightest smile and deadliest dimple. "Nah. Not *me*. He respects *me*. Even told me so. I think we've formed a genuine connection. It's like we're family."

Cutter finally realized she was kidding and laughed. He shot a glance at Phillips, then back at the pretty CO he was hoping to seduce. "You're right, Boyle, I can see that he's truly reformed. Maybe we should let him free, with a stern warning not to rape, mutilate, and murder anyone again."

Jenny quickly glanced at the Bubble. Sparacio glared down, his arms crossed tightly over his chest. Jenny made a point of laughing again. "Hey," she said, "everyone deserves a second chance. Just ask anyone who's already had twenty chances."

Cutter was busy readying Phillips's tray of food.

"What's for lunch?" Jenny asked, "More applesauce?"

Cutter raised his eyebrows a few times and whispered, "Special order." Holding the lunch tray, he turned to face the prisoner who had inched closer and closer and was clearly listening to every word they said. "Okay, Phillips, if you want lunch, you have to be a good boy and move to the extreme back of your cell. You know the drill."

Phillips hesitated, staring hard at Cutter, before he stepped back as directed. Jenny couldn't help admire how the madman controlled his hatred for Cutter, knowing that Cutter would assume Phillips felt intimidated instead. Unlike the overconfident Cutter, she could sense Phillips's silent, patient rage steaming through the plate glass air holes. Cutter removed a key from his duty belt and opened a wicket door slightly bigger than a mail slot, which created a small entrance into Phillips's cell. He slid the lunch tray onto a waiting service rack, and then just as swiftly locked the wicket door and stepped backward.

While Phillips watched Cutter's routine, emotionless, separated only by inches of glass wall, Jenny relished the nervousness in Cutter's face and hand movements reflected on the plate glass. Clearly pleased with yet another smooth transition, Cutter stepped back further and grinned. "Okay, Phillips, lunch is served. Make sure you enjoy your applesauce, buddy. You've officially hooked up with SJ's best chef."

Cutter turned to Jenny and winked. She smiled her approval and made sure she lightly brushed her hands across Cutter's back as he pushed the cart towards the next cell. She knew both Phillips and Sparacio would notice. In fact, she was counting on their attention to detail. Right after she resumed her post, Jenny gently turned her head towards Cutter and then slowly back to her prisoner. She didn't have to look back at the Bubble to know that Sparacio hadn't missed that either. She could almost feel his anger burning through the walls between them. It wouldn't be long before he felt compelled to shake things up. Meanwhile, the young CO watched as Phillips made short work of his boneless chicken breast, overcooked canned-vegetable medley, clump of cold mac & cheese, and stale bread. He gulped his milk in one shot, then angled his spoon over his applesauce and looked up at his observing officer. With the slightest back and forth shift of her head, she signaled a warning, and Phillips threw down his spoon, picked up his tray, strode across the floor, and slung it into the wicket with a loud thump. He swiped his face with a napkin and quickly palmed it in his right hand. Jenny saw him but didn't record the slight-of-hand. She was focused instead on his dilated pupils. This wasn't just an act—the man was criminally insane. He nodded at her, saying "thanks for the heads up" without saying anything. "That red squirrel ain't going to be so lucky when I get out of here" he snarled. "He's gonna learn what happens when you poke the bear."

It took every ounce of will power for Jenny to resist saying, *I know.*

* * *

Jenny had heard footsteps approaching and pretended she didn't because she knew it would be Sergeant Sparacio. He'd been even more obsessed with her since he set up a "DDU Wellness Night" event to watch the Boston Red Sox battle their primary rivals, the New York Yankees. He'd spent weeks making the arrangements and making sure everyone on staff attended. Jenny knew Sparacio set up the whole wellness night crap just so she could be his "date." She schemed-up a preemptive strike, however, by meeting Ronnie Cutter outside Fenway's Green Monster before the game. Then she and Cutter showed up together all laughs and giggles in the section where Sparacio had reserved seats together. It was obvious to everyone that the sergeant had saved a seat for Jenny, next to him, but Cutter sat down in the sergeant's seat and didn't pick up on the sergeant's strong suggestion that he should vacate that seat and move elsewhere. Sparacio had fussed so loudly and persistently that everyone expected him to punch Cutter in the face. If his staff hadn't known before, they knew then that Sparacio had set up the whole event to woo Jenny Boyle—and she'd rebuffed him. She'd even left with Cutter, though she made excuses about other things to do while they were in the subway and quickly dumped him. She knew it had infuriated Sparacio, but she'd played it cool the whole time, as if she were clueless. She knew her latest performance would make him rush down to grill her and she planned to use that jealousy to her advantage.

"What did *he* want?"

"Sergeant Sparacio," she said, gasping as if surprised. "You shouldn't sneak up on someone in this cell block. I could have karate-chopped your throat."

The sergeant made a tsking sound, narrowed his eyes. "What were you two going on and on about? Everything all clear?"

Because her post orders required her to see living-breathing flesh of the inmate at all times, Jenny finished jotting down a note in the activity log before answering: "Prisoner is lying in his bunk with a blanket pulled over his head. His right hand is hanging over the side of the bunk and his chest is rising and falling, as if asleep."

She then turned to look right into Sparacio's eyes. "Just the usual, Sergeant. Phillips was griping about his meal again. He's convinced Cutter is poisoning his applesauce."

Sparacio pointed his chin towards Phillips. "Not *him*. What did that lame ass Cutter want to talk to *you* about?"

The young CO shrugged. "He didn't want anything. He was just shooting the breeze, like always." She enjoyed watching Sparacio process her nonchalance. She knew he'd seen her touch Cutter multiple times that day and he was fuming inside. While Sparacio silently tried to control his temper, Jenny eyeballed Phillips and added to the log: "Phillips seems to be sleeping." She knew the sicko was listening, but she didn't log that in.

After a short silence, Sparacio changed his tone. "You've been doing a good job down here, Boyle. I know it's the bottom of the load, but you've been showing some grit while you've been here with Phillips. Everyone hates being on an eyeball, but you never complain." He paused. "I've been thinking about mixing up your assignments."

Jenny looked up, held his gaze, and smiled broadly—until she knew the dimple was working its charm. "I'm glad you're pleased, Sergeant. It hasn't been very fulfilling working this post, but I was confident you knew what was best for my training, and I've learned so much from you." She paused briefly, drew a breath that made her breasts rise and fall, then looked past Sparacio's busted face into his eyes, which had clearly been staring at her bust. "I hope you know that I'll do whatever you tell me." She watched his eyes light up.

"You've got good attitude, Boyle," Sparacio said, nodding his approval, then furtively looking behind him, and then up and down the cell block. "We should talk more about this, but I don't want to say too much within earshot of the inmates...or anyone who might be skulking around, like that turnip head Cutter."

Jenny brightened, pretended to be excited (if only she could blush on demand). "I agree, Sergeant, we have to be discreet."

Sparacio bent his head to one side, as if to crack his neck, and then tilted his head left and pressed a button on the radio's microphone attached to his uniform's left epaulette, holding Jenny's gaze as he did so. "Sergeant Sparacio to CO Cutter."

A few seconds later Cutter responded. "CO Cutter."

"Report to the Bubble immediately."

"Roger," Cutter replied.

Sparacio released the microphone and then deliberately placed one hand on Jenny's right shoulder and arm before slowly sliding it down to her wrist. Jenny struggled not to jerk away or show any revulsion.

Sparacio briefly grasped her hand and then released it, displaying his lopsided smile as if it were attractive. "I'll see *you* later."

Jenny forced a smile. "Whenever you're ready, Sergeant."

That rape had happened a decade ago. And that's what Jenny Boyle still called it: "that rape" or "the events." She refused to call it "my rape" or even to say "I was raped," as if not saying those words could sanitize what had happened. On good days, she could almost believe it hadn't happened to her; yet on bad days the dark ghost returned, she relived it all again, in living color. The random specifics that she could, and could not, recall from that night still amazed her. Because she'd begged, her older sister had allowed her to tag along when she and her friends went to a college party on Commonwealth Avenue, in Allston or Brighton—*that* she couldn't remember. She did remember arriving at a brick apartment building, one that looked exactly like every other brick apartment building that lined Boston's streets and housed thousands of drunken college students celebrating nothing in particular. It was late fall or early winter. She remembered loud music blaring into the street. She, her sister, and her sister's Lesley

University dormmates had been drinking before they left for the party. Someone had poured a cold beer into a frosty mug and offered it to Jenny, though she was only fifteen. Jenny could still recall that, because it was super frosty on the outside and looked so inviting. She could remember feeling grown up as she reached for its handle. A short while later, they left her sister's cozy apartment for the late-night party. The apartment they entered was so dimly lit you couldn't see much of anything. Everyone already seemed obnoxiously drunk. Frat boys stood in corners eyeing all the girls, or were crammed in together, in the middle of the room, dancing with girls. Empty kegs bobbed in trash barrels of ice water. Tables were stacked with empty beer bottles and abandoned disposable red cups. Jenny remembered feeling awkward, a fifteen-year-old girl dressed in a college sweatshirt, right after having her first beer, accepting a Solo cup from the first handsome guy who approached her. She remembered looking around, and not being able to spot her sister or any of her friends, who had instantly vanished into the crowd.

When she turned back around the random guy gently pushed the drink towards her mouth. "Drink up," he said. He was so drunk he was slurring words, but his tall, athletic physique, chiseled face, and blue eyes held her spellbound. No one as good looking as he was had ever even looked at her. He kept leaning closer and closer to her, trying to talk, but the music drowned him out. Soon, he wrapped one arm around her, brushed back her hair when it fell loose, and nuzzled his face against her cheek, all of which felt equally wrong and thrilling. She drank the liquor, making a sour face when it burned her throat. They swayed to the music as he continued to nuzzle her neck and run his hands up and down her back. At one point he got them more drinks, which they downed. Shortly after the alcohol entered her bloodstream, he grasped her hand and they began threading their way through the crowd. She saw her sister briefly across the room and shrugged her shoulders to let her know she didn't know if she should follow him, or not. Her sister laughed and gave her a thumbs up. "Have fun," she shouted.

The next thing Jenny knew, she and the random guy were in a bedroom and he had closed and locked the door. He pretended that he wanted to show her something, but quickly started pawing her. "Wait, no," she'd said, pulling, and then pushing him away. "I'm too young. I don't want to have sex yet." But he didn't stop. He had one arm tightly around her and the other massaging her breast. "I'm *too young*," she'd shouted, shoving him so hard he stumbled backward.

"But you're so sexy," he'd argued, leaping back to his feet and grabbing her again. "And you've been teasing me for an hour." He insisted she wanted to "do it" too. "You know you do," he said, shoving his tongue into her mouth.

She put both hands on his broad chest and pushed, but she was far smaller than he was. "No, no, I don't want to do it," she'd shouted. "I don't, I don't." She'd balled up her fists to pummel his chest. "Please stop. I'm *only fifteen*. I'm not a college girl. I'm here with my older sister."

But he wasn't listening to her anymore, or if he was, he didn't care. The harder she pushed back, the more she could literally see his face change from drunken happiness to anger. He'd shoved one hand into her pants, jerking her yoga pants and underwear to her knees, which buckled beneath her. Her arms were now locked against him so she had no way to resist as he wrestled her onto a bed that smelled like a sweaty gym bag. She both heard and felt him unzip his pants and felt him shoving himself against her.

"No, no, don't, don't," she pleaded. She knew a scream would never be heard so she gathered all the strength she could and pushed hard against his chest, but he was too strong and too determined.

"Stop fighting and you'll like it," he mumbled. "All the girls say 'no' and all of them end up liking it. They even like it like this, a little rough."

"No, no, no," Jenny cried, "not me, not like this, no,

please." She was sobbing now, but his body had practically smothered her into silence.

He slammed into her and thrust his body against her repeatedly, each thrust slicing through her like a knife. She could feel blood trickling down her right leg, which was already shaking uncontrollably. It seemed to go on forever, but in reality it lasted only a few minutes. When he climaxed, he'd pushed himself off her and jerked up his pants. He'd only looked at her as he pulled up his zipper. "See, that was fun, wasn't it?"

Jenny sat up and swiped one hand across her teary face. "I hate you," she spat.

And he laughed. Laughed so long that she looked around the room for something she could use to smack him hard across the face.

He watched her with an amused look on his face. "Oh don't act like you didn't like it. You wanted it the minute you saw me. I'm a stud, baby."

Jenny stared at him in disbelief, memorizing the features that had first attracted her and now repulsed her. Before she could say anything, he leaned over and actually kissed her on the cheek. "Congratulations," he said, "you've officially hooked up with one of the top college jocks. That should make you a legend in high school." He turned to leave and then turned back and pointed to her bloody leg. "You'll want to clean that up," he said and left, closing the door behind him.

She'd never told anyone, not a single person. She and her sister weren't close and never would be, and she knew her contemporaries would make fun of her if she admitted what had happened. So she insisted *nothing* happened until eventually they stopped asking. But she was forever changed. Once a star athlete and student, she couldn't concentrate and no longer felt comfortable around boys or other jocks. By the time her parents, teachers, and guidance counselors noticed, it was really too late. She barely graduated, foregoing college, and slowly succumbed to a drug- and alcohol-fueled slide that wasted years of her life.

Eventually she sobered up and by twenty-one she started community college, working towards a criminal justice degree. Around the time she was sobering up, Jenny had seen a movie called *The Count of Monte Cristo*, about France during the Napoleonic years. The main character, an ignorant, peasant sailor named Edmund, had been wrongfully accused of treason by his best friend Fernand, because Fernand wanted Edmund's beautiful fiancée. Edmund was sentenced to life imprisonment at the inescapable *Château d'If*—the French version of Alcatraz, where he met a fellow inmate called the Priest, also wrongfully sentenced. Priest educated Edmund, refined his manners, and cultivated his business skills. Best of all, Priest gave Edmund a treasure map before setting the stage for Edmund's daring escape from the *Château d'If*. Edmund re-entered France, educated, cultivated, rich, and above all, respected. Ironically, had he never been imprisoned, he would have been "sentenced" to a life of ignorance and poverty. The *Château d'If* set him free because now he possessed all the tools he needed to exact his revenge against Fernand, take back the life stolen from him, and enjoy a life of privilege reserved for the chosen few. When she thought of it now, Jenny liked imagining that being posted to observe Phillips for four months had become her *Château d'If*. As the months passed, she'd learned everything she needed to know to extract revenge—and now the time had come. Everything was in place, about to go down, just a she'd planned. And then…all would be clear.

"Hey Boyle," Cutter called out. He was making his way down the block corridor. He did not look happy. In fact, he was scowling. Cutter made a hitch-hiking motion toward the Bubble. "Report to *Sergeant* Sparacio. I'm posting up on the eyeball."

Jenny did her best to look surprised. "What did I do?"

Cutter pulled up close to her, leaned in. "You! Nothing. He's got a case of the ass for me for some reason."

He really could be dim, Jenny thought as she lightly touched his arm, knowing the good sergeant would have them under surveillance. "Oh, he probably wants to talk to me about something. I'm sure it's not permanent."

Cutter clearly wasn't appeased and jerked his head toward the Bubble. "Better get up there." He knew the Sergeant had a thing for her and clearly he didn't like the competition any more than Sparacio did.

After a quick glance at Phillips, whom she knew wasn't sleeping, but listening carefully, Jenny handed Cutter the activity log. "He's been lying in his bunk, with his blanket over his head for an hour, right hand hanging out, breathing has been ragged. I think he's sleeping, but he complained about a stomachache, and he's been moaning." She tapped the activity log. "I've written it all down so you can start from *there*."

Cutter shook his head. "Sure makes you feel good to have that wall between you and that slimeball, doesn't it?" Jenny nodded. "Freak can't do anything from there."

"No," she said, looking at Phillips and then deep into Cutter's eyes, "You're right, Phillips can't do anything from there."

Once she entered the Bubble, Jenny was able to closely watch Cutter—and Phillips. She saw the murderer slowly rolling one arm up and down his leg beneath the blanket. He wasn't masturbating, but he was up to something. She knew he'd at minimum kept the napkin, so likely another "ball," but maybe a spit ball this time. She also knew he'd been furious about Cutter putting piss, or something worse, in his applesauce, and Jenny knew he wanted to rock Cutter's world. Luckily, he'd overheard both Sergeant Sparacio and Cutter, who'd both been so self-centered and negligent they failed to remember that Phillips *always listened* to everything. The murderer's worst instincts remained sharp as ever, and he was always coiled to create mayhem. Even if he couldn't escape, he could make their lives miserable—or worse.

Sparacio had pretended to be busy when she'd arrived, but now he had successfully ushered everyone else out of the room and closed the door tightly behind them. "I sent them on errands and breaks, he said. "That should give us a few minutes to talk...privately."

"You should lock the door," Jenny said.

Sparacio laughed nervously. "No, really," she said. "You can keep anyone from busting in on us, say it was routine habit to lock it."

Sparacio spun around, slammed one rod into locking position, and then spun around again, breathing heavily. "We can't, you know, do anything. Goddamn Paredes videotapes everything that goes on in here." He looked around nervously.

Was he sweating? Jenny could feel her heart racing, but not from lust. She'd maneuvered so that she could see what Phillips was doing, while keeping Sparacio's eyes on her. The security control panel to the DDU cells was on a table right behind her. One turn of a key would activate its buttons, and pressing one certain button, such as "Phillips's Cell 23," would spring open its door. Behind her back and out of Sparacio's eyesight, Jenny turned the key, unlocking the control panel, and made sure one finger was on Cell 23's button. Sparacio had been staring at her the entire time, panting with excitement, like he expected her to declare her love for him.

"You were right, Sergeant. I do have something to tell you."

"So tell me already," he said.

"He raped me," she said.

Sparacio shook his head swiftly, as if clearing his ears of water. "*Who* raped you?"

"...Cutter..."

The big man's face wilted and then reddened. Forgetting the videotape, he shouted. "That rat bastard! When? How?"

Jenny used a split second to glance down at Phillips, who was stirring. She knew Sparacio would assume she glanced at Cutter.

"It...it happened a long time ago. But I was only fifteen.

Fifteen, Sergeant, and a virgin. I went to a frat party and he was the big man on campus. He came straight for me and lured me into a room. And then..."

"He raped you," the sergeant shouted.

Jenny gasped, "I fought him. I fought hard, but he was huge and drunk and he...he forced himself on me and brutally raped me. She paused to suck in a shock of air, make sure Sparacio was adequately riled up. He'd scrunched his face so hard all his scars blended together.

Jenny rocked her body slightly forward. "And then, worst of all...he laughed at me and bragged about it afterwards." Tears spilled from her eyes—something she'd practiced for weeks.

Sparacio paced back and forth, slamming his fist into his palm. "So you're telling me—"

She raised her voice, shouted, "Ronnie Cutter *raped me*...when I was *a child*."

Her admirer's eyes filled with fury. "I'll fucking kill him," he shouted.

And then it all happened, better than she even planned...

Phillips bolted upright in his bunk, clutching his throat, his face turning shades of blue and purple, his eyes bulging. A white, foamy paste dribbled from his mouth.

Cutter hit his portable microphone to report a suicide attempt. "Code 99. Code 99. Cell 23. Cell 23."

Sparacio instinctively hit his mike and yelled, "SRT to Cell 23. SRT to Cell 23. Code 99."

"SRT copies," crackled through the system.

"I turned the control panel on," Jenny said, using one hand to grab and stall Sparacio as he raced towards her. Keeping her voice low, she said, "Cutter raped me, Sarge, I was a child and he raped me. He raped us." Sparacio hesitated, huffed out a breath. "He ruined me *for you*," Jenny said. She could see Sparacio's mind whirling in confusion. She held his gaze as a few seconds ticked away. "SRT en route," came over the system.

Just then Sergeant Sparacio's eyes cleared and he reached out and put his hands on both of Jenny's arms to shove her aside. "No," she screamed, "no, don't do it."

As the Sergeant used all his force to forcibly shove the petite CO out of the way, she pushed Cell 23's button. Her sleight of hand hidden from the camera by their tangled bodies. The cell door slid open and Phillips sprang out, spitting out the tissue paper he'd used to choke himself. Sparacio watched helplessly as Cutter tried to turn and run, and saw his feet get tangled up in the stool's legs, crashing him to the cement slab. "SRT, SRT scramble," Cutter and Sparacio screamed simultaneously. As Cutter frantically tried to scramble to his feet, Phillips grabbed Cutter's left foot and dragged him, like an octopus tugging its prey into its den, into the cell. The SRT was seconds away when Phillips' massive hands grabbed Cutter's head and snapped his neck in one quick twist.

Internal Affairs conducted a thorough investigation. It was Lieutenant Vitória Paredes herself who reviewed the grainy video and reported that Sergeant Sparacio had cleared the room after CO Boyle entered. Once alone, he'd locked the door and an argument had ensued about CO Ronald Cutter raping CO Jenny Boyle when she was a child. When the alarm sounded, you could see, right there on videotape, that CO Jenny Boyle attempted to keep Sergeant Sparacio from getting to the Control Board. She was clearly afraid that he'd open the cell door before the SRT arrived, and they all knew that Prisoner William J. Phillips would take out in an instant whomever was posted up on his eyeball. CO Jenny Boyle sat on his eyeball for four months so she knew how dangerous the murderous psychopath could be. When the alarm was sounded, the argument between Sergeant Sparacio and CO Jenny Boyle had quieted down so she couldn't hear what they were saying just before the event. But when Sergeant Sparacio grabbed both of CO Jenny Boyle's arms and threw CO Jenny Boyle across the room, so hard she slammed against the wall, she had been screaming, "No, don't do it." Three days before he was set to go to trial for the murder of CO Ronald Cutter, Sergeant Sparacio shredded his inmate uniform, made a rope out of the long shreds, and used it to hang himself while awaiting trial in a Worcester County segregation unit.

Jenny Boyle didn't get the news about Sparacio right away. She couldn't understand why everyone in the P-trap was quieter than usual that morning. The catcalls, whistles, and being targeted for search of the day had long since ceased. She was just another blue shirt now.

She got the scoop from Lieutenant Vitória Paredes after the P-trap door clanged shut behind them, releasing them into No-Man's. It was deep into February. Hard, foot-rutted snow covered No-Man's scrub grass and asphalt paths. "Your boyfriend hung himself up in Gardner seg, Boyle," Paredes said, emotionless. "God bless him. Saved the commonwealth the cost of a trial." Paredes stared at Boyle for a moment and then grinned. "Eight hours a day for life, my little pretty. Now post up in the usual manner." Paredes turned and walked away, oblivious to the frigid, wailing gusts sweeping over the walls of Sawmill and into its confines. Boyle stood there alone, slowly rocking her scuffed boots toward the DDU. She heard nothing but screaming wind twisting all around her like a tortured spirit. She pinched the collar of her uniform jersey around her exposed neck, leaned against the frigid cold, and stumbled along the paths of No-Man's.

ACKNOWLEDGMENTS

We'd like to thank all of the authors for contributing their time and talent to make this collection come together. And also Eric and Lance and all the good folks at Down & Out.

ABOUT THE CONTRIBUTORS

COLLEEN COLLINS is a multi-published author and private investigator. Since her first novel was published in 1997, she has written 30 books and short stories in the mystery, romantic comedy, and nonfiction genres. Her stories have placed first in the Aspen Gold, Romancing the Rockies, and Top of the Peak contests, and been shortlisted for the Holt Medallion, Award of Excellence, and Romance Writers of America RITA contests. She has taught workshops at regional and national writers' conferences, and written articles for USA Today, Men's Health, PI Magazine, and other publications. Colleen is a member of the Mystery Writers of America, Private Eye Writers of America, and Sisters in Crime. Ellery Queen Mystery Magazine recognized her blog Guns, Gams, and Gumshoes as one of the top three true crime blogs. American Library Association's Booklist site tapped the blog twice as its "Web Crush of the Week" during Mystery Month. Colleen and her husband-PI-partner Shaun Kaufman were the cover story for Westword magazine (For These Married Denver Detectives, Truth Is More Fun Than Fiction), and featured on an NPR broadcast (A Real Life Nick and Nora Charles). Guns, Gams & Gumshoes: https://writingpis.wordpress.com/.

BRENDAN DUBOIS is the *New York Times* bestselling author of twenty-four novels, including *The First Lady* and *The Cornwalls Are Gone* co-authored with James Patterson. His latest, *The Summer House*, was a number one *New York Times* bestseller. Brendan's short fiction has appeared in *Playboy*, *The Saturday Evening Post*, *Ellery Queen's Mystery Magazine*, *Alfred Hitchcock's Mystery Magazine*, and numerous anthologies including *The Best American Mystery Stories of the Century* and *The Best American Noir of the Century*. His stories have thrice won him the Shamus Award from the PWA, two Barry Awards, a Derringer Award, the Ellery Queen Readers Award, and three Edgar Allan Poe Award nominations from the MWA. He is also a *Jeopardy!* game show champion. Website: BrendanDuBois.com.

USA Today and international bestselling author **ALISON GAYLIN** has won the Edgar, Shamus and RT Reviewers Choice awards. Her work has been published in the US, UK, France, Belgium, the Netherlands, Japan, Germany, Romania and Denmark, and she has been nominated for the Macavity, Anthony, ITW Thriller and Strand Book Award. In addition to her novels, she has published numerous short stories and collaborated with Megan Abbott on the graphic novel Normandy Gold (Titan/Hard Case Crime, 2018). Her 12th book will be out from William Morrow in 2021. Website: AlisonGaylin.com.

Award-winning crime novelist **TOM MACDONALD** has Boston in his blood. Born in Dorchester and raised in Braintree, he now works in Charlestown for St. Mary–St. Catherine of Siena Parish as Director of Social Ministries and Director of Harvest on Vine food pantry. He also teaches creative writing at Boston College. MacDonald earned a BA from Stonehill College, an MBA from Boston College, and an MFA in creative wring from the University of Southern Maine's Stonecoast Writing Seminars. MacDonald's fiction writing has been influenced by his work in Charlestown, where he runs a food pantry that serves the largest federal housing project in New England, the Bunker Hill Housing Development. His goal in storytelling is to depict urban life in a believable way, keeping clear of clichés and stereotypes. To accomplish this, he focuses on gritty settings, hard-luck characters, and street dialogue, especially things left unsaid. His stories hinge on neighborhood norms and how these norms influence seemingly ordinary decisions. His four crime novels are The Charlestown Connection (2011), Beyond the

Bridge (2013), The Revenge of Liam McGrew (2015), and Murder in the Charlestown Bricks (2018). His next novel will be titled is Sleep High, Sleep Long. He currently resides in Braintree, Massachusetts, with his wife Maribeth. Website: TomMacDonaldBooks.com.

ANDREW MCALEER is the author of numerous books including the 101 Habits of Highly Successful Novelists (Simon & Schuster), Fatal Deeds, Positive Results, and co-author with Edgar Winner John McAleer, Mystery Writing in a Nutshell. He co-edits with Shamus Award winner Paul D. Marks, the critically acclaimed Coast to Coast crime fiction series (Down & Out Books). McAleer teaches at Boston College, served with the Massachusetts Department of Correction for many years, and now serves as a full-time police officer. He also served in Afghanistan as a U.S. Army Historian. Website: AMcaleer.com.

MICHAEL MALLORY leads multiple creative lives. He is the author of the "Amelia Watson" and "Dave Beauchamp" mystery series, the standalone thriller Death Walks Skid Row, and some 140 short stories, mostly mystery. A recognized authority on the history of film and animation, he has written eleven nonfiction books and hundreds of magazine and newspaper articles on pop culture subjects. As an actor Mike has appeared on many television programs, including Mad Men, Vegas, and the miniseries Mob City. A former radio news reporter, he continues to work as an interviewer for the Academy of Motion Picture Arts and Sciences' Visual History Program. Mike has lived in the greater Los Angeles area for most of his life and can point out classic film locations, and tell you where to find the best Mexican food in the city.

PAUL D. MARKS is the author of the Shamus Award-Winning mystery-thriller White Heat. Publishers Weekly calls White Heat a "taut crime yarn". Betty Webb of Mystery Scene Magazine calls its sequel Broken Windows "Extraordinary". His short story "Ghosts of Bunker Hill" was voted #1 in the 2016 Ellery Queen Mystery Magazine Readers Award. And "Fade-Out on Bunker Hill" came in second in the 2020 Ellery Queen Readers Poll. "Windward" was selected for the Best American Mystery Stories of 2018, was nominated for a Shamus Award, and won the 2018 Macavity Award for Best Short Story. He has written four novels, co-edited two anthologies and written countless short stories, including many award winners and nominees. His short fiction has been published in Ellery Queen Mystery Magazine, Akashic's Noir series (St. Louis), Alfred Hitchcock Mystery Magazine, Hardboiled, Switchblade, Mystery Weekly, and many others. He has served on the boards of the Los Angeles chapters of Sisters in Crime and Mystery Writers of America. Brendan DuBois, NY Times best-selling author, says Paul's latest novel The Blues Don't Care is "finely written" and "highly recommended". PaulDMarks.com.

Formerly a Hollywood screenwriter (*My Favorite Year, Welcome Back, Kotter*, etc.), **DENNIS PALUMBO** is a licensed psychotherapist and author. His mystery fiction has appeared in Ellery Queen's Mystery Magazine, The Strand and elsewhere, and is collected in From Crime to Crime. His series of mystery thrillers (the latest of which, Head Wounds, was named a "Best of 2018" by *Suspense Magazine*) features Daniel Rinaldi, a psychologist and trauma expert who consults with the Pittsburgh Police. Info at DennisPalumbo.com.

STEPHEN D. ROGERS is the author of *Shot to Death* and more than 800 shorter works. His website, StephenDRogers.com, includes a list of new and upcoming titles as well as other timely information.

JOHN SHEPPHIRD is a Shamus Award-winning author and writer/director of television films. Mystery Scene Magazine hails his novel BOTTOM FEEDERS as "A fast-pace, fun read that explores a part of the movie business that often gets overlooked... from 'Action!' to 'Cut' it's a pleasure to read." John is a two-time Anthony Award-finalist and producer of audiobooks. His short fiction has appeared in various anthologies and publications including Alfred Hitchcock Mystery Magazine and Down & Out: The Magazine. As director, titles include Chupacabra Terror, Jersey Shore Shark Attack, I Saw Mommy Kissing Santa Claus and Teenage Bonnie and Klepto Clyde. Check out JohnShepphird.com.

JADEN TERRELL is a Shamus Award finalist and the internationally published author of the Nashville-based Jared McKean private detective series. At the other end of the spectrum, Trouble Most Faire features a Ren-Faire murder and a crime-solving feline. Terrell's short stories have appeared in several anthologies, and she is a contributor to International Thriller Writers' Big Thrill magazine and Now Write! Mysteries, a collection of exercises published by Tarcher/Penguin for writers of crime fiction. She is the recipient of the Killer Nashville Builder Award, as well as the Magnolia Award and the Silver Quill Award for service to the Southeast Mystery Writers of America. She offers live and online workshops, coaching, and courses for writers. Website: JadenTerrell.com.

DAVE ZELTSERMAN is the award-winning author of numerous noir, horror, mystery, and thriller novels, including Killer, Monster, Pariah, and Small Crimes, made into a Netflix Original film starring Nikolaj Coster-Waldau. The Caretaker of Lorne Field is being adapted for film by the production company Stone Village, with script by Black Swan screenwriter Andres Heinz. Dave Zeltserman lives in the Boston area. Dave's shortest short story: She was a dark-haired beauty who almost stole my heart, but I wrestled the knife out of her hand before she could finish the job. Dave's blog: http://smallcrimes-novel.blogspot.com/.

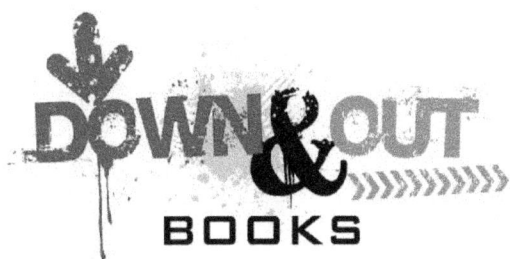

DOWN & OUT BOOKS

On the following pages are a few
more great titles from the
Down & Out Books publishing family.

For a complete list of books and to
sign up for our newsletter,
go to DownAndOutBooks.com.

ALL DUE RESPECT

SHOTGUN HONEY

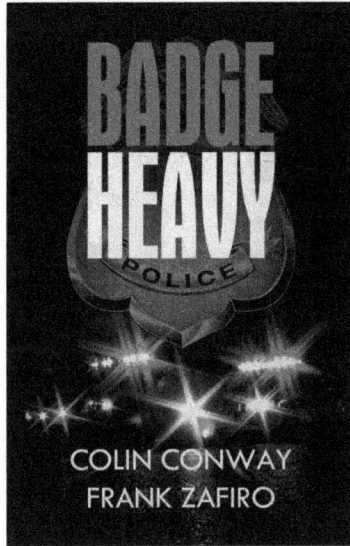

Badge Heavy
A Charlie-316 Novel
Colin Conway and Frank Zafiro

Down & Out Books
September 2020
978-1-64396-152-1

Officer Tyler Garrett's saga continues when he is assigned to the aggressive Anti-Crime Team.

The team's sterling success in battling crime is only matched by the dark agendas surrounding it. The team piles up arrests and seizures, but tension grows as competing goals and loyalties come into conflict.

Something has got to give.

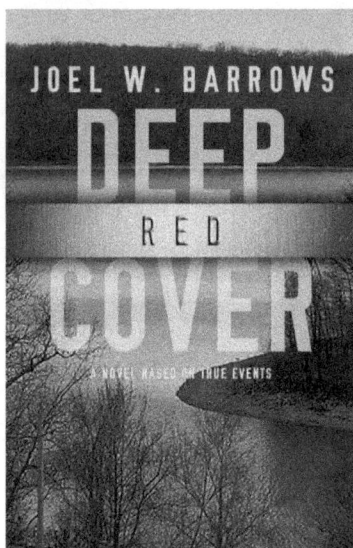

Deep Red Cover
A Cover Thriller
Joel W. Barrows

Down & Out Books
September 2020
978-1-64396-117-0

A body is found on the shores of a Missouri lake, throat slashed. There are few clues, and the trail grows cold for Investigator Morgan Kern.

At the same time, ATF has become increasingly concerned about the growing militia movement. Special Agent David Ward goes undercover to investigate possible illegal weapons trafficking.

Their paths will intersect in a way that neither could have imagined.

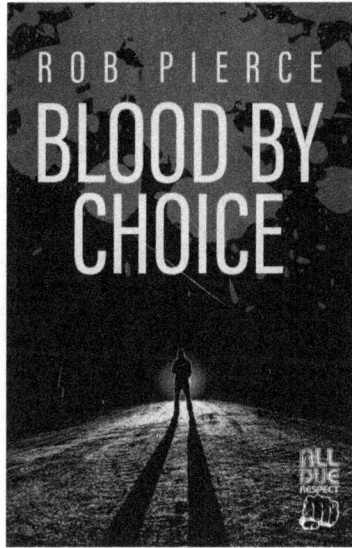

Blood by Choice
Rob Pierce

All Due Respect, an imprint of
Down & Out Books
September 2020
978-1-64396-116-3

Two women and a child are murdered. Dust, who unknowingly set them up, returns to Berkeley to find the killer. With his old buddy Karma in tow, Dust discovers that one of the culprits was Vollmer, a ruthless hired gun working for Dust's former boss, Rico. When Vollmer finds out Dust is in town the hunt becomes mutual.

In this, the third book of the Uncle Dust series, old debts are paid and new ones incurred. Brutish, dangerous men lurk in every corner and slaughter runs rampant.

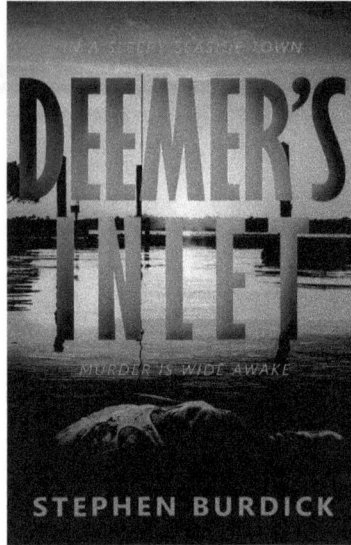

Deemer's Inlet
Stephen Burdick

Shotgun Honey, an imprint of
Down & Out Books
August 2020
978-1-64396-104-0

Far from the tourist meccas of Ft. Lauderdale and Miami Beach, a chief of police position in the quiet, picturesque town of Deemer's Inlet on the Gulf coast of Florida seemed ideal for Eldon Quick—until the first murder.

The crime and a subsequent killing force Quick to call upon his years of experience as a former homicide detective in Miami. Soon after, two more people are murdered and Quick believes a serial killer is on the loose. As Quick works to uncover the identity and motive of the killer, he must contend with an understaffed police force, small town politics, and curious residents.